RADICAL JOURNALISM

This edited volume offers a state-of-the-art synthesis of the historical role of radical journalism, its present iterations, and plans for the future of a journalism that is committed to liberatory movements and politics.

At a time of profound crisis and stagnation for mainstream journalism, radical journalism seems to be riding a wave. New outlets, including those – like Jacobin – with a global reach, have sprung up, presenting a new generation of unapologetically progressive publications with an emancipatory agenda. Understanding the role and place of radical journalism becomes even more urgent given the current political climate in a (post) pandemic world with heightened inequalities and intensified pauperisation.

Drawing on contributions from leading academics, this collection considers:

- How new outlets fit in the genealogy of (radical) journalism and what their flourishing can tell us about the present and future of emancipatory politics and the role of the radical journalist;
- What these new forms and publications mean for mainstream journalism and its persisting problems of financial sustainability and professional journalistic labour;
- Important challenges presented by, for example, the resurgence of fascism, authoritarianism, and the mainstreaming of the far right;
- Essential questions of what radical journalism looks like today, what forms it takes or should take, and what its future might be.

Radical Journalism is recommended reading for advanced students and journalists working at the intersection of journalism, politics, and sociology.

Seamus Farrell holds a Ph.D. from Dublin City University (DCU), Ireland, on the topic of 'A Political Economy of Radical Media'. In addition to research on radical media and politics, Seamus is interested in critical perspectives on Irish development, having worked on the Repast: Conflict in Europe Project.

Eugenia Siapera is Professor and Head of the School of Information and Communication Studies at University College Dublin (UCD), Ireland. She is the Director of the UCD Centre for Digital Policy.

George Souvlis is Adjunct Lecturer in the Department of History & Archaeology at the University of Ioannina, Greece, and a postdoctoral researcher in the Department of Sociology at the University of Crete, Greece. He is the Co-director of the Seminar Series Politics of Liberation.

RADICAL JOURNALISM

Resurgence, Reform, Reaction

*Edited by Seamus Farrell, Eugenia Siapera,
and George Souvlis*

Routledge
Taylor & Francis Group

LONDON AND NEW YORK

Designed cover image: Seamus Farrell

First published 2023
by Routledge
4 Park Square, Milton Park, Abingdon, Oxon OX14 4RN

and by Routledge
605 Third Avenue, New York, NY 10158

Routledge is an imprint of the Taylor & Francis Group, an informa business

British Library Cataloguing-in-Publication Data
A catalogue record for this book is available from the British Library

ISBN: 978-1-032-11841-3 (hbk)
ISBN: 978-1-032-11567-2 (pbk)
ISBN: 978-1-003-22178-4 (ebk)

DOI: 10.4324/9781003221784

Typeset in Bembo
by Newgen Publishing UK

CONTENTS

FIGURES

CONTRIBUTORS

Christos Avramidis is doing his Ph.D. in Political Science and is conducting research at the crossroads of social movement and media studies. He has worked in different research programs about media, social exclusion, and political science. He has published papers in peer-reviewed journals and has given presentations at international scientific conferences. He has worked as a researcher on many projects and he has been working as a journalist for more than ten years in different media of Greece. He is a member of the International Federation of Journalists and he has written pieces for media in other countries. He has collaborated with the European Broadcasting Union, Amnesty International, and Open Democracy. His research interests are Contentious Politics and Media Studies.

Seamus Farrell holds a Ph.D. from Dublin City University on the topic of 'A Political Economy of Radical Media'. In addition to research on radical media and politics, Seamus is interested in critical perspectives on Irish development, having worked on the Repast: Conflict in Europe Project. Seamus is also an active participant in social reproductive struggles in Ireland (anti-water privatization, housing justice, tenants unions, and trade unionism).

Sandra Jeppesen is Professor in Media, Film and Communications at Lakehead University, Canada. She is co-founder of the Media Action Research Group. She held the Lakehead University Research Chair in Transformative Media and Social Movements (2016–2018). She is the co-editor, with Paola Sartoretto, of *Media Activist Research Ethics: Global Approaches to Negotiating Power in Social Justice Research* (2020). Her most recent books include: *Transformative Media: Intersectional Technopolitics from Indymedia to #BlackLivesMatter* (UBC Press 2021) and *The Capitol Riots: Digital Media, Disinformation, and Democracy under Attack* (Routledge, 2022).

Tiago Matos holds a Ph.D. in History and Civilization from the European University Institute. He is Portuguese, but is based in Oslo (Norway). His work has been centred on the intersection between the history of social movements, street politics, riots, and their influence on the institutionalization of democratic practices.

Alexandros Minotakis holds a Ph.D. in Communication Studies from the University of Athens, Greece. Among his research interests are critical/alternative media, critical political economy of media, and fake news. He is currently employed on an Erasmus+ Programme on the integration of socially vulnerable groups.

Yiannis Mylonas is the author of the monograph "The Greek Crisis in Europe: Race, Class, and Politics" (2019, Brill). He has also published various peer-reviewed articles and book chapters on issues related to the cultural politics of the media, concerning the analysis of news representations of ethnicity and class, public memory and the development of informal archives, propaganda and social media, and civic cultures. His research interests depart from the theoretical foundations of Critical Theory and Post Structuralism.

Eugenia Siapera is Professor of Information and Communication Studies and Head of the ICS School at UCD. Her research interests are in the area of digital and social media, political communication and journalism, technology and social justice, platform governance and hate speech, racism, and misogyny. She has written numerous articles and book chapters. Her most recent book is *Understanding New Media* (Sage, 2018, second edition) and the edited volume *Gender Hate Online* (co-edited with Debbie Ging, 2019).

Nikos Smyrnaios is Associate Professor at the University of Toulouse where he teaches theory, history, sociology, culture, and economics of the media and the internet. His research focuses on the political economy of communication, digital journalism, and the political use of social media. He has published numerous articles in peer-reviewed journals and book chapters in English, French, and Greek and gave talks and presentations in international conferences. He is the author of *Internet Oligopoly: The Corporate Takeover of Our Digital World*, Emerald Publishing, 2018.

George Souvlis is Adjunct Lecturer at the University of Ioannina, Department of History and Archaeology, and a postdoctoral researcher at the University of Crete, Department of Sociology. He is the Co-director of the Seminal Series Politics of Liberation. He has published several journal articles and books chapters. His most recent books are *Voices on the Left* (Red Marks, 2019), *Back to the '30's? Crisis, Repetition and Transition in the 20th and 21th Centuries* (co-edited with Jeremy Rayner, Susan Falls, Taylor C. Nelms, Palgrave, 2019), and *Mainstreaming the Far-Right in*

Greece: Media, Gender, Armed Forces and the Church (co-edited with Rosa Vasilaki, Rosa Luxemburg Stiftung, Office in Greece, 2021).

Laurent Thiong-Kay is a researcher in information and communication sciences. His work focuses on the media construction of public problems, online activism, and transformations of journalism. He currently teaches at the University of Lille.

1

RADICAL JOURNALISM AT THE CROSSROADS

Eugenia Siapera, Seamus Farrell and George Souvlis

The first 22 years of the new millennium have been turbulent. The pax Americana that seemed to be the de facto position of the 1990s, following the collapse of the Soviet Union and the end of the Cold War, dissolved in a series of crises: the 9/11 terrorist attacks and the war on terror, the brief interlude of the Arab Spring and the Occupy movements, the financial crisis of 2008 and its aftermath, the return of the far right, Covid-19 and the pandemic and, crucially, the spectre of total environmental collapse. None of these has yet triggered any radical changes in the way in which the world operates, but taken together, they are incrementally destabilising and undermining institutions and practices we took for granted. Protracted political instability, the emergence of new power centres and global alliances, perpetual wars and increasing pauperisation of ever larger parts of the population across the world, create pressure points that might have unpredictable consequences. It is in this historical juncture that we situate radical journalism and its media.

In the beginning of the 21st century, radical journalism entered a new phase, which we can attribute to two main developments. Firstly, the rise of the internet, which provided a means of efficient distribution of content, bypassing the barriers set by traditional, mainstream media. Secondly, the emergence of the anti-globalisation movement which led to a growth in protest reporting, building community-based communication infrastructure and encouraging citizen journalism (Atton and Hamilton, 2008). The paradigmatic radical journalism of the early 21st century is the journalism of Indymedia, a model of federated but autonomous websites that ran on the same principles across the world (Pickard, 2006). Based on user content with an emphasis on action reporting from protests and other local events and actions, Indymedia constituted the experimentation ground for new radical journalism in the internet age. Radical journalism in the Indymedia era included direct frontline reporting from protests, actions and organising, often including visual and narrative commentary and direct proposals, calls for action and support in real time (Siapera

DOI: 10.4324/9781003221784-1

and Farrell, 2019). A precursor to data journalism, radical journalism of this era also included investigative reporting based on information extraction via computer hacking (Pickard, 2006, see also Jeppesen in this volume on radical data journalism). Nevertheless, Indymedia-style radical journalism remained closely associated with the anti-globalisation movement and never scaled or reached broader publics.

The popularity of social media platforms such as Twitter and Facebook entailed the promise of scale and massive reach for radical journalism. The sovereign debt crisis of 2008 and the intense protests and struggles in Greece and elsewhere, the Indignados and Occupy movements, in close temporal proximity with the struggles for democracy in the North Africa and the Middle East, ushered in a new era for radical journalism and media. Protesters and citizen journalists invented new forms of political and media struggles, including citizen witnessing, the use of hashtags and a combination of street action and social media reporting, all of which led to the global scaling and viral spread of political protests in public city squares, linking Cairo, Madrid, Athens, Istanbul and New York in a global wave of protests (Gerbaudo, 2012, 2017; Tufekci, 2017).

The euphoria and new hope of these movements and their media came crushing down with the astonishing wins for reactionary, xenophobic and nationalistic politics in 2016, and in particular, the election of Donald Trump in the USA and the Brexit referendum in the UK, alongside significant electoral gains for the far right in Brazil, Sweden, Germany, Denmark and elsewhere. While centrist liberalism is making a comeback politically, it is significantly weakened and its institutions, including political parties and the media, undermined. For journalism in particular, these developments and the consecutive and overlapping crises have meant that dominant funding models (corporate and public service), political outlooks and functions (watchdog, objectivity, balance) and relationship with publics (trust and credibility) are being challenged. Responses to these crises have typically taken three forms: a techno-solutionist one, looking at technological innovation and entrepreneurship as a means for re-inventing journalism (Anderson et al., 2015); an extreme right form, in which far-right media seek to capitalise on the crisis and recruit supporters (see Siapera, this volume); and a radical one, which considers liberal journalism and technological innovation on its own as inadequate in dealing with the socio-political, economic and ecological problems the world is currently facing, while also building a strong opposition against the threat of the far right. This kind of journalism is at the centre of this volume.

But what does radical journalism mean, more precisely? To address the question of definition, we begin with a historical contextualisation, sketching the beginning of journalism and its radical forms. This is followed by a closer conceptualisation of the term radical as it has been used in the literature, paying close attention to related terms such as alternative journalism. We then discuss theoretical approaches to radical journalism and introduce a brief theoretical sketch that emerges from the discussion, but also from the chapters in this volume. The final part of this introductory chapter will outline the structure of the book and situate the chapters and their contributions.

A Brief History of (Radical) Journalism

The intimate involvement of mainstream media in the legitimation and reproduction of the current political and economic system may be attributed to their origin in the historical salon-based bourgeois public sphere (Habermas, 1989). In early modernity, the media have been at the centre of struggles between the *ancient regime* and the rising middle classes, as the political establishment sought to control and dictate what can and cannot be said in public. The freedom of speech principles in the French National Assembly in 1789 and the First Amendment of the US Constitution in 1791 coexisted with attempts to control the press, for example, through the stamp duty imposed on publishers in the UK, through open censorship, such as the cancellation of the 'privilege to publish' or through self-censorship, undertaken to avoid repression or offending sponsors, advertisers or patrons (Chalaby, 1998). These struggles and the various compromises they involved led to the evolution of the liberal press/media as part of the liberal democratic establishment. The key function of liberal journalism and its media is the provision of accurate information enabling publics to make informed judgements, and the associated use of reason and rational arguments not only to hold accountable but also to legitimate the polity. In Habermas' (1989) historical account, journalism's precursor was art and literary criticism, which socialised the public to reading and debating matters of morality and ethics. From there, the next step was to debate issues of public concern raised in the print media, leading to the formation of a public opinion. The formation of public opinion was the main means by which to legitimate the political system outside elections. Normatively, Habermas (1996) outlined the role of the media in liberal representative democracy in the following terms:

> the mass media ought to understand themselves as the mandatary of an
> enlightened public whose willingness to learn and capacity for
> criticism they at once presuppose, demand, and reinforce; like the
> judiciary, they ought to preserve their independence from political
> and social pressure; they ought to be receptive to the public's
> concerns and proposals, take up these issues and contributions
> impartially, augment criticisms, and confront the political process
> with articulate demands for legitimation.
>
> *1996: 378*

The above quote illustrates the normative role of media and journalism as a 'fourth estate', independent from politics, the market and society, acting objectively and impartially. Habermas' normative ideal is far from the reality of a structurally transformed media sphere, controlled by private interests. His critique is therefore oriented towards the realisation of this normative role. This kind of journalism, which we term liberal, operates on the premise that the structure of society, its institutions, laws, norms and values are fundamentally legitimate. Small adjustments and calls of justification do not aim to transform society but to incrementally improve it.

In contrast to liberal journalism, the radical version of journalism had an altogether different political agenda, focusing on social, political and economic transformation. It peaked and ebbed at various historical moments, for example, during the early part of the 20th century, and then again in the 1960s and 1970s often in close proximity with social movements, such as the labour movement and the civil rights movement. Throughout its existence, it faced a multitude of challenges. Chalaby (1998) details the history of the working class press in the UK of the late 18th to early 19th century, pointing to the important role of the 'unstamped' papers in facilitating class consciousness. These were newspapers that circulated illegally and aimed to represent the interests of the workers. Paradoxically, it was not taxation or repression that eventually led to the demise of the 'unstampeds', but the rise of the popular Sunday market with its cheap apolitical stories. During its peak, the circulation of the working-class 'unstamped' press superseded that of the legal press. Publicists represented their class and sought to analyse and criticise the political process from their class perspective; through this critique and analysis, they cultivated class consciousness and the ability of working-class people to understand politics from their position. Their writing was not only towards understanding but also towards social change for their class and for society as a whole, in a close approximation of Marx's 'Thesis Eleven'.

In parallel with the working class radical journalism, the Black radical tradition of the early 20th century in the USA used journalism to open up a space for political imagination, even if thinkers such as W.E.B. Du Bois were characterised as 'poets' and 'dreamers' (Johnson and Johnson, 1977: 329). It did so in various ways: through articulating a concern with a historical account and reinterpretation of the African diaspora experience; writing and archiving Black history; and providing an outlet for literary expression and cultural development from the perspective of the Black experience, through the publication of short stories and poems (Johnson and Johnson, 1977). The radical politics of the 1960s and 1970s articulated the struggle against racism and added new forms including documentaries, such as The Murder of Fred Hampton (Alk and Gray, 1971), which used original footage documenting the Black Panther movement in Chicago and helped prove the murder of Fred Hampton by the police. The witnessing, documenting and archiving of Black lived experience, including both the brutalisation of Black people at the hands of the police and empowering moments of Black activism, continue to enrich the tradition of Black radical journalism and media (Richardson, 2020). The expansion of political imagination along with the documentation and archiving of political action are two further elements of Black radical journalism.

In a similar manner, the feminist press of the 1960s and 1970s pursued the emancipation of women not only through journalism, but also through reimaging journalism from a feminist perspective. For instance, *Spare Rib* magazine, launched in the UK in 1972, sought to give voice to the feminist movement and advance its political position of linking the personal to the political, publishing first-person accounts, satire and do-it-yourself guides and validating the experiences, emotions and struggles of women with a view to challenging and ultimately destroying patriarchal gender relations (Waters, 2016). When the feminist movement was openly challenged by women occupying intersectional identities, for example, Black feminists or Irish feminists during the Troubles (Boyd, 1983; Mohanty, 1988), the magazine sought to shift perspective, incorporate and address the concerns and viewpoints of these women. Inclusivity and challenging of the form of writing as part of feminist praxis are therefore two additional key elements of feminist radical journalism.

Has radical journalism led to social and political transformations? Undoubtedly, this journalism provides direct evidence of the tensions and struggles in particular historical times. It has helped social movements find their voice and articulate their demands publicly. The combined efforts of political struggle and public interventions including via radical media have directly contributed to important social, cultural and political advances and to the establishment of labour rights, civil rights and women's rights.

This brief discussion of the historical emergence and evolution of radical journalism points to its origins in political struggle, its close connection with social movements and some of its struggles with various obstacles, ranging from overt repression to co-optation and the dissipation of social energies. This discussion, additionally, sought to outline the specific and historically located attributes of radical journalism, which we will now employ in defining it with more precision.

Defining Radical Journalism

'Radical' remains an elusive and open confused term in contemporary public discourse. A radical idea is one that is far reaching, innovative or even dangerous. In some cases, radicalism is attributed to left politics, but in others it is synonymous with extremism and can be used to define or typecast the left and the right through the political theoretical lens of horseshoe theory (see also Siapera in this volume). When we try to define the kind of journalism that operates outside of the mainstream of the modern mass media, other terms also leave us with definitional problems. Alternative, progressive, socialist, grassroots, oppositional, community, minority, DIY, citizen media are worthy describers of new, non-traditional forms of journalism and media but their interchangeability and lack of definitional clarity remain a challenge for the field.

The origins of the use of the concept 'radical' are outlined in Raymond Williams' (2014) *Keywords*. He points out that 'radical' was used to discuss progressive social movements which aspired for reforms, such as the Chartist and English Whigs, as well as revolutionary republicanism such as Jacobinism. Similarly, writing in the context of social movements and liberation struggles, Angela Davis (1990) understands radical as involving the uprooting of oppression in its whole and the complete transformation of society. Echoing these analyses, Fenton (2016, p. 9) traces the concept 'radical' to its original Latin meaning of root, alluding to 'the grass-roots' and to the 'nurturing and sustaining of an ecosystem'. These meanings of radical all converge on the idea that it goes beyond small or superficial differences and that it concerns a comprehensive social transformation.

While here we refer to radical journalism and its media, the literature often describes such media as alternative or oppositional, decentring the term radical. To some extent, this can be explained by the political climate in the late 20th to the early 21st century; however, such different terms often reflect the different inflection of specific works and their different focus. For example, in one of the most influential publications in this area, Chris Atton (2001) refers to alternative media. In particular, Atton (2001) considers radical more narrowly and focuses on the wider expressions of non-mainstream media under the category of alternative media, as this can then include, for example, fanzines and similar kinds of media that are not necessarily radical but still stand separately and occasionally in opposition to commercial media. In an equivalent manner, Curran's (2002) historical account understands the Chartist press as a radical project, but addresses modern media in terms of countervailing power.

Fuchs and Sandoval (2015) choose the term alternative media instead of radical media, considering it more generally used and understood and therefore more useful for their modelling of an ideal anti-capitalist media. Jeppesen (2016) places radical within a subset, as autonomous and radical, narrowing its definition to focus on a smaller specific type of anarchist and autonomous media, within a broad alternative media which includes critical, DIY and community forms. Is alternative a better concept to use than radical, or should radical be considered as a minor force within a broader alternative media field?

There are a number of reasons why radical can be considered a better framework to analyse the media that operate outside of and opposed to the mainstream and corporate media, as well as the political right-wing media. Firstly, radical offers a clear normative stance and positive assertion of what media is and what its values are, while alternative does not. As noted, radical refers to radical change at the roots, change that is politically progressive in pursuit of emancipation. In these terms, radical media have to be seen as part of left politics and put forward proposals for what a transformed society might look like: a society emancipated, liberated from harm, restraints and oppression, and liberated in the fullest sense, implying economic, social and political freedom.

Alternative, by contrast, is defined as different from the dominant capitalist and media material and ideological practice. At its best, this difference can be a statement of media plurality and diversity against the historic development of oligarchic media ownership, in favour of all voices being heard. At worst, it can be a statement of the 'two extremes' argument, with alternative referring to everything that is outside the mainstream, from far-right hate speech to radical left politics. Neither plurality nor the 'two extremes' offer a clear, positive normative value for an understanding of media that has a stated ideological and moral position on what it analyses and how it interlinks with politics.

As we have also seen, radical journalism and its media are clearly historically grounded, while the historical use of alternative is more limited. Radical movements, radical media and radical politics have a long history, from the peasant revolts of late medieval times through to early working-class and emancipatory revolutionary traditions, socialism and anarchism, and into the New Left of the 1960s and 21st-century socialism. Alternative, by contrast, is squarely dated within a counter-cultural pattern of consumption, and subcultural politics, developing particular resonance within the late 1990s and early 2000s. Indeed, it emerged out of alt-rock, an initially anti-corporate rock counter-culture, punk and then a more general alternative cultural aesthetic in the 1990s (Hesmondhalgh and Meier, 2014). Considering the two terms, radical and alternative, from a historical materialist perspective, radical is a concept with a long history of use, referring to a range of dynamics, theories and models, publications and practices, while alternative is narrowly positioned as a specific subcultural, particularly 1990s, practice (Hesmondhalgh and Meier, 2014). Additionally, the consumerist co-optation of alternative media and the emergence of the alt-right raise serious questions over the continued use of alternative media as an overarching category that includes both far-right and progressive media. That alternative that has increasingly been integrated into consumerist society makes its value as an outsider and anti-capitalist expression diminished: it is merely another option to be consumed or used, without posing a fundamental challenge to capitalism. The alt and far-right use much of the aesthetics and anti-corporate language of the alternative media period, redirecting its energy into the substantiation and development of a new (or a resurgence of an old) political force on the right. In the USA, this has focused on emboldening white supremacy, with organised neo-Nazis and the remains of the Tea Party acting as a pressure force moving conservativism to the right. Similarly, Identitarianism in Europe and a range of far-right parties and youth organisations have adopted an alternative aesthetic (and language) as part of recruitment and development (Holt, 2019; see also Siapera in this volume for a discussion of the challenges of the far-right media). Notwithstanding these criticisms, there is still scope to use the term alternative to approach media and journalistic practice that walks along the path of radical journalism in supporting progressive politics, but is not always and necessarily radical in all its dimensions (see, for example, Thiong-Kay and Smyrnaios on environmental journalism in this volume).

Applying the term radical to journalism as a field foregrounds the question of its relation to radical and transformative politics, alludes to its historical links and continued contribution to progressive struggles for emancipation and liberation. We can therefore define radical journalism as the kind of journalism that emerges from radical politics and supports its political project. For radical journalism, however, to be truly and comprehensively radical, it must not only carry contents that propagandise for radical politics; it must also involve an entirely different set of relationships between journalists and their labour, and between journalists, their output and readers/publics. Using the example of Brecht's theatre, Benjamin (1970) argued that radical media should radicalise the form of writing and should actively involve readers as producers of journalistic and media works. Radical journalism and media should also explore and apply models of ownership and management of journalistic labour that are very different from those of for-profit mainstream media, countering alienation and providing an example of worker-organised and managed enterprises (Downing, 2000; Fuchs and Sandoval, 2015). As we will discuss below, these form the basic premises of theoretical approaches to radical journalism.

Theorising Radical Journalism

Understanding radical journalism requires not only an examination of the historical conditions of its emergence, but also a focused analysis of its socio-cultural and political economic dynamics. Theoretical approaches to radical journalism therefore range from historical to political and political economic, and from sociological to cultural. In particular, political economic and sociological frameworks are significant for the analysis of radical media as part of a media field/system as a whole. Social movement theory approaches journalism as activism and examines the use of media by activists. Journalism studies examine micro and meso-dynamics of labour production and content, while cultural studies focus on content and representation. Political, sociological and cultural approaches can also be used to understand the relationship between radical journalism and its publics and the role of these publics as co-producers and users of the knowledge generated by radical journalism.

In particular, political economic frameworks place emphasis on the analysis of 'systems' as a whole (Mosco, 1996). Within this, journalism is examined in the context of the wider operation of economic production dynamics and political structures that shape communication and media. Radical journalism can be seen as operating under the constraints of capitalist political economy while also carving out political opposition and transformative modes of production. Political economic approaches have become an important framework for the analysis of communication and media, particularly re-emerging in the late 1990s and 2000s (e.g. Golding and Murdock, 1997; Mansell, 2004; Wasko et al., 2011; Fuchs and Mosco, 2015). Mosco (1996) identified four defining characteristics of the political economy as an analytical approach. Firstly, it is grounded in a comprehension of history and historical context should be central in terms of method and outlook; secondly, it focuses on the totality of analysis (multileveled, multi-layered and multidisciplined); thirdly, it is normatively underpinned by principles of social justice, holding that a vision for a better, more equitable and just, world should motivate inquiry, analysis and solutions; finally, praxis is central, as the analysis is closely linked to application. Since radical journalism is animated by the same concerns and principles, a political economic analysis is a privileged point of departure for understanding it.

But political economy, notwithstanding Mosco's call for multi-layered and multidisciplinary analysis, tends to focus on structural elements, and in particular on media ownership, labour processes and revenue models and their impact. Useful as these elements are, they are short of the full picture. Connecting the broader context with meso and micro dynamics at play could offer a more holistic analysis of the ways in which journalistic norms and conventions emerge and are negotiated, their links to contents and the role of the public. Cultural Studies approaches and frameworks such as the circuit of culture (Du Gay et al., 2013) can offer insights into how processes of production, regulation, identity, representation and reception/use are bound in a cycle, feeding into each other and co-determining outcomes. For radical journalism, this framework can be usefully employed in order to understand both the agency of radical journalists and media and also the structural constraints that circumscribe their efforts. This approach can also be used to understand journalistic output (contents or representation of issues) as the outcome of a complex interplay of processes of production, identity, reception/use and regulation. Radicalising the form of journalism therefore is not simply a matter of greater creativity or imagination but also a struggle against the ways in which these processes forge specific paths that must be followed. This is especially the case when radical journalism operates under conditions of full or quasi authoritarianism (see Mylonas, this volume on left journalism in Russia).

Given the close links between radical journalism and activism, social movement theories can shed light on this particular dimension. Specifically, while liberal journalism operates with norms of objectivity, detachment and impartiality, radical journalism is already positioned and uses the perspective of those marginalised (in terms of class and other oppressed subject positions) to understand, intervene and report on the world. A body of research examines the links between political activism and journalism. Cammaerts (2012) has theorised the relationship between media and activism in terms of the mediation opportunity structure that identifies the ways in which socio-political actors circumvent and bypass obstacles set by the mainstream media in order to directly reach publics. This activist role was evident in the Arab Spring and Occupy era using social media platforms to publish first-hand witnessing accounts of street events, to organise protests and coordinate action and to amplify the voices of those present in street protests (Gerbaudo, 2012; Tufekci, 2017). The citizen journalism that emerged in this context could be seen as a form of radical journalism to the extent that it supports social transformation towards the goals of social justice and equality (Pain, 2018).

Citizen and community journalism and more broadly the close connection between publics and radical journalism reflects the prioritisation of the needs of groups and communities that tend to be marginalised or invisible to professional journalism and mainstream media (Rodriguez, 2000). Crucially, it also shows the grass roots, bottom-up emergence of radical journalism and its organic connection to communities and the socio-political projects that represent these communities and their needs and interests. Often, such journalism emerges precisely because political projects for emancipation are misrepresented or silenced in the mainstream public sphere. It facilitates the public discussion of points of concern and supports the construction and articulation of demands that can then reach the mainstream (see Matos in this volume). Because of this connection, radical journalism is not following the professional norms of detachment, objectivity and neutrality. While therefore the focus of journalism studies on professional journalism and its practices, especially around labour and representation, can be useful in identifying some of the reasons behind the blind spots of mainstream media when it comes to marginalised communities and the working class, it doesn't necessarily provide any insights into the practices of radical journalistic projects in all their forms and complexity.

When it comes to the forms that radical journalism takes, there has been a lot of emphasis on formal innovation, on the upending and radicalisation of the traditional, reverse pyramid, 'balanced' forms of news reporting and journalism encountered in the mainstream. Benjamin (1970) referenced the theatre of Berthold Brecht as an example of radical innovation of form, whose principles could be extended to journalism. Drawing in audiences/users/readers as authors in radical journalism aims to develop new forms of journalism that are not beholden to the professional versions of how journalism should look and enable different voices, perspectives, views and experiences to be heard. The use of first-person perspective is part of this, along with an obvious and clear positioning when it comes to writing about and understanding the world. Documentary forms, which introduce new formal elements, are also seen as part of the radical tradition (Siapera and Papadopoulou, 2018). On the other hand, radical journalism could make use of professional journalistic forms, such as investigative journalism, and put these to radical ends. The use of investigative journalism to expose corruption, wrongdoings, injustices or the impact of certain policies on the working class and other marginalised communities can fit this purpose (Huerta Zapién, 2021). In the same vein, Jeppesen (this volume) explores the extent to which data journalism can be made part of radical journalism.

In theoretically understanding radical journalism, therefore, it may be more fruitful to rely on approaches that combine insights from a variety of disciplines and avoid the somewhat narrow focus on journalism on its own, cut off from its social, political, economic and cultural context. Taken as a field, radical journalism may be considered as structured by tensions between radical, mainstream and far-right journalism and media; tensions between radical journalism initiatives with different foci and inflections; tensions within radical journalistic outlets and media, especially in terms of organisation, labour and sustainability; tensions between radical journalistic initiatives, state authorities, regulatory systems and, recently, corporate social media platforms, which exercise a form of control over the digital public sphere since they facilitate or hinder content distribution (Siapera, 2013); and finally, tensions within the left and its relationship to political parties and to broader socio-political and historical developments (see Souvlis, this volume). Theorising radical journalism therefore requires a more holistic view, contextualisation and attention to structural and systemic dimensions, as well to the historical context.

Secondly, considering the difficulties and debates around what constitutes radical journalism, it may be more fruitful to consider acts of journalism alongside specific journalistic or media outlets as part of radical journalism. Theorising radical journalism in this manner counters more 'purist' perspectives that consider that radical journalism must be radical in all its dimensions, from its business model and labour conditions to its forms, contents and relationship with publics (Downing, 2000). Including acts of radical journalism alongside radical journalistic outlets and media contributes to a more comprehensive view of the field as it is shaped not only by structural forces but also by the agency and actions of people and by the products of these actions that in turn give shape to and influence future actions and eventually structures.

In short, a theory of radical journalism pays attention to the past and the history of not only radical journalism and media but also the history of struggles and movements to take society towards more just and equitable forms of organisation. Understanding theoretically radical journalism further requires paying attention to the multiplicity of its forms and contents, and their connection to communities, classes and identities. Thirdly, it requires an understanding of the tensions that run through radical journalism and its various relationships: with political actors, with the profession of journalism, with publics and communities, and within the field, with other radical media initiatives. Finally, it requires paying attention to social and political struggles that form the context within which radical journalism and its media take shape and form, struggles in which they participate directly. Such struggles are evident in the recurring crises that we are experiencing. As we write this introduction, more crises are looming, with reports of a coming recession, a global housing and food crisis, the threat of a generalised war triggered by the war in Ukraine and the ever present ecological deterioration. It is evident that we have reached a crossroads. Historically, journalism and media provided the means and platform for the public use of reason, which was linked to social progress and freedom. Radical journalism sought to expand this use of reason and create a platform for the voices and views of excluded and oppressed social groups and communities, with the ultimate goal of freedom and equality for all. What role might radical journalism play now? How can its different forms support and facilitate a radical politics? What may be the obstacles in its way? These are the central questions that animate this volume. In the following section, we present the structure of the book and summarise the various chapters and their key contributions.

Understanding Radical Journalism

It should be clear from the preceding discussion that we consider historical analysis as key for understanding the contributions, actual and potential, of radical journalism to the project of emancipation. On the one hand, the book is preoccupied with radical journalism in the context of contemporary crises; on the other, progressive politics always operates within a temporal horizon: action in the present can address injustices of the past and lead to a better future. We therefore used temporality to structure this volume: the past, the present and the future. These temporal lines provide specific discrete contexts for the study of radical journalism, delineating the forces and struggles prevalent historically.

Chapters 2 and 3 focus on the past, analysing the role(s) of radical journalism, its relationships with various political actors and its struggles, tensions and eventual (partial) resolutions. This discussion foregrounds the significance of radical journalism at key points in history. In Chapter 2, George Souvlis examines the history of radical journalism as part of the history of the left, focusing on key moments, associated with the publication of the Communist Manifesto, with Lenin's What is to Be Done, Gramsci's focus on hegemony, the New Left's journals, the recent example of Jacobin. His conclusion is that radical media of the left work better when they are organically connected to movements, serving both as platforms for debate and as a means of disseminating information. A historical analysis of radical journalism and its connection to movements is instructive not only because it is linked to key debates within the left, such as reform versus revolution, but also because of journalism's key role in constructing understandings and framing action. For example, today's Norway is one of the most developed nations in the world, and one of the few that retains significant elements of social democracy. In the 19th-century Norway, however, when Oslo was known as Kristiania, the city was in upheaval: riots were common events, triggered both by street brawls and by perceived injustices as well as by worker strikes. Framing these riots and their principal political actor (the crowd) was politically significant since it was used to legitimise and delegitimise actions, and in this manner contribute to collective understandings but also actions resulting from these understandings. Chapter 3 by Tiago Matos captures what was at stake: frames found in radical socialist media were oriented towards creating solidarity, exposing police brutality and connecting the riots to demands for justice. The lesson for contemporary radical journalism, argues Matos, is to be fully cognisant of the stakes involved in developing frames, especially when it comes to street politics.

Street politics and protests guide the second, and longest, part of the book, which focuses on the present and contemporary forms of radical journalism, in different countries, all caught up in the throes of the various crises described earlier. In Chapter 4, Seamus Farrell focuses on what he terms the 'Anglo sphere', an English language cross-national (if not international) space between the USA, the UK and Ireland. Tracing the complicated history of radical media in the 20th century, and the various attempts to conceptualise radical journalism, Farrell describes the current radical media field as structured by a key tension between quasi-professional radical media and small, fragmented, 'grassroots' initiatives, found dispersed across corporate digital platforms. While the quasi-professional forms need the imagination, experiences and community connections of the smaller forms, the latter require the financial acumen and strategies of the former in order to sustain themselves without exhausting the social energies that feed into them. At the same time, both forms must disengage from the corporate digital platforms and reduce their dependency on them. While Chapter 4 looks at the radical media field in English language countries, Chapter 5 focuses on the emergence of a new kind of radical journalism that navigates and perhaps creates a new terrain, straddling the borders of professional journalism and activism in order to address and counter ecological catastrophe. In Chapter 5, Laurent Thiong-Kay and Nikos Smyrnaios examine the contents of this new kind of journalism and speak to some of its actors in order to gain insights into the emergence of a new journalistic identity. They identify key dynamics within the profession, such as its labour process, as well as aspects of symbolic capital, prestige, recognition but also criticism, which contribute to the development of a specific identity and approach to (radical) journalism: a combination of professional techniques, borrowing from investigative journalism, with political perspectives and subjective elements. All these coexist in tension and structure this new form of 'committed journalism'.

While the first few chapters focus on some of the core Western countries, Chapter 6 focuses on the European south and in particular on Greece during one of the most serious crises it faced in its 200-year existence. The crisis years, roughly from 2008 to 2015, shook the foundations of the country, leaving deep marks and trauma that still reverberates. Christos Avramidis and Alexandros Minotakis tell the story of ErtOpen, the brief period during which the Greek public service broadcaster was occupied and run by its employees. The worker-managed public service broadcasting revealed the potential for a radical media to operate at scale, but also showed that a radically different organisation of work in worker-managed media can successfully produce large-scale media outputs. While ErtOpen was a short-term experiment born out of exceptional social and political circumstances, Avramidis and Minotakis clearly show that the social energies expended and uncompensated labour take their toll on workers and compromise the long-term sustainability of such projects.

Greek society and media had to deal with a political and economic crisis caused by the advancement of neoliberal capitalism in its post-2008 iteration. Russia, on the other hand, can be seen as in a state of crisis since the collapse of the Soviet Union. In Chapter 7, Yiannis Mylonas is charting the uncertain territories that left wing, potentially radical, media are navigating in clearly capitalist but other-wise confused political landscape that merges elements of autocracy and authori-tarianism with representative democracy. Mylonas shows clearly the problems with using concepts that developed in specific historical and cultural contexts, such as the public sphere. He further shows the limitations of polarised approaches to Russia, which view it mainly through the authoritarianism versus (representative) democracy lens. His interviews and analysis demonstrate the difficulties of radical socialist media in Russia which have to create a space for themselves in between virulent antifeminism and empty nostalgia for the past.

The chapters on contemporary forms of radical journalism focused on specific national contexts but future challenges for radical journalism may come from out-side and beyond the local national political contexts. Chapters 8 and 9 examine two challenges of very different kind. In Chapter 8, Sandra Jeppesen looks at data jour-nalism, and the extent to which it is compatible with progressive radical politics. As the dataification of everything proceeds unhindered, colonising more and more areas of the lifeworld, what space is there for radical data journalism? Borrowing from critical data studies and data feminism, Jeppesen shows the potential of radical data journalism to serve the political goals of equality and social justice. To do so, it must address data inequalities, it must work alongside communities for the cre-ation of datasets from below, able to tell different stories, for example the story of how Airbnb changed housing or how Covid-19 has had different, more damaging, effects on working class communities, ethnic minorities and women. There is little doubt that the radical journalism of the future will have to be data literate. Finally, in Chapter 9, Eugenia Siapera looks at a challenge of a different kind: the challenge posed by the far right and its media. As far right, 'populist' politics gains more ground internationally, often mobilising its media for recruitment, organising and framing issues from a right-wing perspective, progressive radical media are faced with three challenges: to address the 'horseshoe' or 'two extremes' theories that equate progressive radical media to far-right media; to reinvent and reclaim critique, especially media critique, that has been usurped by the far-right media; and to shift the media agenda towards progressive frames, countering the convergence of the mainstream and the far right on matters such as migration.

As we theorised earlier, above all, this volume's chapters show the various tensions that end up structuring the field of radical journalism; they illustrate the ways in which radical journalism acts, actors and media manage these tensions and participate in ongoing struggles; and identify both lessons from the past and challenges for the future. These still leave a number of unaddressed and unanswered questions. First and foremost, the book only covered the context of Europe. The great tradition of radical media in, for example, South America has not been explored. While some lessons and challenges may be applicable more widely, future discussions of radical media in Africa, Asia and South America may reveal different trajectories, tensions and struggles for freedom and equality, leading to different lessons for radical journalism. What we hoped we have achieved with this volume is to restart a conversation on radical media which will continue in the years to come as societies grapple with the inevitable crises that capitalism entails.

References

Alk, H., & Gray, M. (1971). The Murder of Fred Hampton, Facets Multi-Media Chicago Film Group, MGA Inc., available at: www.youtube.com/watch?v=d-7JIR1u9qw

Anderson, C. W., Bell, E., & Shirky, C. (2015). Post-industrial journalism: Adapting to the present. *Geopolitics, History & International Relations*, 7(2), 1–122.

Atton, C. (2001). *Alternative media*. London: Sage, 1–172.

Atton, C., & Hamilton, J. F. (2008). *Alternative journalism*. London: Sage.

Benjamin, W. (1970 [1934]). The author as producer. *New Left Review*, 1–62 (July–August), available at: www.marxists.org/reference/archive/benjamin/1970/author-producer.htm

Boyd, R. (1983). Race, place and class: Who's speaking for who. *Spare Rib*, 133.

Cammaerts, B. (2012). Protest logics and the mediation opportunity structure. *European Journal of Communication*, 27(2), 117–134.

Chalaby, J. (1998). *The invention of journalism*. Basingstoke: Palgrave.

Curran, J. (2002). *Media and power*. New York & London: Routledge.

Davis, A.Y. (1990). *Women, culture & politics*. New York: Vintage Books.

Downing, J. (2000). *Radical media: Rebellious communication and social movements*. Thousand Oaks, CA: Sage.

Du Gay, P., Hall, S., Janes, L., Madsen, A. K., Mackay, H., & Negus, K. (2013). *Doing cultural studies: The story of the Sony Walkman*. London: Sage.

Fenton. (2016). *Digital, political, radical*. Cambridge: Polity Press.

Fuchs, C., & Mosco, V. (2015). *Marx and the political economy of the media*. Leiden: Brill.

Fuchs, C., & Sandoval, M. (2015). The political economy of capitalist and alternative social media. In C. Atton (Ed.), *The Routledge companion to alternative and community media* (pp. 165–175). London: Routledge.

Gerbaudo, P. (2012). *Tweets and the streets: Social media and contemporary activism.* London: Pluto Press.

Gerbaudo, P. (2017). The indignant citizen: Anti-austerity movements in southern Europe and the anti-oligarchic reclaiming of citizenship. *Social Movement Studies, 16*(1), 36–50.

Golding, P., & Murdock, G. (Eds.). (1997). *The political economy of the media* (Vol. 2). Brookfield, VT: Elgar.

Habermas, J. (1989). *The structural transformation of the public sphere* (T. Burger, Trans.). Cambridge, MA: Massachusetts Institute of Technology Press (Original work published 1962).

Habermas, J. (1996). *Between facts and norms: Contributions to a discourse theory of law and democracy.* Cambridge: Polity Press.

Hesmondhalgh, D., & Meier, L. M. (2014). Popular music, independence and the concept of the alternative in contemporary capitalism. In J. Bennett & N. Strange (eds.), *Media independence* (pp. 108–130). London: Routledge.

Holt, K. (2019). *Right-wing alternative media.* London: Routledge.

Huerta Zapién, R. I. (2021). *Reframing investigative journalism in Mexico: Towards a transformative practice* (Doctoral dissertation, Goldsmiths, University of London).

Jeppesen, S. (2016). Understanding alternative media power: Mapping content & practice to theory, ideology, and political action. *Democratic Communiqué, 27*(1), 54.

Johnson, A., & Johnson, R. M. (1977). Away from accommodation: Radical editors and protest journalism, 1900–1910. *Journal of Negro History, 62*(4), 325–338.

Mansell, R. (2004). Political economy, power and new media. *New Media & Society, 6*(1), 96–105.

Mohanty, C. T. (1988). Under western eyes: Feminist scholarship and colonial discourses. *Feminist Review, 30*, 61–88.

Mosco, V. (1996). *The political economy of communication: Rethinking and renewal* (Vol. 13). Thousand Oaks, CA: Sage.

Pain, P. (2018). Educate. Empower. Revolt: Framing citizen journalism as a creator of social movements. *Journalism Practice, 12*(7), 799–816.

Pickard, V. W. (2006). United yet autonomous: Indymedia and the struggle to sustain a radical democratic network. *Media, Culture & Society, 28*(3), 315–336.

Richardson, A. V. (2020). *Bearing witness while Black: African Americans, smartphones, and the new protest# journalism.* New York: Oxford University Press.

Rodriguez, C. (2000). *Fissures in the mediascape: An international study of citizens' media.* Cresskill, NJ: Hampton Press.

Siapera, E. (2013). Platform infomediation and journalism. *Culture Machine, 14*, 1–28.

Siapera, E., & Farrell, S. (2019). Activist and radical journalism. *International Encyclopaedia of Journalism Studies*, 1–7. https://doi.org/10.1002/9781118841570.iejs0115

Siapera, E., & Papadopoulou, L. (2018). Radical documentaries, neoliberal crisis and post-democracy. *tripleC: Communication, Capitalism & Critique. Open Access Journal for a Global Sustainable Information Society, 16*(1), 1–17.

Tufekci, Z. (2017). *Twitter and tear gas: The power and fragility of networked protest.* New Haven, CT: Yale University Press.

Wasko, J., Murdock, G., & Sousa, H. (Eds.). (2011). *The handbook of political economy of communications.* Malden, MA: Wiley.

Waters, M. (2016). 'Yours in struggle': Bad feelings and revolutionary politics, in *Spare Rib*, *Women: A Cultural Review, 27*(4), 446–465. DOI: 10.1080/09574042.2017.130113

Williams, R. (2014). *Keywords: A vocabulary of culture and society.* Oxford: Oxford University Press.

2

FROM THE COMMUNIST MANIFESTO TO JACOBIN MAGAZINE

Towards a Historical Sociology of Radical Journalism

George Souvlis

This chapter aims to examine the relationship of the political left with journal-istic practices from the mid-19th century to the current conjuncture. My argu-ment is that this type of relationship is not defined so much by relevant economic or technological determinants but rather by the nature of politics that different political lefts endorsed through the time. In other words, the special features of knowledge, propaganda and self-representation that the political left aimed to pro-mote through its journalistic practices was defined by the wider politics to which its subscribed. This practically implies that the content and the aims of journalism that the political left developed reflected – most of times in a direct way – the type of politics it promoted. For example, the type of politics that *L' Ordine Nuovo*, the weekly newspaper that Gramsci set up in 1919, promoted was quite different from that of *Pravda* during the era of Stalinism. The degree to which promoted politics was emancipatory or not, the openness of the on-going debate, the cause of inter-nationalism, the challenge of the patriarchal order, the specificities of the discussion on the social transition, the relation of the promoted Marxism with other political ideologies, the politics of everyday life and other issues found in the different forms of radical press in different historical periods and geographies were structurally linked to the political party, social movement or governmental formation to which the press was affiliated. This phenomenon should be explained with reference to the fact that the political left since the French Revolution did not aim just to interpret the world but also to change it. Thus, the journalistic practices and the institutions that accompanied it have always a prescriptive character in terms of which direc-tion the social change will orient itself and how this will happen. The key target of the radical journalism of the political left is the capitalist system and its economic, political and ideological parameters. In this sense, radical journalism functions as an antagonistic form of public discourse against capitalism itself. Though, given what has been already said, even the way that it conceptualizes and perceives the existing

DOI: 10.4324/9781003221784-2

system of exploitation is defined by the politics within which it is inscribed. I will demonstrate my argument by presenting key examples of radical journalism that have been formed from the 1850s until today.

Historically, radical journalism is a phenomenon that emerged with the outbreak of the French revolution. This event gave birth to some of its historical preconditions. First of all, in the French Revolution someone can detect the emergence of the modern political ideologies, part of which is the political left. Additionally, it established the Freedom of the Press as an organic part of The Declaration of the Rights of the Man and of the Citizen giving for the first time voices to the subaltern classes and the political powers that were aligned to them (Popkin, 1990). In other words, the event of French Revolution opened the historical preconditions for the emergence of an alternative, radical public sphere that was not under the direct control of the propertied classes. The event itself that offered a radically different organization of the political enabled the emerging political imaginaries to think of radical social change as a historical possibility. In this sense, the type of journalism that emerges in this context includes forms that perceive the reality as something that can radically change through political action. Thus, the act of writing in newspapers, leaflets, reviews, magazines and other forms of printed communication transformed from an act of legitimization of the political power to an intellectual enterprise that included challenges to this political power. This does not mean that most of the journalistic outlets in Europe during and after the French Revolution functioned as radical intellectual alternatives of the political realities of the time. Rather, this period saw the mergence of some of the key historical conditions of possibility for radical journalism. On the contrary, during the 19th century, the majority of the press publications were owned, written on behalf of and for the emerging bourgeoisie and the collapsing aristocracy. The serious challenge of hegemony's dominant press from the political left will take place only when the latter will develop robust organizational forms, something that only happened during the 20th century. Another important change that the events of 1789 triggered, and which directly affected the way in which journalism was structured, was to whom it was addressed, its new audience. The change of the way in which the political was constituted having now as point of reference "the people" and not metaphysical forces defined its new audience. The "people" – those who constituted the new nation states – were the new target of the press (Skocpol, 2014). Of course, the new nation states in practical terms did not include everyone since not everyone could participate in the political sphere nor could everyone read, write and buy newspaper copies. Though, as the franchise was expanding and more people gained the right to educate themselves through the emerging national institutions of education, more and more people could become the possible audience of the different news forms of journalism let alone its radical version. A last aspect connected to the launch of political modernity and journalism is that the French Revolution demonstrated the impact of the press in mobilizing the masses. The Napoleonic era was the most indicative time period when the mass propaganda through the press had a direct impact in the political sphere. The dominant classes and authorities of Europe after the defeat of Napoleon would be very careful with the freedom of speech fearing that it could produce events of equal importance and subversiveness with this of French Revolution. Thus, the history of journalism in the counter-revolutionary era will be developed in relation to the different trajectories that political liberalism followed, something that affected its radical version as well. In other words, there was not a linear progressive development of the democratization of the different forms of communication but rather a war of manoeuvers and intense continuous struggles over freedom of the press as a non-given right.

The new expanding audience of the press implied also the use of a new language that would be accessible to those considered to belong to the nation. Thus, several newspapers from this point on will be written in the vernacular languages that were understandable to the growing reading national community. Because of this, the press retained its relative autonomy from the political but started to become steadily an integral aspect of it. Thus, we can observe a parallel trajectory of the democratization of politics along with the widening of journalistic practices. This historical process functions also a way of self-consciousness of the society itself and its distinctive modern character. In other words, the press of the period after the French Revolution contributed in a substantive way to the realization that capitalism was a distinct historical formation offering a different experience of historical time and sense of belonging. It was one of the key factors that embedded the self-understanding of the modernity's subjectivity, or as Fredric Jameson (1984) has put it, functioned as facilitator of "the cognitive mapping" of modernity (89).

The reaction that followed after the fall of Napoleon Bonaparte and the attempt by the dominant press to develop a counter-revolutionary discourse against the gains of the French Revolution from the 1850s onwards were substituted by a systematic discourse that propagated the ideology of the bourgeoisie. The bourgeoisie was now not just financially dominant but politically as well (Hobsbawm, 1975). This period was also a formative one for the working class as well; it saw the gradual transition from the artisan/craftsman to the factory worker (Marx, 1976). In the first decades of the 19th century, radical journalism in terms of content reflects this slow and painful transition. There was not an explicit class-oriented analysis that informs the analyses of the radical outlets because it is a historical process in the making and it is accompanied by several antinomies. Thus, the political lines of left journalistic understanding of the capitalist society in the making remained blurred. Class-based analysis will emerge as an ongoing practice on behalf of the radical journalists only after the revolutions of 1848 when the distinctions between classes will become clearer and the working class will differentiate its political identity from this of bourgeoisie (Dowe, 2000). Parallel technological innovations of the time such as the telegraph, the telephone, the typewriter, the trans-Atlantic cable, the rotary press and photography proved decisive for the massification and commercialization of the press. The proliferation of advertisements in the pages of the press transformed most of it outlets to commodities of the expanding market economy. The fact that most of the outlets of the press at that time were organically linked to the capitalist market while its radical forms attempted to improve or in some cases overthrow capitalism became one of the key distinctions between the two forms of journalism.

This is the historical point from which starts the history of radical journalism that I will narrate. This is a conscious choice. The 1840s is a turning point because 1848 was the year when *The Communist Manifesto* of Karl Marx and Friedrich Engels was published. This pamphlet introduced an explicit class analysis and launched a Marxist understanding of society linked to the First International and its successors. In other words, *The Communist Manifesto* launched a specific theoretical and political tradition that would define the latter trajectory of the global left. Journalists – who were at the same (time) activists – like Thomas Paine and William Cobbett and movements like Chartism were very important in their time but did not have the global impact of the politics and theoretical work of Karl Marx and Friedrich Engels.

It is especially noteworthy that Karl Marx worked for almost all his adult life as a journalist, writing for different German, British and American newspapers analysing different events of political and economic significance that he further used in his philosophical or economic writings. In this sense, Marx's works have been formed by, and to a certain extent are products of, the analyses that he offered in his journalistic pieces that launched penetrative insights into the developments in the globe for the second half of the 19th century. Thus, Marx's Marxism is an extension and re-elaboration of key events of his time. This was not something that he did only in order to earn money but perceived it as a task of understanding the historical specificities of his time, a precondition for his theoretical works that were naturally more abstract. This work by Marx has been underestimated by his analysts with the exception of few recent studies that have been engaged with this aspect (Marx the Journalist, 2018).

Additionally, Marx's writings on newspapers aimed to do political propaganda. This is a feature that informs *The Communist Manifesto* as well. The writing, conception and publication of this pamphlet demonstrates a wider political transformation for the trajectory of the workers movement itself. Its composition signalled the transition from a clandestine form of political action to a legal one. This shift is crystallized as well in the transformation of the League of the Just – in which Marx and Engels participated – from a secret radical organization to a legal political society renamed as The Communist League (Hobsbawm, 2012). The pamphlet of *The Communist Manifesto* was the political guide of the League aiming to appeal to the masses of workers to participate in an organization that would be open and legal. In this sense, *The Communist Manifesto* signalled the rejection of the Blanquist tactics that considered the communist cause to be in the hands of small illegal violent organizations and the emergence of mass politics that had the need of propaganda (Greene, 2017). This document could be interpreted as implicit acceptance of modern politics and the way that has been organized since the French Revolution. Political modernity in its ideal form, among others, implies free political antagonism between different political formations, the use of propaganda in order to appeal to voters, legal political entities that function as the basic elements of the aforementioned antagonism and political ideologies that speak in the name of the people (Rosich & Wagner, 2016). With the writing of *The Communist Manifesto*, Marx and Engels come to approve these realities as inseparable aspects of modern politics. This argument does not suggest an ahistorical conception of Marx and Engels' politics; rather, it proposes that in their understanding, the hegemonic consensus, a concept that will become later known in the Marxist terminology through the work of Antonio Gramsci, was an unavoidable aspect of the modern form of the political.

Beyond the programmatic aims of the League, this pamphlet proposed a materialist understanding of historical process putting in its epicentre the concept of class struggle. The phrase "The history of all hitherto existing society is the history of class struggles" encapsulates the political and to a certain extent the theoretical analysis that informed Marxism from this point on (Marx & Engels, 2012). It is an epistemological claim that has a teleological character and perceives the historical process as the history of class struggle and seeks to reconstruct it under this perspective. In this sense, the approach they propose has an explicit presentist character.

In political terms, this historical document suggests the historical praxis as the way through which the working classes will promote their interests. Workers should unite on the basis of their objective class interests derived from the specific social position they hold within the capitalist social formation. *The Communist Manifesto* though is not just a descriptive but also a prescriptive text aiming to contribute to the transformation of the working class from a class in itself to a class for itself, something that has not been achieved when the pamphlet was composed but was posed as one of the key aims of the communist movement since then. Thus, propaganda means such as *The Communist Manifesto* were considered to be intellectual vehicles through which the workers could gain class consciousness. This attempt though was not just the product of a genius duo but the outcome of the collectivity: The Communist League.

The next episode in the history of the relationship of the political left and the means of communicational propaganda is the period between the formation of the First and the Second International during the late 19th and early 20th centuries. During this period, there were wider transformations that defined the political left and consequently its relation with the different forms of journalistic practices. Two key historical transitions which are interlinked to this period are the slow transitions from empires to nation states (Breuilly, 2017) and the liberalization of the political sphere through the implementation of constitutions throughout Europe (Rapport, 2012). This affected drastically the socialist movements of the period since they accepted and exploited this structural framework to adjust their political action. A political party that was linked to a union or unions aiming to achieve significant social reforms for the working classes within an expanding liberal political framework became the canon for the western and central Europe since then. The reformist parties of the Second International are those that attempted to achieve the expansion of the democratic framework of the nation states within they are acting by attempting to enlarge the franchise to the male members of the working classes. In addition to the right to vote, they attempted also to give social content to democracy (Eley, 2002).

The Social Democratic Party of Germany that was the most massive among the socialist parties of the period crystallized all the aforementioned developments. The outlets that were politically linked to it proved to be a key instrument in the party's identity building. Through the pages of its theoretical journal *Die Neue Zeit* that was published from 1883 to 1923, Marxism became the official ideology of the party (Dorrien, 2019). The debates it hosted formed a version of Marxism that was compatible with the political choices of the party: an adherence to the institutional framework of the emerging national bourgeois societies and its perception as an accepted social and political reality within which they can function, the rejection of Marx's idea that the capitalist system tends to produce recurrent financial crisis, a progressivist understanding of the historical process, the nation state as an indispensable point of reference of its action and the class-based analysis in which the working class is the political motor of the history securing its strongholds in the society through its union-based organizing (Sasson, 2010). The diffusion of these ideas to the wider working classes was achieved through the newspapers of the party. The central organ was *Vörwarts*, a newspaper founded in 1876 and which still exists, but it was not alone. As the social historian Geoff Eley notes, in 1913 there were 94 party newspapers, 90 of which were daily with a circulation of 150,000 sheets (Eley, 2002, 44). These impressive numbers can be explained with reference to wider historical transformations that occurred in the period of the foundation of the Second International (1889) until the eve of WWI. These can summed up as forging the irreversible passage to modernity: massive factories, urbanization, working class communities with their discrete spatial existence and the expansion of capital to all forms of social life. This implied a transformation of the working class from a class itself to class for itself, something that included a distinct way of life and distinct self-identity (Eley 2002, 59). The formation of reading groups with material the newspapers of the party was contributing to and was forging these shifts. These changes of course did not happen only in the German version of socialism but also in different parts of Europe. This made necessary the multiplication of efforts to propagandize the communist ideology throughout the world. Indicative of this focus was the translation of *The Communist Manifesto* in more than 30 languages until 1918 (Eley, 2002, 43).

However, the reformism associated with the Social Democratic Party was not destined to remain the key doctrine of the socialist movement. The geopolitical shifts that emerged with the break-up of WWI posed new political dilemmas, gave voice and formed new political actors and rearranged significantly the priorities and character of the socialist movement. Against the predictions of Marx that a successful revolution will occur in the developed countries of the West where social polarization was intense and the working class transformed to a massive political force leading the events, this happened to the dissolving empire of the Tsarist Russia where the proletariat was a minority compared to the rest of the working people who were peasants. The agrarian population of Tsarist Russia was not at all familiar with the Marxist ideology and its organized politics. However, a combination of structural and conjunctural reasons contributed to the formation of the first Socialist state there with the success of Bolshevik revolution (Smith, 2002). In the conjunctural reasons that could interpret this event one cannot omit, reversing Hegel's famous phrase, the "Cunning of Politics" that can be summed in the political practice of Dual Power. This term, coined by the Bolshevik leader Vladimir Lenin in a homonym article in the newspaper *Pravda* in order to conceptualize the antagonism between the Social Democratic Provisional Government and the Bolshevik Soviets, which endorsed the latter as the political vehicle through which the socialist transition should be achieved (Sotiris, 2014). Rejecting an understanding of a transition in stages, that implied for the case of Russia a successful Bourgeois Revolution that sought to be established with the February Revolution, Lenin propagated the slogan "All power to the Soviets" considering that the conditions were mature enough for a successful revolution after July's events.

Lenin's use of the socialist press in order to propagate his analysis of the direction the revolutionary practice in the conjuncture of the revolutions of 1917 was not an one-off action. Lenin was involved both as journalist and editor of socialist newspapers throughout his life. He was an avid reader of the bourgeois press and his contributions to the socialist newspapers and the writing of pamphlets aimed, among others, to combat the ways in which the social and political developments of his time were interpreted, offering alternative counter narratives of them. In one of his pamphlets, *What Is to be done?*, that formed decisively not only his politics and this of Bolshevik tradition, but also the history of the communist movement in its entirety, he described the establishment of a newspaper as one of the key tasks of socialists (Lih, 2008). In this sense, the vanguard party of revolutionaries that he suggests in this work as the key organization through which the revolutionary politics would be conducted was inconceivable without its own newspaper. Given this importance assigned to the press, Lenin participated in the editorial board of *Iskra* that was the official organ of the Russian Social Democratic Party, a newspaper which he will quickly abandon (1903) due to the reformist politics it endorsed (Lih, 2008). From this point on, Lenin's politics as promoted in *What Is to be Done?* will constitute one of the key political targets of the newspaper perceiving them as terrorist actions that undermine the socialist cause which could gain leverage only through implementation of political reforms. This debate is suggestive of the role that the press, even in its clandestine form, played in the Russian socialist movement: forming and delineating the discrete political identities and ideologies of the different traditions that co-existed within it. The propaganda of the socialist cause was not the sole role that Lenin assigned to the press. According to him, "the newspaper is not only a collective propagandist and a collective agitator, it is a collective organizer" (Lenoe, 2004, 27). With this phrase, the Bolshevik revolutionary meant that press was not only an institution that could diffuse the ideas of the movement but also could be used as an organ that will facilitate the self-consciousness of its existing members creating a robust political identity necessary for the clarification of the tasks that the revolutionaries have to undertake.

This understanding proved very crucial in the events of the Russian Civil War. The success of the Bolshevik propaganda was one of the features that could account for the victory of the Red Army in the Russian Civil War.

The success of the Russian Revolution did not only change the history of the country itself but also the political landscape of the 20th century as a whole. It set an example of how a revolution can be successful in overthrowing a previous political order and the ideal type of the revolutionary party: a group of disciplined ideologues that are specialists in the art of modern politics combining in a successful way the war of manoeuvers with the wars of positions. The Russian Revolution formed also a distinct tradition in the political left that rejected bourgeois parliamentarianism, the pro-imperialist stance of Social Democracy that was endorsed during WWI and the idea and tactics of progressivism. WWI and the contradictions that it produced proved the cataclysmic event that defined the political physiognomies of the different political lefts for the rest of the century (Hobsbawm, 1994). In the aftermath of its break up, the events of WWI created the conditions for the expansion of the "virus" of revolution outside the Russian territory in the heartlands of the European continent. Germany and Italy were two of the countries that seemed to meet the conditions for a successful repetition of the Bolshevik takeover of the power (Anderson, 1979). The reaction that both attempts confronted from the political establishments along with a series of mistakes in the political calculations and the tactics that the respective communist movements made proved fatal for the success of these experiments. After these defeats, the Bolsheviks remained isolated, something that in turn defined to a certain extent the political nature of the regime. From this point on, the European bourgeoisie will form its identity and politics in opposition to the Bolshevik experiment.

In the Italian case, the uprising took place in the north-west part of the country with the Red Biennium of 1919–1920 and took the form of occupations, strikes and experiments of self-management of the factories organized by the workers of Milan and Turin areas. Following the example of Soviets in Russia, Workers Councils emerged claiming a different way of running factories putting in the epicentre of its action the democratic control of them by the workers themselves transforming the existing model of their governance characterized by a clear dividing line between employers and employees (Williams, 1975). This reality though did not lead to an overthrowing of the Italian political system since the political leadership of the left (PSI and CGL) did not play an equivalent role to the Bolsheviks, refusing to lead a direct confrontation with state apparatus and thus leaving the revolutionary transformation of the country an unfulfilled potentiality. Interestingly, the industrial unrest was accompanied by rural uprising in the area Po Valley refuting Marx's understanding of peasants as a reactionary group, an argument found in *The 18th Brumaire of Louis Bonaparte* where he described them as a "sack of potatoes" (Cowling & Martin, 2002, 100). Thus, the historical framework of massive unemployment, political instability, soldiers' desertion and a massive socialist political agitation that was created in the years after the end of WWI was not exploited by the political representatives of the Italian working class in order to establish a socialist success story in Western Europe. The Italian case of worker and peasant revolts and their self-organizational models further demonstrated the rejection of representative parliamentary politics and the adoption of a more direct and substantial democratic governance of the political and economic sphere.

The movement of the Workers Council very quickly found its theoretical though organic voice in the pages of the weekly newspaper *L' Ordine Nuovo* that was established on May 1919 headed, among others, by Antonio Gramsci, Angelo Tasca and Palmiro Togliatti, members of the Italian Sociality Party. The newspaper, despite its initial cultural orientation, quickly understood that the stakes of the time given the worker mobilization were mainly political and thus turned its focus to the ongoing struggles developing an organic relationship with the participants of the events:

> On 1 November *L' Ordine Nuovo* reported how a meeting of delegates from 25 factories representing 50,000 workers discussed putting the ideas into practice. The next week its sales shot up to 10,000 as it carried the programme of the first assembly of Turin factory councils.
>
> *Harman, 2003*

Taking this into account, it is evident that in the case of *L' Ordine Nuovo*, journalism was used as a means to shape and articulate the demands of the Italian working class. Interestingly enough, the newspaper opposed the decisions of the leadership of the socialist movement that refused to polarize further the social struggle leading to a revolutionary change.

One of the editors of *L' Ordine Nuovo* would become later one of the most important figures of the communist movement in the 20th century: Antonio Gramsci. His interventions radically changed the way socialist strategy was perceived, offering an analysis with different emphases on the ways it should be pursued in the context of the robust bourgeois states of the West (Riley, 2011). While the Bolsheviks successfully took control in a very quick and abrupt way without a lot of resistance from the Tsarist political establishment, the Italian Communists believed that this could not happen so easily in West Europe. This is because the Western states were more robust compared to their Russian counterpart not only because their repressive apparatus was more effective but also because they exercised more successfully the hegemonic consensus within the European societies. For Gramsci, this meant that in Western societies, it was not enough for socialists to attack the state apparatus but they should also gain hegemonic consensus among different social groups as a political precondition for a successful post-bourgeois transition (Riley & Souvlis, 2016). In this sense, ideological preparation was equally important to political organizing and the war of manoeuvers. Given this understanding, journalism and the press for Gramsci were conceived as an organic part of the ideological struggle that the socialists should conduct in order to appeal effectively to the working classes.

It is not accidental that Antonio Gramsci before *L' Ordine Nuovo* had worked for several years as a journalist for left-wing newspapers such as *Il Grido del Popolo* and *Avanti* and then founded the historic newspaper of the PCI (Partito Comunista Italiano), *l'Unità* in 1924. These choices were indicative of Gramsci's prioritization of the need for a robust socialist press as a means to diffuse and make familiar socialist ideas to wider masses contributing to their ideological formation. André Tosel has defined this type of journalism as an "integral" one, given that it was considered an organic part of the ongoing hegemonic struggle on behalf of the socialists (Tosel, 2005, 67). Thus, for Gramsci the communist press was a vital element to the war of position by offering a counter-hegemonic narration of events combating those produced by the bourgeois newspapers. In his writings, Gramsci attempted to combine the particular (of the ongoing events) with the general (the socialist point of view) contributing in that way to the formation of a worldview that would interact in a dialectical way with the philosophy of praxis (Thomas, 2015). The understanding of the centrality of the party as a key institution through which the political struggle will be conducted did not mean for him that the party was the sole actor that would define the ideological debate in the pages of the newspapers and the magazines related to it in a top-down relationship (Rüdiger, 2018). He was more in favour of a multipolarity of influences by and exchanges with different political, social and cultural actors that would contribute in their own ways to the general intellect that would form the antagonistic worldview to the bourgeois conceptualizations of the world.

This openness of perspective would stop to be the canon in the communist movement after the domination of Stalin in the ranks of the CPSU (Communist Party of the Soviet Union) something that affected the global trajectory of Communism along with the developments in the internal political life in Russia. The catastrophic tactics of the CPSU from 1928 onwards, which are summed up in the phrase of "class against class", considering social democratic organizations as an enemy of the Communist movement led it to significant defeats, of which the emerging far right took advantage (Worley, 2017). The defeat of Biennio Rosso in Italy had already allowed Mussolini to take the power with the help of the political and economic status quo of the country establishing the first among many authoritarian regimes that would follow up during the interwar years. The fascist phenomenon of the interwar years can be interpreted, as Dylan Riley has suggested, as the inability of the political systems of the period to articulate the emerging demands from below, a historical chance that fascists took advantage of and captured political power (Riley, 2019). These developments did not allow communist journalism to function in a way that would promote the revolutionary cause since in most countries it became a clandestine activity and where it was legal, it propagated the line of Stalin's policies. This changed only after the conquest of the power by the NSDAP (Nazi party) in 1933 that worried the Soviet Union and made it adopt the tactics of the Popular Front where broader alliances with liberal and social democratic parties pursued (Horn, 1997). This experience defined many communists that perceived it as the most viable solution not only when it was the official line of the CPSU but also during the WWII and the decades that followed it. Radical journalism during the WWII proved a very useful weapon for the communist international for organizing the common people, boosting their morale and diffusing useful information for the different fronts of war (Dell, 2007).

The post-world war conditions brought a series of changes that radically changed the globe (Romero, 2014). The first significant change was the division of the world in two antagonistic camps: the Western and the Eastern bloc. This dividing line would hold until the collapse of the Soviet Union. The second significant change was the decision on behalf of the economic and political elites of the time to expand the welfare state in the most part of the Western world as antidotes to the financial realities and their political repercussions during the interwar period (Emigh, Riley, & Ahmed, 2016). From the mid-forties until the mid-seventies, this reality remained unchallenged. The emergence of welfare institutions in the Western world meant that for the first time in history for a part of the world the employment of its population was secured through state intervention, that the same population gained access to a wide gamut of social rights and that the economic elites consciously decided to reduce the financial gap between the different social classes. One of the many implications of the historical shifts was that the working classes in the West experienced a significant improvement in their living conditions, making insurrectionary moments of the interwar period seem like a distant and unnecessary reality. The postwar economic advancements of the Soviet Union played a significant role in pushing towards the development of similar regulatory regimes in the West. The third development was the anticolonial struggles that emerged from the 1950s onwards in Africa, Asia and Latin America (Rothermund, 2006). The fourth development had to do with the success of the Chinese Communist Revolution (Souvlis, Rodriguez, & Smith, 2018). These historical shifts destabilized certainties of centuries and made the revolution still a historical possibility, but this time, its geographical point of reference was neither in Russia nor in the advanced capitalist societies but in the peripheries of capitalism. Last but not least, the popularization of television as a mean of communication radically changed the ways in which propaganda, advertising and entertainment were conducted (Williams, 2003).

This historical context was the structural substratum of political developments during the following three decades. In the terrain of left-wing politics, the leak of secret speech by Nikita Khrushchev denouncing the Stalinist policies of terror had a great impact on most of the communist parties of the world (Bracke, 2007). It triggered several splits in its ranks with the key issues including the denouncement or not of the new reality, the relation of the Communist Parties with the CPSU, the desirable form of the communist party and the nature of the Soviet Union and its role to the communist cause. A few months later, the Soviet invasion of Hungary confirmed that CPSU had followed a path that was distant from the initial aspirations of its founder Vladimir Lenin (Lendvai, 2008). Indicative of the impact that these events had on European Communists are the words of Stuart Hall (2010): "'Hungary' brought to an end a certain kind of socialist innocence" (177).

In the United Kingdom, the Communist Party was, in terms of membership and influence, a rather small organization compared to its continental counterparts. Nevertheless, it exercised significant influence on intellectuals and unionists. The former reacted to the political developments in Eastern Europe and attempted to raise them as significant issues for debate. The debate regarding these issues was conducted, among other outlets, in the pages of the journal *Reasoner* that was founded in 1956 by the two historians: E. P. Thompson and John Saville (Kenny, 1995). The Stalinist leadership of the party though did not welcome this publication and the wider political initiative by the two dissidents expelling them from the party. They did not remain passive, and after the events in Hungary, they decided to launch a new journal with the name *New Reasoner* gathering different intellectual figures related with the CPGB, aiming at "the re-discovery of our traditions, the affirmation of socialist values, and the undogmatic perception of social reality" (Davidson, 2019). Most of the intellectuals who participated in this initiative were historians coming from the Communist Party Historians Group, a rather heterodox enclave of historians who offered new and radical readings of British history, putting at its centre the "British people". This can be explained with reference to the fact that during the Popular Front era, class was substituted by the nation although in a critical way since different nations were struggling to defeat the Nazis and their allies. For Hobsbawm, another historian who was part of this milieu, in this historical moment there was a clash between the forces of enlightenment and counter-enlightenment (Souvlis, 2019). This experience had significant impact and affected the way people perceived not only their present but also their past. This tendency is reflected also in the historical writings of E. P. Thompson, where there is a conscious attempt to create, along with the other historians in the CPGB, a counterhegemonic, invented tradition of the British nation, which could challenge the dominant narrative and be politically inspirational in the postwar British context. Thompson's most significant contribution in theoretical terms was that of socialist humanism, offered in the pages of *New Reasoner*. It was his theoretical reply to the Stalinist orthodoxy with explicit political implications. Thompson was inspired theoretically by the early writings of Karl Marx and politically by the anti-Stalinist struggles that were occurring at that time in Eastern Europe. This approach did not inform only his historical writings but also the forthcoming politics of the British New Left that attempted to formulate a political identity that opposed both against the Soviet Union and against Western Imperialism. The *New Reasoner* initiative was one of its key components. The movement around which the first British New Left was built was the Campaign for Nuclear Disarmament that was the key institutional vehicle of peace activists from 1958 to 1965. In terms of the relation of the British Communist dissidents and journalism, their journals formed the key outlets around which they sought to articulate their disagreement with Stalinist policies, to suggest a different narration and epistemology on the way they imagined left theory and politics and these became a key intellectual source through which the New Left of the 1960s was structured itself as opposition to this tradition.

The 1960s were different from the previous decade to the extent that material achievements of the welfare state had been established and the generation born the during the first years of the postwar period had come of age in a context of, for the first time in history, material security and access to newly obtained social rights, albeit limited to a certain part of the Western world. This generation – the baby boomers – had significantly different experiences from their parents and those who fought in WWII and thus had very different social expectations. Their key opposition to the previous generation that grew up in the interwar fascist Europe was the conservative culture inherited during the cold war period. This new generation revolted for almost a decade from the mid-1960s to the mid-1970s in different parts of the world claiming a different way of life away from the mentalities of their parents. However, it did not assume a "hippie" orientation, as some have claimed. The 1968ers conducted struggles that followed explicit anti-imperialist, feminist and socialist directions challenging basic underpinnings of the capitalist realities of the time. The victory of the armed struggle in Cuba and the defeat of the American troops in Vietnam became two of the key points of reference in the struggles of the 1968ers creating, as Goran Therborn (1968) has argued, a dialectic of events between the metropolis and the ex-colonies. Another structural development that affected this generation was the expansion of higher education both as a need of the restructuring of the capitalist economy and as an expansion of the right to education. The student population multiplied throughout the world. Thus, for first time in history, the youth had the opportunity to spend its student years without the necessity to earn a living, and to be formed as a distinct social group with its own identity. A parallel significant change was that the world became much "smaller" given the development of technologies of communication and transportation facilitating the development of networks between people in different parts of the world and the development of a more international or global sense of "we".

One journal in the English-speaking world that encapsulates these developments was the *New Left Review*. It began its life as the intellectual vehicle of the British New Left including personalities such as E. P. Thompson, Stuart Hall and Raphael Samuel. Very quickly, both its political and theoretical position changed when Perry Anderson and a younger group (Robin Blackburn and Tom Nairn) of socialists undertook its editorship aiming to imitate the French journal *Les Temps Modernes* that was initiated by Jean Paul Sartre, Simon de Beauvoir and Maurice Merleau-Ponty. The focus now was more global covering developments outside Britain and with an epistemological emphasis on sociology and political theory. *New Left Review* played a very significant role translating in English significant essays from the Western Marxist tradition (Frankfurt School, French Structuralism and Existentialism, Antonio Gramsci and György Lukács) and introducing for the first time the works of these writers to the English-speaking world. The political focus expanded outside the Western world covering the guerrilla wars in Latin America during the long 1960s with a special emphasis on Cuba. The armed struggle considered now as a legitimate way to take power projecting it as a necessary step for the leftists of the Western world. The shifting point for the New Left Reviewers came with the student revolts in 1968. The journal rejected parliamentarianism and reformism as a legitimate way for the left to take the power and endorsed the insurrectionary politics of the Leninist tradition. Many from the editorial board became members of the International Marxist Group, the section of the Fourth International in Britain reaffirming the tendency of radicalization that became a canon for the youth. Western Marxism and its politics were rejected as theories that do not promote the theory with praxis as the Marxist tradition promoted until the defeat of the German Revolution. Thus, this was considered as a limitation that the Marxists of their time should overcome. Summing up, for the next decade *New Left Review* returned to classical Marxism in order to get theoretical inspiration rejecting the theoretical traditions of socialist humanism and Western Marxism. Revolutionary insurrection was considered as the only method that could lead to dictatorship of the proletariat both in the east and west. Thus, it focused its political attention on the struggles occurring in Latin American and Asia where the insurrectionist moments of the local movements were renewing their political hopes.

Despite the suggested revisionisms compared to the older left and these of the Communist Parties of Europe, *New Left Review* did not succeed in bridging the gap between theory and praxis, remaining a theoretical journal of analysis that contributed valuable insights though disconnected from the struggles of the time (Souvlis, 2020). Its editorial board followed the professional trajectory of many New Leftists, working in academia, away from the needs and the visions of the working class. The paradigms of *L' Ordine Nuovo* and the clandestine newspapers of the Russian revolutionaries that were organically linked with the cause of revolution remained examples that were not followed. On the contrary, the *New Left Review* followed in terms of content the trajectory of its editorship becoming more academic and less optimistic about the possibility of a revolutionary rupture that will overturn capitalism.

The revolutionary 1960s and 1970s were followed by a conservative revolution in the 1980s crystallized in the governments of Thatcher in Britain and Reagan in the United States, respectively. The latter functioning as counter-revolutionary hegemon contributed, among others, to the establishment of Augusto Pinochet's dictatorship in Chile. The break-ups of the Soviet Union and Yugoslavia as developments allowed the United States to be the sole world superpower. This counter-revolutionary shift was completed when the prospects of democratic renewal in ex-Soviet countries proved to be an illusion, with their political systems to be dominated by corrupt oligarchs.

More generally, the neoliberal right became dominant worldwide and the liberal left (including social democracy) lost any potential autonomous presence as it completely caved to neoliberal dogmas. Meanwhile, the left was unable to offer any long-term vision or practicable economic and political solutions alternative to the neoliberal status quo. Books like *The End of the History and the Last Man* that championed these shifts became the common sense of the period.

Karl Marx's Old Mole appeared though again in the 21st century, this time not with the version of a revolution as the communist philosopher expected but with the Pink Tide and the global financial crisis of 2008 that radically changed the sphere of politics. The extreme centre destabilized by forces coming both from the left and the right of the political spectrum leading to a series of shifts creating openings for political players that the liberal analysts of the previous era could not image as a historical possibility. Austerity imposed throughout the globe as an antidote by the forces of extreme centre to the ongoing economic crisis destabilizing further the political systems of the west. From the left, the response was the emergence of anti-austerities parties (Syriza, Podemos, Corbyn's Labour Party and Bernie Sander's movement) that considered that it was possible to implement progressive policies without further ruptures with the capitalist establishment, an illusion that led to a series of defeats with the most impressive one to be with the case of Syriza. Alexis Tsipras rose to power promising a progressive governance that would refute the neoliberal policies that had been implemented by the previous austerity government. In reality, what happened after its reelection in September 2015 was the implementation of one of the hardest neoliberal political programmes that a government had ever put in action.

The left-wing parties and movements that emerged since 2010 develop their own media but this time it was through online formats since the internet dominated the globe in the sphere of communication. The anti-globalization movement in the beginning of the 20th century also used alternative online media to organize political mobilizations, using them as a source of information. The multiplication of users, the emergence of social media and the global character of the crisis of 2008 gave another leverage to the dialectic between the internet and political organizing.

One of the most successful examples of online left-wing media that emerged in the aftermath of the global financial crisis was the Jacobin magazine. It was established in 2010 by Bhaskar Sunkara declaring that his political aim and the reasoning behind its foundations was:

> I felt like there was a huge amount of intellectual space there that wasn't being filled. Other publications like the venerable Third Camp journal *New Politics* were born out of different generations that had a different style of engagement, so we felt that there was room for a new batch of young writers to engage in these ideas. Within the left, I wanted to assert the primacy of class analysis and some of the oft-maligned "old ideas," especially among young writers and academics who are usually culturalist in their orientation. But it wasn't just that, because I also thought that socialist ideas could still have broad appeal beyond the left and beyond academia. So *Jacobin* was set up to be a popular venue that would reach not just a few thousand people, but hundreds of thousands if not millions of people eventually.
>
> *Souvlis and Sunkara, 2016*

Its global scope covering developments throughout the globe, the understandable style of the articles away from the academic jargon, the combination of a non-dogmatic robust theoretical and political content along with attractive aesthetics has functioned as an ideal platform for the diffusion of radical ideas and alternative narrations. In terms of politics, Jacobin was linked first with the Occupy Movement and then the movement around Bernie Sanders in 2016 and his presidential campaign attempting to function as a space of open discussion for the political direction of the movement, popularizing its reasoning. This involvement had as an outcome the significant increase of subscriptions to its print version and its site visits. The politics endorsed are not all of the same variant – meaning social democracy. It has endorsed, among others, both in Latin America and in Europe ongoing struggles whose political connotations are far from the typical social democratic version of politics. The support or not of specific struggles has to do not so much with an a priori theoretical or political commitment but more with a conjunctural understanding of the context and the balance of forces in each country. Recently, there were foreign language editions of the magazine in Italian, German and Spanish. A limitation that can be detected is its strong emphasis on class issues undermining sometimes issues related to gender and race and other forms of oppression. Its achievements though are far more important than its limitations succeeding to introduce theoretical insights and political analysis to a global progressive audience that is searching for information in order to understand the complicated world within which we live and to orient accordingly its political action.

Alternative radical media platforms are necessary more than ever for the global left. The dominance of the neoliberal media and the representation of the capitalist realities as the only alternative should be radically challenged. The examples had been set – not only with outlets such as *Jacobin* but also outside the Western world with the media initiatives of the Kurdish movements and those developed in Latin America. Their importance has been great in the growing of a movement, as the recent Jean-Luc Mélenchon's pre-electoral campaign demonstrated in the most emphatic way. However, as it has been argued in the article, communication has proved useful for the struggles of the left when the media have been organically connected to them. This is the stake we have to confront for the future: non-dogmatic, accessible and informative media that will be informed and will inform the different projects of the left.

References

Anderson, P. (1979). *Considerations on Western Marxism*. London: Verso.

Bracke, M. (2007). *Which Socialism? Whose Detente? West European Communism and the Czechoslovak Crisis of 1968*. Budapest: Central European University Press.

Breuilly, J. (2017). Modern empires and nation-states. *Thesis Eleven*, 139(1), 11–29.

Cowling, M. & Martin, J. (Eds.). (2002). *Marx's 'Eighteenth Brumaire': (Post) Modern Interpretations*. London: Pluto Press.

Davidson, S. (2019). 'An outrageous expansion': Soundings, the New Left and the boundaries of politics and culture. *Eurozine*, available at: www.eurozine.com/an-outrageous-expansion/

Dell, S. (2007). *The Image of the Popular Front: The Masses and the Media in Interwar France*. London: Palgrave Macmillan.

Dorrien, G. (2019). *Social Democracy in the Making: Political and Religious Roots of European Socialism.* Yale: Yale University Press.

Dowe, D. (Ed.). (2000). *Europe in 1848: Revolution and Reform.* New York: Berghahn Books.

Eley, G. (2002). *Forging Democracy: The History of the Left in Europe, 1850–2000.* Oxford University Press: Oxford.

Emigh, R. J., Riley, D. J., & Ahmed, P. (2016). *Changes in Censuses from Imperialist to Welfare States: How Societies and States Count.* London: Palgrave Macmillan.

Greene, D. E. (2017). *Communist Insurgent: Blanqui's Politics of Revolution.* Chicago: Haymarket Books.

Hall, S. (2010). Life and times of the First New Left. *New Left Review*, 61, 177–196.

Harman, C. (2003). L'Ordine Nuovo: paper of the Italian revolution. *Socialist Worker*, available at: https://socialistworker.co.uk/features/l-ordine-nuovo-paper-of-the-italian-revolution/

Hobsbawm, E. (1994). *The Age of Extremes: The Short Twentieth Century, 1914–1991.* London: Michael Joseph.

Hobsbawm, E. (1975). *The Age of Capital: 1848–1875.* London: Weidenfeld & Nicolson.

Hobsbawm, E. (2012). Introduction. In Marx. K. and Engels, F. (Eds.), *The Communist Manifesto*, pp. 1–30. London: Verso.

Horn, G-R. (1997). *European Socialists Respond to Fascism: Ideology, Activism and Contingency in the 1930s.* Oxford: Oxford University Press.

Jameson, F. (1984). Postmodernism, or the cultural logic of late capitalism. *New Left Review*, I/146, 53–92.

Kenny, M. (1995). *First New Left: British Intellectuals after Stalin.* London: Lawrence Wishart.

Lendvai, P. (2008). *One Day That Shook the Communist World: The 1956 Hungarian Uprising and Its Legacy.* Princeton: Princeton University Press.

Lenoe, M. (2004). *Closer to the Masses. Stalinist Culture, Soviet Revolution, and Soviet Newspapers.* Cambridge, MA: Harvard University Press.

Lih, L. T. (2008). *Lenin Rediscovered: What Is to be Done? In Context.* Chicago: Haymarket books.

Marx, K. (1976). *Capital*, vol. 1. London: Penguin Books.

Marx, K. & Engels, F. (2012). *The Communist Manifesto.* London: Verso.

Marx the Journalist. (2018). An interview with James Ledbetter. *Jacobin Magazine*, available at: https://jacobin.com/2018/05/karl-marx-journalism-writings-newspaper

Popkin, J. D. (1990). The press and the French Revolution after two hundred years. *French Historical Studies*, 16(3), 664–683.

Rapport, M. (2012). 1848: European revolutions. In Isakhan, B. and Stockwell, S. (Eds.), *The Edinburgh Companion to the History of Democracy*, pp. 282–292. Edinburgh: Edinburgh University Press.

Riley, D.J. (2011). Hegemony, democracy, and passive revolution in Gramsci's *Prison Notebooks. California Italian Studies*, 2(2). https://escholarship.org/uc/item/5x48f0mz

Riley, D.J. (2019). *The Civic Foundations of Fascism in Europe: Italy, Spain, and Romania, 1870–1945.* London: Verso.

Riley, D. J. & Souvlis, G. (2016). Fascism and democracy: An interview with Dylan Riley. *Jacobin Magazine*, available at: https://jacobin.com/2016/08/trump-clinton-fascism-authoritarian-democracy

Romero, F. (2014). Cold War historiography at the crossroads. *Cold War History*, 14(4), 685–703.

Rosich, G. & Wagner, P. (Eds.). (2016). *The Trouble with Democracy: Political Modernity in the 21th Century.* Edinburgh: Edinburgh University Press.

Rothermund, D. (2006). *The Routledge Companion to Decolonization.* London: Routledge.

Rüdiger, F. (2018). Trotsky, Gramsci, and communist journalistic thought between the World Wars. *Medien & Zeit: Kommunikation in Vergangenheit und Gegenwart*, 33(3), 28–38.

Sasson, D. (2010). *One Hundred Years of Socialism: The West European Left in the Twentieth Century*. London: Tauris.

Skocpol, T. (2014). *State and Social Revolutions*. Cambridge: Cambridge University Press.

Sotiris, P. (2014). Rethinking political power and revolutionary strategy today. *Viewpoint Magazine*, available at: https://viewpointmag.com/2014/09/08/rethinking-political-power-and-revolutionary-strategy-today/

Souvlis, G. (2019). The Popular Front and Marxism in Eric Hobsbawm's historical works. *Práticas da História, Journal on Theory, Historiography and Uses of the Past*, 7, 105–131.

Souvlis, G. (2020). The antinomies of Perry Anderson. *Jacobin Magazine*, available at: https://jacobin.com/2020/08/perry-anderson-marxist-historian

Souvlis, G., Rodriguez, A. Z., & Smith, S. A. (2018). Interview with S. A. Smith, *Revolutionary Russia*, 31(2), 208–225.

Souvlis, G. & Sunkara, B. (2016). Marxism, culture and class analysis for the 21th century: An interview with Bhaskar Sunkara. *ROAR Magazine*, available at: https://roarmag.org/essays/jacobin-bhaskar-sunkara-interview/

Smith, S. (2002). *The Russian Revolution. A Very Short Introduction*. Oxford: Oxford University Press.

Therborn, G. (1968). From Petrograd to Saigon. *New Left Review*, I/48, 3–11.

Thomas, P. D. (2015). Gramsci's Marxism: The 'Philosophy of Praxis'. In McNally, M. (Ed.), *Antonio Gramsci. Critical Explorations in Contemporary Political Thought*. London: Palgrave Macmillan.

Tosel, A. (2005). La presse comme appareil d'hegemonie selon Gramsci. *Quaderni*, 57, 55–71.

Williams, G. A. (1975). *Proletarian Order: Antonio Gramsci, Factory Councils and the Origins of Italian Communism, 1911–1921*. London: Pluto Press.

Williams, R. (2003). *Television: Technology and Cultural Form*. London: Routledge.

Worley, M. (2017). *Class against Class: The Communist Party in Britain between the Wars*. London: Bloomsbury Publishing.

3

RIOTS AS POLITICS

Socio-Political Context, Demands, and Media Translation – The Case of 1890s Kristiania

Tiago Matos

Introduction

Since 2008, the broad flora of action repertoires on the left has become increasingly visible through mainstream and social media. The development of new unapologetic and progressive media outlets has showed how journalists and journalistically minded activists have been instrumental in spearheading deeper contextualized analysis of social movement actions and in the creation and dissemination of frames of understanding that can challenge those narratives offered by mainstream media – and as such, play important roles in movement building. However, leftist media are not a be-all pursuit; to state the obvious, radical media can serve a purpose for political and social action, and leftist and radical media have an unbreakable interdependency with on-the-ground action. However, the creation of lasting social movements and countercultures – and community beyond the immediate – are dependent on the formulation of a common project of which the media are an indispensable vehicle.[1]

This chapter is based on a study of how socialist media approached coverage of riots in Norway's capital Kristiania – which was Oslo's name at the time – in the late 19th century, with a particular emphasis on a set of riots in April and May of 1893.[2] Within this context, I will concentrate on two processes in framing street politics and protest as seen in the socialist press. First, it is important to identify how riotous crowds and crowd behaviour could be described, and how those descriptions were common tropes used to create connotations such as order and disorder, legitimacy and illegitimacy relative to the ideology of those in power and expressed within a liberal public sphere. Secondly, due to its expressive form of action and connection to street politics, crowd behaviour and riots took on a particular role in both creating and disaggregating demands, actions and collective frames of understanding.

DOI: 10.4324/9781003221784-3

These processes are, of course, not exhaustive of the analysis of the interaction between media and street politics. They do, however, represent some of the more important traits of framing within the Kristianite and Norwegian context and more broadly of group-making and organizational legitimacy of the labour movement. They show the importance of how the interplay between riotous crowd behaviour and activists' media can represent examples of the ways in which hidden transcripts, pre-existing attitudes of opposition and feelings of injustice were made public, in turn bringing social demands into the agenda of their contemporary radical left.

As such, this chapter looks beyond the categorization of crowds within the variants of the dichotomy of order-disorder and investigates the role of crowds and riots in the development of demands and frames of understanding through late-19th-century socialist media.[3]

The Newspapers

The newspaper we will be following in our analysis is the socialist party newspaper, *Social-Demokraten*. However, while we are primarily concerned with the framing processes in this relatively radical publication, it will have to be viewed in the context of a contemporary public sphere and a broader media landscape. Here, that landscape will be embodied by the liberal *Dagbladet* and the conservative *Morgenbladet*. Information about riotous events have also been cross-referenced with judicial and police sources, and in some instances with census data on arrested protesters.[4]

The City

In the late-19th-century Kristiania, there were still many small workplaces that adhered to the master-apprentice principle. Many of the larger workplaces were paternalistic in structure, although some industries had already started to undergo restructuring process that led to proletarianization of workers. The 'social question' – in Norway dubbed 'the workers question' – was uttered with both benign and fearful concern. Up until the early 1900s, however, there was no workers' representation in formal politics, and while there were locally organized workers' insurance funds, most measures to solve 'the workers question' was top-down politically driven poverty relief, private sector philanthropy and sometimes came in the form of a Billy club. When formal recognition and political representation finally came about, it was on the back of organizing efforts that started in the 1880s and did not happen in a sweeping motion. The last two decades of the 19th century saw the advent of mass labour and workers' organizations, the founding of the Norwegian Labour Party (1887), the party adhered to the second international and joined the global Mayday demonstration for the 8-hour day, landmark strikes and so on – and, of course, based on agitation and framing by a relatively radical party press.[5] Meanwhile, alongside this development, riots were almost a yearly event in Kristiania; there was clearly many protest-willing people who did not have an organizational expression or affiliation through which to do so, or who protested in a way that the organizations did not always see as beneficial.

The Riots

In the years between 1878 and 1917, there were riots in 16 different years and sometimes there were several riots in the same year. They could have had various triggering causes – from labour disputes to large street brawls over arrests for public drunkenness.[6] What they all seemingly share is a pattern of escalation, from initial conflict through to catcalling, whistling, shouting and verbal protests, culminating in rock and bottle throwing, property destruction and clashes on the street between said protesters and police.[7]

Before we move on to the analysis of the processes of framing and upscaling within this case, a short overview of the various riots in 1893 is in place. While some of these cases are known to Norwegian historians, they have both been treated independently, played roles of different narratives of Kristiania's (Oslo's) history, but never as part of a history of riots and crowd behaviour, and never with an individual emphasis on the riotous behaviour and street politics of each case.[8] Therefore, what has been missed is the fact that all cases in 1893 happened between 27 April and 10 May – some overlapping, other seemingly relaying from one place to the next. Looking closer at how the newspaper media covered the period, we see how the reoccurring riots and unrest were both lumped together and split apart, depending on what that coverage and political inclination of the newspaper was set to achieve.

In 1893, there were riots in all the central and eastern working-class neighbourhoods with diverse triggering causes. The cases were as follows:

1. On 27 April and 28 April, a group of people assembled outside one of the many orphanages in the city. This particular orphanage and its manageress Johanne Sophie Fougner had been subject to an investigative piece in one of the city's newspapers that alleged that there had been severe mistreatment and abuse of girls between the ages of two and 17. When the story broke, people gathered in curiosity outside the orphanage – now dubbed "The Torture institution in Pilestredet" – but it all soon escalated to protests and clashes with police that lasted for two days. Fougner was not a nobody either: her brother was the mayor of Kristiania's neighbouring county, and her father had been a member of parliament, which placed her in proximity to the ruling class. Furthermore, the board of the orphanage was headed by a local parish priest with the support from several of the city's banks.[9]
2. A few days later, a brawl broke out during the assembling and line-up of the International Workers' Day march between a group of Anarchists ("Libertas") and the police. The previous year, in 1892, the small anarchist group had their banner confiscated and were denied the right to participate in the march by the authorities. The brawl in 1893 was very much a rematch. Libertas had announced their intent to participate in the march, but were attacked by police

as soon as they entered the Anker square where the labour movement was gathered for Mayday. Clashes ensued while the police attempted to confiscate their banner, which in turn drew in many other participants. One of these was the head of the labour party who was subsequently also arrested for inciting a riot. In the judicial aftermath he was acquitted, while one of the anarchists was sentenced to serve eight months on bread and water.[10]

3. Later that evening and during the night, on 1 May and 2 May, riots erupted in a neighbourhood not too far away – Vaterland – and spread to other adjacent neighbourhoods eventually covering the Vaterland, Grønland and Fjerdingen neighbourhoods. These riots lasted for a full week. Especially the former neighbourhood had a poor reputation as being the site of dingy taverns, illegal alcohol trade and brothels. None other than Abelone Christensen, "The Queen of Vaterland", embodied this illicit business more. She was the proprietor of a tavern, which also served as a brothel, that was central to the escalating riots this spring; on the evening of 1 May, she was involved in an attempt to defraud a customer that ended in a brawl inside her establishment. During the brawl, the customer shot and killed her husband. Following the event, a riot broke out in the neighbourhood almost immediately *directed at* the now widowed Abelone Christensen. The aim of the riots were the talk of the town, and there was outcry for more missions, more control with serving licences and calls for demolishing parts of the neighbourhood. However, during the burial of the Christensen's husband, a new crowd formed and followed the casket procession shouting, whistling and throwing rocks. It was rumoured that there was a police officer amid the procession, a friend of 'The Queen', who was then followed to a police station nearby and the protest escalated to clashes with the police outside the station.[11]

4. Any strike during the 40 years around the turn of the century had the potential of developing into a riotous situation due to the fact that they involved striking workers, strike breakers and the police as protectors of private property rights and the so-called "right to work". The strikes that were ongoing at the time riots were breaking out around the city in 1893 were no different, and unsurprisingly, brawls and riots broke out in connection to three strikes in May 1893. They were of varying magnitude and intermittently distributed between 2 May and 9 May connected to a strike at a tailor's workshop, at a glove factory and, lastly, at an iron works. These strikes had been going on for various lengths of time, though only the last couple of weeks of April saw all of them coincide.[12] There were stale fronts between both workers and employers with accusations of scabbing and threats of violence, and solidarity seemed to have broken down amongst workers as different groups of workers were put up against each other in negotiations. The strikes clearly functioned as a tense backdrop to the atmosphere in the city as they were visible in several neighbourhoods and in marches through the city. Their direct connection to riots around the factories and adjacent neighbourhoods – and the other riots in the city – was, however, as we will see, contested.[13]

5. On 8 May, a crowd of people clashed with police over rumoured mistreatment of a grocer's assistant in the neighbourhood of Grünerløkken. The crowd got wind that a shop keeper had mistreated or beaten a boy in his employment because he had complained about his working conditions (more specifically, his room and board) and reacted by breaking the windows of the store, before it developed into a street fight with the police.[14]
6. At the same time, there were riots in the Kampen neighbourhood. These clashes between demonstrators and police were a reaction to a situation where a newly appointed poverty relief fund manager told an old lady to do something better than to burden the fund.[15]
7. On the outskirts of the city the following day, in the neighbourhood of Ekeberg, a group of youth were involved in clashes with police over a forced eviction of a family.[16]
8. Finally, on 10 May 1893, another brawl was brought on by the mistreatment of a young boy by a coal dealer at Grønland. While this case was also referred to as a riot in the newspapers, drew police and media attention, the coverage seemed to come as an attempt to jump on the bandwagon of sensationalism and media's inclination towards continuing the coverage of riots.[17]

These riots were of various magnitudes, had varying impact and received differing media attention; some were highlighted, some were mentioned only once. In the following sections, I will turn my attention to (1) how the designation of crowd actors and dichotomies functioned to underscore the political illegitimacy of the crowd and (2) how crowd behaviour and riots functioned to create or disaggregate collective frames of understanding.

The Framing

Framing has an intuitive meaning; framing is a collective narrative that helps us locate, place and decipher meaning in the world, and leads us to "justify, dignify, and animate collective action."[18] Furthermore, framing does not happen in a vacuum, and as such, is actively constructed to accommodate and include local cultural symbols, existing or past conflicts, accessible repertoire of action and understandings of local social relations. Riots and crowd behaviour can function as moments where hidden transcripts are made public, and thus also represent moments where framing development occurs.[19] These local frames of understanding also exist in relation to various frames of understanding at different geographic and conceptual levels. In order to make sense of one framing level in relation to another other, central actors, activists and journalists will often have to act as 'mediators' or 'translators' to translate unfolding events and actions and potential demands to a political language that is understandable to subjects and to political adversaries.[20] This mediating exercise has been called 'scale shifting' by Doug McAdam, and essentially denominates a process in which a frame of understanding is upscaled (or, I would add, downscaled) in order to bridge identities and claims that may seem incompatible at a base level or categorize local adversaries with a more generalized group or category of adversaries.[21]

While historians and social scientists have made the understanding of crowd behaviour and riots more nuanced, this distinction is still difficult to recognize in the public sphere, and output is still often based on archaic notions inherited from crowd psychology.[22] The public discourse on crowds and riots has a long history with few nuances. An important observation about our sources is that, in Kevin Passmores words, "cultural approaches show that conservatives (and their opponents) shared many analytical categories and participated in a common political culture, yet used its categories differently."[23] This draws our attention to the fact that any contemporary actor will have an accessible, though limited, political language to comment on crowd behaviour, but may or may not use that language in different ways and for different aims. In continuation, the scope of what is legitimate political protest – and reasons thereof – will be contained within a narrow spectre.

The 19th-century socialist media came into existence within a set public sphere and was thus tasked with both reporting on ignored/neglected points of view and creating a coherence between existing protest frames at the base and a socialist world view. Ultimately, the role of media is not only as mediators towards an existing world, but also to help create a new one.

One of the most prominent features within these perimeters is the use of dichotomies with connotations of what is legitimate and what is illegitimate, what is accepted and what is not. The overarching dichotomy, with various connotations, is one which puts order against disorder. Other examples that we need to be attentive to are those that put public against private, male against female, adult against child, individual against collective, rational against irrational and level-headed against emotional. The use of these dichotomies is central to any framing of crowds and can be used to promote negative or positive connotations as well as promote or negate the image of independent and able political agency. For the socialist media in the late-19th-century Kristiania, navigating this linguistic landscape became a tricky tightrope walk, where clashes and riots were often, if not always, contrasted against the strike. The need to establish legitimacy for the strike, the wage workers' strongest weapon against owners and employers, could seemingly only be achieved if it was shielded and defended from the negative connotations of riotous protest, which very often were conflated with the strike by both liberal and conservative media.

The Disorderly Actors: The Crowd as Poor, as Young, as Female and as Drunk

Investigating how crowds and riotous behaviour are discussed publicly in a society is an investigation into the power structures of that society. Collectively, descriptions of the crowd in Kristiania could come in many variations: For example, the crowd involved in the riots around the orphanage case were described as "riff-raff of the

city's big mob (…) the confluence of masses (…) denoting their path with van-
dalism and violence (…) the scores with lust for strife".[24] As we can see, the crowds
have many names: 'riff-raff', 'the masses' and 'the mob'. Crowds could also be
denominated as 'the hordes', 'the rabble', even 'the people' and 'the public opinion'.[25]
All of these could be used to describe or refer to the same group of people in the
same situation and served to evoke both negative and positive connotations. In
order to make these monolithic descriptions efficient, however, it was necessary to
conflate the crowd with a heterogeneous category of actors, and to reduce nuances
to a minimum.[26]

These categories could be based on economic, judicial, spatial and social aspects,
which in turn brought the description of certain types of protest in line with a
hegemonic world view that upheld the constitution of political rights. Regardless
of gender, age or state of mind, being in a crowd made you an illegitimate political
actor – and being in a category with few or no political rights made you prone to
conflation with the crowd.

For example, if you lived in Vaterland and did not have trading and merchant
rights, meaning you had a different legal status, you represented an antagonist to
the city's burghers through various regulations and the lack of patrician privileges.[27]
Traveling by road, or even arriving at port, helped create these 'other' places that
swelled with local, regional, national and international migration to the city. The
suburbs of the city were liminal spaces, and few neighbourhoods represented this
better in Kristiania than Vaterland, an old suburb that exemplified how spatiality
interplayed with judicial, economic and social aspects to create this 'othering'. In
the 18th- and 19th-century Kristiania, the suburbs maintained a close relationship
with rural life due to interchangeable seasonal urban and rural work. In turn, this
made suburbs look different not only due to different building regulations and
cheaper building materials, but also due to the more rural way of life. The denigra-
tion was based on the legal context, which ultimately also affected the social and
economic relationship between 'the others' (e.g. the Kritianite suburbs) and the city,
and between disorder and order.

Vaterland had developed to encompass varied trade, sometimes illegal due to
lack of merchant rights, and attracted many dayworkers, handlers, middlemen – in
general, informal trade and an informal labour market. If you did trade outside of
city regulations, you were considered a thief. In fact, the objectification of those
who lived outside the city was an easy task due to different legal status of suburban
inhabitants, and in continuation enforced a regulatory regime that connected low
socio-economic standing to poor moral judgement. To the burghers of the city,
Vaterland was filled with 'prostitutes', 'pimps', 'moonshiners', 'crooks', 'fraudsters',
'brothels' and 'shady taverns'.[28] When the city expanded and incorporated these
suburbs, and other industries became dominant, this view was inherited by the new
industrial capitalists.[29]

Vaterland was often regarded as being home to the rabble, and thus the rabble
was defined in opposition to city burghers. Rabble could therefore be used to
denominate 'everybody else', especially those who did not have a merchant or

trade rights within city regulations. Ultimately, in a world where only a figurative handful of people had political and economic privileges, it was an easy task to create a monolith impression of the crowd. Those who protested, riotous or otherwise, were very often 'the others' described as the poor, as female, as young, as drunk or as thieves and rabble. However, these descriptors tell us very little about the actual crowd. Rather, because they are proxy words for politically illegitimate actors, they say something about the frame of understanding any given newspaper attempted to promote. As we will see, while these words were used most often by liberal and conservative media, it was not an exclusive to those publications. In fact, these tropes and words also played a role in narratives created and disseminated by the social democratic paper.

The Rumours: Examples of Popular Local Frames

An example of crowd actors own local framing of conflicts comes in the form of rumours. However, they clearly also play a central role in the description of the riots. They can have various roles. First of all, the claim of the existence of rumours in the media can play a role in undermining the legitimacy of riotous (or other) protests.[30] Tropes regarding conflicts, protest and riots and their escalation and development are accessible, understandable and accepted by readers. By using rumours as an attribute of the lead up to a riotous protest, it creates the connotations that connect the riots with disorder and imply crowd actors' ease in dealing with truth and 'objectivity'. This does not harmonize with the order of a society in which 'objective' knowledge is formalized by certain actors (and not others). Causes for the riots are thus often accused of being caused by "untruthful rumours", "unfounded rumours", "simple rumours" or "false rumours", and thus can be considered delegitimising slurs used to falsify popular accounts of conflicts.

Secondly, the possible existence of rumours should also be viewed as serving a purpose to those who share them: Rumours tell familiar stories and represent street-level dissemination of knowledge; they cast the roles of adversaries, transgressors, create a drama and can contain within them descriptive, normative and prescriptive elements. Their existence, regardless of their truthfulness, and the willingness to share them as explanations of the world, however tiny that world may be, indicated how they both have an explanatory and a justifying effect. Their existence and circulation show some people's willingness to believe them, meaning they say something about what they think is likely to be true. They offer a glimpse into riot participants' motivation, the causes for riots and how events are framed. While they may be true, judging their truthfulness can be a secondary task. Real triggers at the onset of a riot may be important, but equally so are the narratives and frames that sustain the riot.

What do rumours tell us about Kristiania in the 1890s?[31] What information are people acting on? And how does that connect to the context and to a frame of understanding at a more abstract level? Perhaps what stands out the most is that all the riots seem to cast transgressors as someone above themselves in socio-political hierarchies. There was a willingness to believe that those who were better off were capable, if not likely, to have mistreated the weak and innocent. This is true for shopkeepers, poverty relief fund managers (officials) and especially police. No example from 1893 shows this more clearly than the riots connected to the mistreatment case at the orphanage. During these riots, in addition to what had been published in the exposé, there were rumours circulating that dead children had been carried off on a chariot bed in the middle of the night, and that teenage girls were sent to America and forced into prostitution. We know this because these rumours were printed in *Social-Demokraten*.[32] The rumours were not dismissed as untrue. Rather, they were used as reasoning to demand further investigations into that particular orphanage.

Rumours could also prompt and sustain strikes, such as the case was with the glovemakers and the cast iron workers' strike, where rumours circulated that a different glove factory had fired a union worker while retaining a non-unionized worker at below agreed-upon pay, or in which the prevalence of strike breaking was toned down or amplified, and through which threats may or may not have been uttered. *Social-Demokraten* published strike breakers' names, confirming, and attempting to 'objectify' and 'formalize' much of that knowledge by spearheading it into the public sphere upheld by the printed media.

All the strikes were highly visible in the media, particularly in *Social-Demokraten*, as they also would be in their respective neighbourhoods. Neighbourhoods, however, had local identities, and rallied around striking workers often on the basis of social and geographical proximity or the workplace's embeddedness in the neighbourhood topography. What we see in Kristiania in the late 19th century is that while neighbourhoods could have rivalries, class identity would transcend these rivalries in conflict situations. This base-level solidarity could however not occur without the dissemination of knowledge of a conflict through the media. That is not to underestimate the power of word-of-mouth or turnouts in the immediate surrounding areas, but no one had the same reach as the newspapers.

From Police to Class Society: Upscaling Protest Frames

The process of using rumours to disseminate knowledge, either on the street or through the newspapers, must be viewed as a two-way process. Information that originated from crowd actors themselves, true or hearsay, at a street level could be recounted in newspapers, either to legitimate or delegitimate triggering and sustaining causes of protests. At the same time, the newspapers would, in return, interpret and reformulate the content of rumours to fit a larger narrative. In the case of the socialist newspaper, causes for most riots were translated to demands put forward in the political language of the time that could be adopted – or re-adopted – by readers. To further highlight how upscaling could successfully occur, it is helpful to contrast how cases of police brutality were framed in the liberal leaning *Dagbladet* with how police brutality was framed by the socialist *Social-Demokraten*.

The main and primary distinction we observe is how police brutality was framed as an individual experience and as a collective problem, respectively. In fact, much like *Social-Demokraten*, *Dagbladet* ran multiple articles condemning the city's police for excessive use of force in dealing with the riots; the riots were not to be accepted, nor did they have legitimate causes, but the police did not have to crack down on them so indiscriminately and harshly. The complaints were mainly individualized and the problem with the police was framed in such a way that was not apt to aid the formation of a subjective collective narrative; the police were not the problem; it was poor leadership; and it was poor training of street officers. Furthermore, this poor training led individual officers to transgressions and excessive use of force, which in turn would go without consequences for individual officers.

The socialist paper chimed in with the liberal newspaper that the police were excessive in their use of force against the protesting crowds. *Social-Demokraten*, however, went further. The police were also the main instigators of violence; the responsibility of the police's lack of leadership was political; the police were like they were because the political leadership willed it. In fact, the fault of the police's brutality was not only placed with the mayor's office, but was also connected to a general subjugation of the working class by the bourgeois society, a society that was upheld by the judicial system, church and capital. This was especially explicitly expressed in the articles discussing the orphanage case – where victims were female children – but only after 1 May. It was by connecting it to the Mayday march brawl that this generalized way of understanding protest and society could be formulated.

As we might remember, the board of the trust that ran the orphanage was composed of both clergy and banks. Using the police's conduct as a bridge between the two cases allowed for a connection to be made at the top level between the judicial system, the church and capital. Connected with people's willingness to believe various rumours about what the extent of the orphanage case was could thus be used to emphatically criticize the police, the judicial system and the church.[33] At the same time, a connection could also be made between the labour movement, the protesting and riotous crowd and the victims of the abuse at the orphanage under the working-class umbrella, as the subjugated collective.[34]

This generalized narrative created the postulate for solidarity; while these transgressions had affected the anarchists during the International Workers' Day march, who could say who would be next?[35] In some cases, the socialist newspaper went as far as to regard the riotous crowds as 'assemblages of people'. This allowed the narrative to encompass all the crowd events and riots, turning their repression to a generalized attack on the right to assemble and a denial of constitutional rights for the working-class population, while also contesting the defining rights of formal organization and assembly. The accusation that it was the police who were a threat to order was reiterated over and over.

During the aftermath of the anarchist clashes on 1 May, the immediate discussion surrounded a situational tactlessness of police. However, when it became clear that the judicial repercussions of the brawl were particularly hard, the socialist press condemned the police as the henchmen of class justice. The state repressive system was cast as barbaric – in opposition to the civilized socialist project – and the true agents of disorder were in fact the police and those who gave orders. In sum, the blame was first moved onto the police – they acted like uncivilized barbarians – then the police institution and ultimately the whole of bourgeois society. For a readership that was willing to periodically believe rumours that the police killed drunks in holding, covered up abuse of working-class orphans and protected local powerholders, a biased judicial system that targeted poor and working-class people was not a difficult narrative to sell.

Furthermore, class society and class justice were connected to the lack of voting rights in attempts to delegitimize their existence: The mantra was that workers take no part in creating the laws but get punished under them; the ruling class break their own laws and do not get punished.[36]

During the riots against the poverty relief fund manager at Kampen, the riots were said to have worked because the lady who had been subject to cuts in her support had regained the full amount. Furthermore, the case was used to show how

> [o]ne cannot expect any change of the current miserable administration [of poverty relief funds] until there is universal suffrage at the municipal level, and above all, that the workers become conscious of their citizenly rights (alt. trans. civil/civic position) and learned the causes of the prevalent need and misery.[37]

The sentencing of one of the anarchists later in May became further proof that it was impossible to achieve real freedom within current society. The strength of rumours is evident during the coverage of the Mayday march clashes. In the following days, rumours circulated that the military and the navy were mobilized against the labour movement in the city. This process of upscaling centred the workers, as a class and as a movement, in national politics as a challenge to power by the powerless. In such a narrative, the anarchists were only scapegoats created to distract from the real demands of the working class and their actions as prerequisite for only the suppression of the labour movement. There was some truth to the mobilization of troops, but that they actually were mobilized was not confirmed before much later, and the reason for their mobilization was not the labour movement – at least not exclusively. However, the socialist press was eager to connect the brawl between the anarchists and the city's police to the suspicion of an impending crackdown and to the upper classes and police's disregard for constitutional rights of workers.[38] The actions of the police and the judicial system went far beyond any common people's sense of justice, which placed *Social-Demokraten* as the vehicle for 'public opinion' and people 'beyond the ranks of the socialists'.

The Strike: Disaggregating and Sequestering Different Protest Actions

Alongside the process of upscaling frames and mediation/translation of political demands, *Social-Demokraten* reported on the ongoing strikes in a different way. For various reasons we will return to briefly, the newspaper was compelled to admit that there had been riots around the factories subject to strikes and their adjacent neighbourhoods, but the workers on strike had not been involved whatsoever. In fact, they were behaving in an 'ideal' and 'orderly fashion'.[39]

From our viewpoint as historians, however, it is difficult to argue that the strikes and the riots in their immediate spatial proximity were separated insular events.[40] The socialists press was, however, weary of explicitly connecting the two together, because it would leave them and the strikes (specifically and conceptually) vulnerable to attack from the conservative and liberal media. Especially the conservative *Morgenbladet*, who positioned itself firmly on the side of employers, was eager to connect the strikes and the riotous behaviour, grabbing onto any opportunity they saw to attack and delegitimize the actions of the striking workers. They accused the workers at the factories of threatening the owners and managers, and anyone who broke picket lines. However, conservative media was careful never to say that the striking workers were directly involved in the riots, but still connected the two: the riots were, instead, "in occasion of the strike".[41] By doing so from a position of power and influence within an established public sphere, *Morgenbladet* could promote illegitimacy of protest actions and strikes and their condemnation through connotations and implicit conflation of the two.

In this situation, the socialists had two challenges. First, they needed to sequester the strike from the riots in order to legitimate and create acceptance for the strike. This was done with the accepted political language and within the logic of the political establishment. The socialists needed to gain formal recognition and legitimacy for the strike vis-à-vis their employer counterparts facilitating negotiations by achieving equal standing between opposing parties in industrial struggles. Meanwhile, and secondly, they could not – as we saw above – completely alienate riotous people, presumed or possible supporters, nor could they deprecate their causes and perceived demands. For these two tasks to be compatible, *Social-Demokraten* helped foment the strict delineation between the riots and the strikes.

In line with the first task, the newspaper became focused on underscoring the order of socialist and labour relevant events. The International Workers' Day was always 'perfectly ordered and disciplined' – in 1893 as well.[42] *Social-Demokraten* only made the workers directly involved in the strike visible as idealized versions. Workers who were on strike were reported to be disciplined, calm, sober, controlled and orderly; they held meetings every day and no one was exempt.[43]

In this imagery, there was no room for riotous workers – and so they were not present or involved. When the riots were put in connection with the strikes, *Social-Demokraten* was quick to refute those accusations. In those instances, they would double down and emulate conservative language describing the crowds as 'driven by desire and totally without foundation'.[44] They were disorderly and not a part of the workers repertoire. This created some inconsistent approaches to the riots; riotous outbursts were, in some cases, warranted, such as they were in the orphanage case, while they were destructive in cases and neighbourhoods where a strike was in effect. They could argue that the police's actions were more blameworthy than any riot in one moment, only to say that they understood that rioters were arrested in the next.

Regardless of the truthfulness of the idealized strike – because it might be true if we include only those workers with a strict connection to the labour organization responsible for the strike – it does not make visible the agency of all workers at a workplace and extinguishes the possible actions of solidarity expressed by those who were affected by the strike, but who did not have a direct connection to the workplace. For example, early unions could bar young or female workers; these categories of workers could be transient or temporary. Additionally, neighbourhood and familial solidarity, their involvement and how the community at large was affected falls far into the background of the strike in the strict formal sense.

We do know, however, how common clashes between striking workers and their neighbourhood allies and strike-breakers were – and *Social-Demokraten* even printed names of scabs with addresses.[45] However, the labour movement and socialists sought to uphold the distinctions between riots and strikes and made use of familiar language to do so, including denouncing information about their overlap as rumours. During the glovemakers' strike, for example, the strike-committee accused people who lived in the neighbourhood of perpetuating rumours that the workers were involved in the riots – and encouraged people to stay neutral to the strike if they could not find better ways of supporting the strike than to riot.[46] It is not without importance that this was published in the liberal newspaper, not in the socialist paper. It was intended not only for the neighbourhood, but to harness support for the strike in liberal readership within the working class.[47]

Conclusion

This chapter shows how one socialist newspaper aimed to redefine or transcend the hegemonic hold of liberal media (as ideal), and its intrinsic relation to the emergence of liberal democracy and a bourgeois public sphere. The example here shows how difficult it is to break such a hegemony, and how the mediation of radical street politics is a tightrope walk if the aim is to legitimize radical action *within* the logic of the current system. Mainstream media – from left to right – will more-often-than-not be quick to reject radical street politics, lock stock and barrel, and in doing so, purposefully, or inadvertently, delegitimize it. In fact, the tension between the coverage of institutionalized politics and of street politics as mutually exclusive has a long tradition, and knowledge of its history is paramount for the continued success of radical journalism.

I have shown how crowd behaviour and riots were translated into the contemporary political language by the emerging socialist media and the labour movement, and how activists and journalists navigated around the tension between institutional legitimacy and street politics.

While riotous crowds were often treated as expressions of disorder, archaic, juvenile and feminine by both mainstream media on the left, centre and right, these riots were nonetheless integral to the formulation of demands and conceptualiza-tion of larger goals by radical contemporary activists within their media outlets.

The strikes that were ongoing as the riots broke out in late April 1893 show us how disaggregation of protest could work as a defence against attacks from both liberal and conservative voices. However, sequestering the strike from its geo-graphic and social context also had its backsides; it put the socialist press in line with the liberal and conservative press in reproducing and communicating tropes that had connotations to disorder, ultimately aiding in solidifying the dichotomy between crowd behaviour and the strike.

Finally, there is a point to be made that there is a lot to be learned from past experiences such as these. Clearly, there was a dialectical process between street pol-itics and framing in the media. Understanding media as part of a dialectical relation with street politics shows how new possibilities became visible, how some actions were legitimized and other were not – and how ambiguity could be a necessary strategy – but ultimately, how framing of certain demands and collectives helped foment solidarity and disseminate a radical leftist point of view. Anyone under-taking the role of framing agent for a movement or political leaning needs a con-sciousness of this fact at the outset.

Notes

1 Andersen, Sven Aage (1982). "Forholdet mellem arbejderklassens kultur og arbeiderbevægelsens kultur – delkultur, subkultur og modkultur" in *Tidsskrift for Arbeiderbevegelsen Historie (1)*. Oslo: 35–36; Dahl, Hans Fredrik (1979)."Arbeiderbevegelsen og Offentligheten. En introduksjon" in *Tidsskrift for Arbeiderbevegelsen Historie (1)*. Oslo: 5; Tjelmland, Hallvard (2003)."Aviser som Produsent og Produkt av Fellesskap – eksemplet Nord-Norge" in *Arbeiderhistorie*. Oslo: 157–161.

2 Matos, Tiago (2020). Beyond Order and Disorder – Crowd Behaviour in Kristiania in the 1890s. PhD-dissertation. EUI-HEC. Florence, Italy.

3 Thompson, E. P (1991). *Customs in Common*. London: The Merlin Press; Brubaker, Rogers (2004). *Ethnicity without Groups*. Harvard University Press, Cambridge, MA and London; Passmore, Kevin (2008)."A Gendered Genealogy of Political Religions Theory" in *Gender & History*, Vol. 20, No. 3: 646 and 663–664; Matos (2020): ch. 1.

4 Bjørgen, Hildegunn (1997). *17. maifeiring som politisk redskap?: en studie av nasjonaldagsfeiringen i Kristiania 1879–1905*. Oslo: Hovedoppgave; Høeg, T. A. (1973). *Norske Aviser 1763–1969 – En Bibliografi*. Oslo: UBs hustrykkeri; Matos (2020); In depth, see Chapters 1 and 2.

5 For a history of the working class, see volumes 1 and 2 of the history of the Norwegian working class: Bull, Edvard 1(1985). *Arbeiderklassen blir til (1850–1900)*, Volume 1 in *Arbeiderbevegelsens historie i Norge*. Oslo: Tiden Norsk Forlag; Bjørnson, Øyvind (1990). "På Klassekampens Grunn".Volume 2 in *Arbeiderbevegelsens historie i Norge*. Oslo: Tiden Norsk Forlag. For labour history, see, for example, volume 1 of LOs history: Olstad, Finn (2009). *Med Knyttet Neve*.Volume 1 of LOs Historie (Bergh, Trond, Terje Halvorsen, Finn Olstad and Inger Bjørnhaug [eds.]). Oslo: Pax.

6 For an outlined categorization of riots, see Matos (2020): 25–41.

7 The choice of 1893 as a case study is due to it being a particularly riotous year and because it presents us with an opportunity to investigate the broad array of triggering causes and how these were apt to serve many different media narratives. For a more

detailed and critical view on this monocausal and lenear presentation of riots, see Matos (2020): 84–85.

8 History of Oslo, see Myhre, Jan Eivind (1990). Oslo bys historie. Volume 3: *Hovedstaden Christiania*. Oslo: Pax (3rd edition; 2000) and Kjeldstadli, Knut (1990). Oslo bys historie. Volume 4: *Den delte byen* Oslo: Pax (3rd edition; 2000) and Kjeldstadli, Knut and Jan E. Myhre (1995). *Oslo – spenningenes by*. Oslo: Pax. History of the police, see Valen-Sendstad, Farstein (1953). *For Lov og Rett – Oslo Politikammer 200 år* (Oslo Politis Historie). On social control, see Kjeldstadli (2018b). "Strategier for kontroll i storbysamfunnet Kristiania rundt 1900" in *I Dørstrekken fra Europa – festskrift til Knut Sprauten i anledning 70-årsdagen 22. juni 2018* (Alsvik, Ola, Hans P. Hosar and Marianne Wiik [eds.]). Oslo: Nasjonalbiblioteket.

9 *Social-Demokraten* 29 April 1893; *Social-Demokraten* 1 May 1893; *Social-Demokraten* 9 May 1893.

10 *Social-Demokraten* 6 May 1893; *Social-Demokraten* 24 June 1893; *Social-Demokraten* 7 October 1893; *Dagbladet* 2 May 1893; *Dagbladet* 5 May 1893; *Dagbladet* 9 May 1893; *Morgenbladet Aften* 9 May 1893.

11 *Morgenposten* 20 June 1893; *Morgenposten* 12 May 1893; *Morgenbladet Morgen* 2 May 1893; *Morgenbladet Morgen* 5 May 1893; *Morgenbladet Aften* 7 May 1893; *Morgenbladet Aften* 8 May 1893; *Morgenbladet Morgen* 9 May 1893; *Dagbladet* 4 May 1893; *Dagbladet* 5 May 1893; *Dagbladet* 6 May 1893; *Dagbladet* 9 May 1893; *Dagbladet* 11 May 1893; *Social-Demokraten* 6 May 1893.

12 The glove-makers strike would eventually go on to be the longest running strike in Kristiania up until that point.

13 The unfolding events of the strike at Kværner can be followed almost daily in *Social-Demokraten* between late March 1893 and July 1893. *Social-Demokraten* 6 April 1893; *Social-Demokraten* 8 April 1893; *Social-Demokraten* 15 April 1893; *Social-Demokraten* 16 April 1893; *Social-Demokraten* 5 September 1893; *Social-Demokraten* 24 October 1893; *Dagbladet* 3 May 1893; *Dagbladet* 9 May 1893; *Dagbladet* 10 May 1893; *Morgenbladet Morgen* 9 May 1893; *Morgenbladet Morgen* 10 May 1893.

14 *Morgenposten* 12 May 1893; *Dagbladet* 9 May; *Dagbladet* 10 May 1893; *Dagbladet* 11 May 1893; *Morgenbladet Morgen* 9 May; *Morgenbladet Aften* 9 May; *Morgenbladet Morgen* 10 May 1893; *Morgenbladet Morgen* 11 May.

15 *Dagbladet* 9 May 1893; *Dagbladet* 10 May 1893; *Morgenbladet Morgen* 9 May 1893; *Social-Demokraten* 25 May 1893.

16 *Dagbladet* 10 May 1893; *Morgenbladet Morgen* 10 May 1893.

17 *Dagbladet* 10 May 1893.

18 Tarrow, Sidney (1998). *Power in movement*. New York: Cambridge University Press: 21. See also 13–19.

19 Matos (2020); McAdam, Doug, Sidney Tarrow and Charles Tilly (2001). *Dynamics of Contention*. New York: Cambridge University Press; Tarrow (1998); Scott, James C. (1990). *Domination and the Art of Resistance: Hidden Transcripts*. New Haven: Yale University Press.

20 Matos (2020).

21 McAdam et al. (2001): 339; 331.

22 Matos (2020); Since the 1950s E. P. Thompson, Charles Tilly, George Rudé and Eric Hobsbawm have contributed with important work in the field. Schweingruber, D. and R. Wohlstein (2005) show how crowd behaviour is discussed in the public sphere is based on the traditions of Le Bon and Tarde, which have created 'mythical' characteristics of the crowd that include *irrationality, emotionality, suggestibility, destructiveness, spontaneity, anonymity* and a *myth of unanimity*.

23 Passmore, Kevin (2012). *The Right in France from the Third Republic to Vichy*. Oxford: Oxford University Press: 11.

24 *Morgenbladet Aften* 3 May 1893: *Christiania 3die Mai. Gadeuordner;* (…) griber den store Hobs slettere Elementer med Glæde Anledningen (…) afholder dette ikke de sammenløbne Masser i at molestere det uskyldige Børnehjem og senere forurolige en anden Privatbolig, overalt betegnende sin Vei med Hærværk og Vold. (…) de ufredslystne Skarer (…). See also Matos (2020): 91.

25 *Social-Demokraten* 1 May 1893; *Social-Demokraten* 10 October 1893.

26 Matos (2020): 5; Thompson (1991). Thompson calls for caution when studying categories, such as 'the crowd', 'the working class' or 'popular culture' because one may inadvertently obscure the diversity within them.

27 Melvold, Erik Oluf (1978a). "Det Gamle Vaterland" in *St. Hallvard: Illustrert tidsskrift for byhistorie, miljø og debatt* 2/3–78. Selskapet for Oslo Byes Vel: Oslo: 95, 101.

28 Melvold, Erik Oluf (1978b). "Det Gamle Vaterland – 1800-tallet" in *St. Hallvard: Illustrert tidsskrift for byhistorie, miljø og debatt* 3/3–78. Selskapet for Oslo Byes Vel: Oslo: 203–205.

29 Melvold (1978a); Melvold (1978b): 203–205.

30 Matos (2020): 228–229.

31 Matos (2020): 225–231.

32 *Social-Demokraten* 9 May 1893; *Social-Demokraten* 13 May 1893.

33 *Social-Demokraten* 1 May 1893; *Social-Demokraten* 10 October 1893.

34 *Social-Demokraten* 1 May 1893; Matos (2020): 221–222.

35 *Social-Demokraten* 20 May 1893.

36 *Social-Demokraten* 10 October 1893.

37 *Social-Demokraten* 25 May 1893.

38 Matos (2020): 225–229.

39 *Social-Demokraten* 1 May 1893; *Social-Demokraten* 16 May 1893; *Dagbladet* 11 May 1893.

40 I have argued for at least some possible ways in which strikes and simultaneous riots were connected in Matos (2020): chapters 1, 2, 9 and 10.

41 *Morgenbladet Morgen* 10 May 1893.

42 In addition to the brawl between anarchists, labour movement and labour party activists and police, there were accusations printed in Morgenbladet that howling youth had rushed towards the soapbox, and someone had shouted 'long live anarchism' outside city hall.

43 *Social-Demokraten* 1 May 1893.

44 *Social-Demokraten* 13 May 1893.

45 *Social-Demokraten* 8 April 1893; *Social-Demokraten* 16 May.

46 *Dagbladet* 11 May 1893; *Social-Demokraten* 16 May.

47 *Dagbladet* 11 May 1893. An additional point of context was that the socialists were in the middle of a power struggle for domination of the workers' associations and societies most of which were still under liberal party influence in 1893.

4

RADICAL MEDIA IN THE ANGLOSPHERE

Seamus Farrell

Introduction

A set of interlocking crises, social reproductive, economic-financial and ecological, frame the emergence, or resurgence, of critical publications. This chapter examines these publications as radical media, focusing in three countries, Ireland, the UK and USA in the period 2014–2019. Its aim is to conceptualise radical media and its historic development and to map the shifting contours of its publications and politics in the 21st century. Researching the field of radical media has value as it constitutes an underexamined form of political communication. Additionally, understanding radical media from a normative perspective widens and enriches our views of the social and political role of journalism. In an era of digital corporate media dominance, what can be learned from past and present radical media that can be used to transform media and communication generally, in the direction of social justice and equality?

The first half of the chapter focuses on definition, theory and historical practice of radical media. Raymond Williams (2013) is drawn on to consider 'radical' as a word defined by its cultural and material use over time. Examining Marxist theories of communication this chapter then explores radical media as it has been theorised in relation to power. Finally the particularities and contradictions of the concept 'Anglosphere radical media' are considered and the history of radical media practice is briefly sketched in Ireland, the USA and UK.

The second half of the chapter examines in more detail 21st-century radical media in these three countries. The use of the concept 'radical media' has taken on a new meaning in this era and the dynamics of media power have shifted in important ways particularly with the emergence of digital dimensions of capitalism. The practice of radical media is the main focus and is divided into three parts: the Indymedia era through to the financial crisis and Occupy which saw important

DOI: 10.4324/9781003221784-4

experimentation in radical digital media, the re-emergence and reorganisation of a radical media from 2010 to 2014 and the social democratic wave of 2014–2020. Finally this chapter looks to the future of radical media. What can we learn from the definition, theory and history of radical media, and what we learn from recent shifts and developments to help us proactively support and build radical media as part of a wider radical, transformative and liberating politics?

Anglosphere Radical Media: Definitions, Theory, Politics and History

Defining Radical Media

R. Williams (2013), Davis (1990) and Fenton (2016) trace the etymology of radical to – change at the roots. According to R. Williams (2013) 'radical' had two early political uses: it was associated with the English reform movement, in which efforts were made to extend voting rights, reform the House of Lords and develop popular civil participation in democracy. 'Radical' was also associated with Jacobinism and revolutionary republicanism in England during the Napoleonic Wars. In the 20th century R. Williams (2013) argues that 'radical', as well as 'radicalise' and 'radicalism', has a more complex and mixed political use. In French parliamentary politics 'radical' came to be used by liberal, secular and republican parties, by conservatives as a concept of the radical right and additionally, by left-wing parties contradictorily both by social democrats to distinguish themselves from revolutionary, socialist and militant politics but also interchangeably with these traditions (R. Williams 2013; Dewey 1963).

In considering concepts of radical change, Marx lay new ground by distinguishing between social and political emancipation, the transformation of the whole social being and the transformation of an extracted political subject (Marx and Engels 1965; Marx 1972). Bernstein (1993) and Luxembourg (2007) elaborated the political strategy dimensions of emancipatory radical change: social transformation entailing revolution (Luxembourg) and political emancipation through reforms of a satisfactory radical change in society (Berstein). In the late 20th century Davis (1990) located 'radical' as that which positions far-reaching change at the roots of society. Davis draws on an analysis of classic Marxism, third world liberation movements (Freire 1971; Fanon 2007) and the 1960s Black liberation and feminist movements in the USA who explored and used the concepts radical change emancipation and liberation as demands, processes and goals in which all systems of oppression are dismantled and the fullest freedom of collective economic, political and social relations is created (Evans 1980; Freeman 1973; Haider 2018).

In *Digital, Political, Radical* Fenton (2016, p. 9) traces the concept 'radical' to its Latin origins in terms of roots, with radical, 'of the grass-roots' and 'nurturing and sustaining of an ecosystem'. Here Fenton (2016) understands radical as politically progressive and left-wing. Fenton also locates this progressive 'radical' in multiple sites: the 'high' politics of parliaments, the street politics of movements and the politics of everyday experience and social relations. Within the consideration of radicals as broadly progressive, it is also worth noting variations and narrower usage within social movement theory (Fitzgerald and Rodgers 2000) and egalitarian theory (Baker et al. 2006). In both theoretical frameworks 'radical' refers to the organisation and bodies of people who go further, push boundaries and demand major system change. This is in contrast to moderates, who accommodate, compromise and aim for concessions. While radicals' and moderates' tactics are distinguished from each other as different tendencies, they are both considered broadly progressive.

Media provide a particular form for and application of 'radical'. If radical refers to change at the roots of society, progressive politics and emancipation, how do these take place in and of media, in and of communication systems? Mosco (2009, p.1) considers a political economy of communication in terms of 'the social relations, particularly the power relations that mutually constitute the production, distribution, and consumption of resources.' Building on Mosco (2009) in defining radical media then, we need to understand how communication power relations have been assessed in and of social and economic relations as a whole; i.e. how does radical media power constitute and organise itself within society and economy as a whole and in doing so relate to and contribute to radical politics more generally?

Anglosphere Radical Media

Drawing on the work above radical media can be understood in terms of how the word use has developed culturally (R. Williams 2013; Davis 1990; Fenton 2016) and in terms of how media have been theorised in relation to political and cultural power. These understandings of radical media use and relationship to power can be used to frame the analysis of particular sites of radical media and politics. The UK, USA and Ireland are key sites of (so defined here as) the 'Anglosphere' (Vucetic 2020; Wellings and Mycock 2019) and its media. Anglosphere media are used in this chapter to apply to English language publications and communication mediums and the particular influence of UK and USA media on the global media sphere. It also refers to a range of secondary sites of English language media, Ireland, Canada, Australia and New Zealand, as well as the proliferation of the English language, US and UK media in other countries, where English may not be the primary language.

In the 1800s English-speaking bourgeois media publications and wider bourgeois culture emerged as part of capitalist class formation in Britain (Curran 2002). The Victorian era was the height of British state and capitalism global power and reach (Wood 2002; McVeigh and Rolston 2021). The 'virtues' of the British ruling class, the empire and 'free' enterprise were triumphant ideological pronouncements of the British media. The vice of the common people and the incivility of the colonial subjects of the new empire were important frameworks for justification of a class structure and empire (Wood 2002; Randell-Moon, 2017). The USA media modelled the British system (Hallin and Mancini 2011) retaining the dynamics of British bourgeois liberalism, capitalist triumphalism and colonial representation

(Meyer 2009). Ireland was a battle ground, with the imposition of both the English language and customs as well as the media model accommodated to and contested in a colonial context (Lloyd 2001; Foley 2004; McVeigh and Rolston 2021). Anglosphere media historically then can be understood as serving an ideological function as part of wider cultural and political hegemony: sustain and strengthen the British and US bourgeois, subdue and contain 'commoner' and working-class cultural and political activity and erase and destroy the colonial subject, marginalised and racialised other.

In the 1900s as radio, television and then digital media emerged, the USA emerged as the dominant political and economic force reinforced by US mass culture, including its media (M. Cox, 2002; Arrighi 1994). The British empire gave way to the modern British state, which carried over many of its 1800 features, while compromising with the rising power of British labour and the demands for a welfare state post-World War II (Arrighi 1994) . The British Empire, outside its border, gave way to the Commonwealth and the White Dominan in which English language publications remained as neo-colonial and post-colonial mediums from which power and culture were constituted in newly independent states (McVeigh and Rolston 2021). Ireland contained a duality in the 20st century: a powerful post-colonial force integrated with the USA and elements of the British ruling class as well as global capital, as well as a context partition colonial island, with segregation in the Northern Irish statelet and conservative Catholic hegemony in the southern Irish state. Media, as in Law, and state institutions retained elements of the British perogies culture while attempting to form its Catholic, Irish bourgeois culture form (McVeigh and Rolston 2021).

Radical media have existed as part of a wider radical politics which set out its opposition to these social, political and cultural power structures. Radical media have been embedded in emancipatory radical movements that have particularities of the local, national and regional as well as international crossover and convergence. The influence of the UK and the USA on emancipatory radical politics more broadly is hard to overestimate and the dominance of the analyses and literature from these countries attests to this. The British Chartist press in the 1840s was formative for British radicalism and the shaping of British media and politics more generally (Curran 2002). The chartist press, counting millions of readers, acted as a precursor to both British labour press and working-class radical publishing. At the same time in the USA, abolitionist, racial justice and feminist publications in the 1800s were a precursor to significant strands of thought, globally, in the 20th century (Streitmatter 2001). The socialist and anarchist press of the First International, publishing in both countries, were significant components of a global emancipatory formation. In the late 1800s in both countries, London and Northern US cities were also centres of black radicalism, pan African thought and black radical publishing which would influence anti-colonialism and black radical thought in the 20th century.

The Russian revolution shifted the centre of global emancipatory politics to the East. That said, World War I and the interwar period were significant for communism revolutionary publishing and socialist publishing on both sides of the Atlantic. The US civil rights movement, Black Power and anti-war movements (Streitmatter 2001) and British trade unionism (Harrison 1974) shaped radical publishing globally in the second half of the 20th century. Radical media in the 1960s, in the USA more than the UK were framed by (white) counter-culturalism on the one hand and a globalised anti-colonialism, and racialised liberation struggles, including reopening the erased experiences of Native Americans and African Americans, fusing frameworks and opening up new mediums of publishing and experimentation on the other. Meanwhile academic and scholarly radical currents, facilitated by the expansion of university education in the West saw full-time professional intellectuals writing to engage and shape the New Left and their publications, such as *The New Left Review*, which moved beyond and drew on currents of thought on either side of the Atlantic, redrawing Marxist theory and the understanding of global radical politics more generally.

Ireland occupies a unique position in the Anglosphere. It is both against English language mediums and a great contributor to its canons, both anti-colonial and integrated with empire, both racialised and white, both economically dependent and the site of capitalist experimentation. As such, it presented fertile grounds for the formation of radical political thought and media, hybridising and borrowing from different emancipatory movements. The particular way in which Irish republicanism and the Irish radical press flowed through a diaspora embedded in the UK and USA, taking away lessons from British and US trade unionism and socialism and applying them to the particular conditions of Irish independence and post-colonial struggle is a case in point (Lane 1997; Whelan 2004). In the 1800s, Irish radical publishing particularly associated with fenianism influenced anti-colonial thought opposed to and fighting the British Empire, in particular in India, as well as challenging the British labour movement itself to oppose the empire. In the Irish revolutionary period (1913–1923) a diverse set of republican, socialist, feminist and trade unionist publications made up a rich radical media ecosystem, as again was the case in 1968, influenced by the US civil rights movement and liberation struggles, but positioned in a context of a civil and military conflict in the north of Ireland and social unrest in the south of Ireland which would last for 30 years.

Anglosphere Radical Media in the 21st Century

The use of radical media as a concept, referring to media as part of change at the roots of society, progressive politics and emancipation shifted in the 21st century with more emphasis on 'alternative' as a way framing the counter-hegemonic and counter-cultural media form which overlaps with the 'radical'. Downing's (2000) radical alternative media model positions radical media as a sunset of radical culture, its variety of forms, news, plays, theatre, music and op-eds, its prefigurative organisation and its relationship to social movement politics. Atton (2002) preferred the term alternative media altogether emphasising the oppositional and experimental dynamics, the distributive technological forms and both the cultural and political influence of said media. Curran (2002) conceptualises a countervailing media power, with an emphasis on ownership of media production (by journalists and wider working class and non-elite social forces). Fuchs and Sandoval (2015) also refer to alternative anti-capitalist media, with the ideal such media being non-commercial, collectively owned and organised by prosumers (producer–consumers) and having a critical (radical) analytic framework. Jeppesen (2016) defined alternative media in terms of four types: DIY media, focused on sub-cultural expression and self-organisation, critical media focused on and embedded as socialist analysis and non-commercial ownership, community, focused on participation, cooperative structures and organisation of oppressed voices and radical media specifically as that which is focused on protest and direct action. Finally Farrell (2020) combines these models in a typology of radical media outlining four dimensions of radical media: radical critical, community, institutional and activist media.

As the use of the term 'radical' has shifted, and the terrain of media power has shifted in the 21st century, so has radical media practice and politics. After a period of retreat, radical media re-emerged as part of challenges to corporate, globalised and neo-liberal order in the USA, UK and Ireland and in line with the concept of digital utopia. Here modern Anglosphere radical media practice and politics is split into three phases to explore them and articulate the key shifts that have occurred: the Indymedia period in the early 2000s, the reorganisation of radical media after the financial crisis of 2008 and radical media orbiting the social democratic wave from 2015 to 2020. Finally the chapter ends with an identification of key lessons from the period, and with a more normative goal, potential directions for Anglosphere radical media, which can additionally be considered for radical, emancipatory media across the globe.

Indymedia and Anti-globalisation

Indymedia was the most important and significant site of digital radical content in the late 1990s and early 2000s. Indymedia would begin as the Independent Media Centre in 1999 and would operate in Ireland, the UK and the USA. The Independent Media Centres were both physical sites and new digital communities (Wolfson 2012). Indymedia was anti-corporate and anti-capitalist. The radical press from the 1800s right through to the 1970s had reported on the impact of capitalism in people's everyday lives, as well as on protests, actions and insurrections. Indymedia advanced this using digital media and communication to platform instant reporting and analysis. Specifically, Indymedia groups would report and give live feed updates from protests, particularly during the large-scale G20 protests in Seattle in 1999 and Genoa in 2002. Indymedia fused traditional beat reporting with street agit-prop to expose police brutality and the struggle of anti-capitalists on the streets in real time. There would be live footage and instant reporting of police activities and security measures, including the use of baton charges, kettling, tear gas and rubber bullets.

The ideal of developing and platforming voices from below, the voices of the oppressed and marginalised, came to the fore in the late 1990s and early 2000s as part of the radical media ecosystem. This influence came from the Latin American left, based on the theoretical frameworks of radical Latin American sociology, critical communication research and development studies as part of a re-interpretation of global development, colonialism and neocolonialism. New radical media frameworks of citizen and community radical media, which produced radio and digital content, centred the lives and culture of the oppressed and marginalised. Media here were seen as part of a critical pedagogy (Freire 1971; Fanon 2007). The goal was to use media to empower people to learn and develop their own consciousness and agency (Kidd 2013; Howley 2009). In the USA *Democracy Now* combined this approach with investigative journalism and reporting, while Near FM, Dublin Community Television and the Community Media Network in Ireland and community media in the UK began to adopt these methodologies (Dublin Community Television 2010).

The publications and platforms of the early 2000s emerged as part of a radical political opening: the push back against free trade agreements which gave more powers to transnational corporations at the expense of ordinary people. A new production method, digital communication, was available, allowing a 'scaling up' of production and an expanded reach to new audiences. Anarchism, alive in environmental, racial justice and other movements from the 1980s and 1990s, was able to offer and cohere a mode of political organising, horizontalism and direct action, and connect it to the new radical digital media platforms (Kauffman 2017). In addition, digital media offered a real sense of hope; corporate mediators and filters could be bypassed and people could organise laterally against capital and the state.

For radical media, the energy and utopianism of Indymedia began to run out by the mid-2000s. Corporate social media quickly adopted key methods, the forums and discussion sections, comments and the ability of users to upload their own content, commodifying this process and expanding it (Fuchs 2012). Radical media content shifted from platforms owned by networks of radical activists to those owned by multi-billion-euro corporations (Fuchs 2012).

New Emergences and Reorganisation

If corporate digital media and the decline of the anti-globalisation movement created an important set of challenges for radical politics and its media organisations and expressions, then the financial crisis of 2008 opened up an entirely new paradigm of corporate attack and radical political reorganisation. The financial crisis of 2008 was a moment of crisis with undermined the authority of capitalism in general and financial speculation in particular and in doing so created a new audience for radical progressive ideas, which radical media could fill. The growth of radical media in this context is not a given; it is dependent on the capacity of radical media in that moment and the specific actors and organisations within it to develop themselves and the field more generally. Publications like *Democracy Now* boomed during the financial crisis, with their analysis reaching larger and larger audiences, but the main radical media re-formation, centred on Occupy. *The Occupy Times, Occupy*

Chicago Tribune (Kampf-Lassin 2011), *Occupy London Times* (Reinecke, 2018) and occupy publications in Ireland drew on the prefigurative dynamics of Indymedia but with a spatial concentration in and of occupy encampment.

Despite new 'occupy' publications, investigative journalism and a pickup in audience engagement with pre-existing radical media, radical content volume and the scholarly analysis of radical media largely focused on the wider ideas of hybrid digital activism, media practice and digital social movementism and hashtag activism, often on large corporate media platforms instead of radical publications (Costanza-Chock 2012, Juris 2016, Fuchs 2014, Kavada 2020). The defeat or collapse of Occupy encampments and movements saw a decline of the media projects associated with them but opened up new paths for radical political organisation and media building, prefigurative radical politics, rooting politics and organising in communities and workplaces, social movementism and professional left journalism and previous iterations of mass socialist publishing considered in the contemporary era.

Using Farrell's (2020) typology a range of radical 'critical' media emerged or were reinvigorated post-occupy. They were generally explicitly socialist, focused on analysis, critique and propaganda as content form, with a clear ideological goal (to popularise socialist ideas) and flexible in content form (video, short form and long form writing). *Jacobin* is a key critical publication in this genre. Founded in 2011 (Sunkara 2014), *Jacobin* has expanded with multiple titles, including *Catalyst, Tribune and All Italia*. Sunkara in a *New Left Review* article in 2014 argues that radical media should have a firm business model, with financial sustainability, a clear political orientation – which he argues in the USA should be based on rigorous class analysis and democratic socialism which allows for multiple tendencies and points of debate, aesthetic quality – and internationalism, connecting and analysing struggles across the world and the role of the US left in these struggles. Sunkara was a member of the small youth section of Democratic Socialists of America. He saw *Jacobin* as a broader project, even though a core of its members were young DSA members. Sunkara credits dissatisfaction with Occupy as moving a key subset of young radicals towards Marxist and socialist politics. *Jacobin* also has publishing deals for pamphlets, journals and books and has collaborated on conferences such as the annual Socialism and Historical Materialism (Sunkara 2014; J. J. Williams 2017).

Other critical publications vary in self-description; some are small publications connected to socialist parties such as the *Irish Marxist Review* in Ireland, linked to People Before Profit. Others engage in broad socialist or intersectional analysis, such as *Red Pepper in the UK* and *In These Times in the USA and the New Left Review*, while others occupy political or stylistic niches such as *Salvage* in the UK, which engages a 'radical pessimism' in their words. *Red Pepper*, founded in the 1990s, and *In These Times*, founded in the 1970s, are examples of older publications which were reinvigorated by the financial crisis, occupy and post-occupy socialist organisation and movement. They both had origins in versions of the New Left, combining professionalised editorial board and staff writing with an orientation towards reporting on and understanding social movements. These publications all adopted some form of subscription model, drawing on the socialist paper and cooperative paper traditions of the 1800 and 1900s, with *Jacobin* the most sustainable and commercially viable in this regard (Farrell 2020).

A range of radical media publications are categorised by Farrell (2020) as radical institutional media: They retain the journalist norms and observe outlooks, investigative journalism, reporting and analysis with more emancipatory, participatory and left perspectives. Television broadcasting, extended to YouTube and other platforms as in the case of *The Real News Network and Young Turk* are important examples of this. These have converted aspects of the 24-hour news cycle approach, talk show panels and radio shows into a social justice and partisan counter-institution with a wide reach. Public service broadcasting models (Enli 2008) have been expanded by *Democracy Now* to include the reporting on and analysis of class, race and structural inequality, the impact of US foreign policy and the lives and experiences of social movements and people in struggle (Goodman 2016).

Post-occupy prefigurative publications also fused with investigative journalist spaces. A number of publications within the institutional-type group, such as *TruthDig, AlterNet and Open Democracy*, began in the 1990s and early 2000s as independent and alternative publications blending anti-corporate, investigative journalism and counter-cultural politics. Finally in the UK, a range of left tabloid-style publications emerged – such as *Evolve and The Canary* emerged in the UK after 2014. They combine the concept of truth and speaking truth to power while containing these traditional journalistic forms with an agitation-propaganda model that blends a tabloid-style shock-and-horror content style with strongly partisan pro-left political content (Scott 2015). Institutional publications to a degree seemed to proliferate for three reasons: they contained an existing mainstream media and journalism set of practices and contents that could be used by and developed by socialist and social democratic actors (investigative journalist, tabloid), they possessed financial support from unions or subscriptions from members and they had a new-found critical mainstream audience after a period of crisis (the audience gave to meet them where they were, or publications were developed to engage this new audience).

After 2008 and Occupy, new social movements emerged and re-emerged: Feminism in all three countries (Fraser, Arruzza, and Bhattacharya 2019; Ishkanian and Peña Saavedra 2019; Mullally 2018), Black Lives Matter in the USA (Taylor 2016), student (Cammaerts 2013) and housing movements in the UK (Gray 2018; Lima 2021), and the Scottish independence movement (Lynch 2015), and in Ireland, anti-austerity shaped powerful housing (Gray 2018; Hearne, O'Callaghan, Kitchin, and Feliciantonio 2018), water charges (L. Cox 2017) movements. These movements expanded far beyond the occupation of one space, in a city or a town, in a stand against financial profiteering, expanding the range of radical politics into everyday life and direct material and social exploitation and oppression. These movements have produced a considerable degree of content, with movement literature circulating rapidly online, with interactive debate and many mediums and forms. Despite this the majority of said content has circulated on corporate social media and there has been a smaller range of publications emerging related to this terrain of radical politics.

Sub Media, It's Going Down and *Solidarity Times* are three examples of movement-focused, activist radical media. Their about sections describe their focus as one of reporting on, participating in and live action analysis of protests and other political actions. *Labor Notes*, a long-standing US-based socialist trade unionist publication, specifically focused on the rank and file strategy within the trade union movement, set out its role as an organising facilitator and point of exchange. Its website focuses on telling the stories of ordinary workers in struggle and connecting them online and at troublemaker schools, in which hundreds of union organisers and rank-and-file members are brought together to share skills and train. Jeppesen (2016) identifies a range of activist orientation platforms and productions, activist documentary making, filming and protest reporting, hacktivism and leaking documents, as well as reflective grassroots publishing. These often sit somewhere between movement and formalised media, dictated by the motions of the movement; the need for infrastructure then scaffolds the 'struggle' and nurtures it.

Radical community media-type publications such as the *Manchester Mule and Bristol Cable*, as well as *Dublin Digital Radio and Near FM*, share a common belief in empowerment and a focus on experiences and collective identity. They also vary in terms of degrees of formalisation of structure, ranging from collective grassroots structures to formal co-operatives. Here in community media, as the 1990s and early 2000s are examples of grassroots sustainable funding models tied to worker, journalist or community ownership models. Jeppesen (2016) identifies a range of such community and pirate radio, documentary, art and radical cultural forms, which speak to and explore identity, oppression and lived experiences as part of a community building process that are below and outside of institutional or capitalist power additionally.

Orbiting the Social Democratic Wave

In the European periphery particularly Syriza, Podemos (Kioupkiolis and Katsambekis 2018), closed one chapter of left government experimentation and retreat only to see a new and similar process emerge in the Anglosphere with Bernie Sanders campaign for US president in 2016 (Schulman 2016; Dorrien 2019), Jeremy Corbyn's election as leader of the British Labour Party (Seymour 2017) and Sinn Fein and the left's breakthrough in Ireland (Coulter and Reynolds 2020). These new dynamics created new contexts for radical media to operate and produced important shifts as a result.

During a period of post-occupy reorganisation of radical media, publications such as *Jacobin and Novara Media* faced and overcame the challenge of building a sustainable funding structure while publications such as *In These Times and Red Pepper* faced and overcame the challenge of reinvigorating their media in the context of new audiences, new interest in socialist politics and new social movements and the left government programmes of the Anglosphere challenged the strategy of the new radical media publications. On the one hand, radical politics is centred on contributing to an electoral strategy to win a majority to progress radical politics, gain state power and then transform power from the inside. On the other hand, there is a social movement strategy focused on building power and putting pressure on the state and capital from the outside. Even more immediate to radical media producers is the question, will elections which propagate radical, progressive, ideas increase the audience for radical media and the radical consciousness more widely or are social movements a more effective audience and radical consciousness creator?

In Farrell's (2020) analysis radical media actors in *Jacobin, In These Times* and *Red Pepper* differ in the weight they give to these two strategies and these two understanding of the source of and creation of radical audiences. Uetricht places more emphasis on elections, giving considerable weight to campaigns such as Sanders' 2016 campaign for inspiring and building a socialist consciousness, which in turn allows for the radical political organisation Democratic Socialists of America to be built and progressive seats at local and national level in the USA be won. Burns from *In These Times* places more emphasis on movements. Nelson in *Red Pepper* tries to engage and sustain a position between the two, with the radical media as a kind of forum. In practice, this means trying to retain a balance between the socialist Labour Party led by Corbyn and the social movements that continue to exist and struggle against racial, environmental and gender injustice outside of the Labour Party. A twofold dynamic seemed to emerge as such: New Social Democracy, particularly in the USA and UK, became an orbit for radical politics at an organisation level, which became an audience and funding source for radical media, which in turn meant that radical media journalists and producers also became radical political actors in these projects, campaigns and elections.

As the more professionalised radical media publications and their producers, actors and writers began to orbit social democratic electoral campaigns, while other radical media projects operating in more activist and community settings saw mixed outcomes. Publications of the anti-austerity era in Ireland, such as *Rabble Magazine and Dublin Community TV*, declined or closed. Radical publications connected, for example to the International Socialist organisation closed as their organisation folded, under allegations of abuse within their party. Community publications outside of the London core, the *Bristol Cable and Bella Caladonia*, saw gradual growth by contrast and platforms such as *Black Power News* in the USA represented a degree of infrastructure development out of the Black Lives Matter and the struggle for Black liberation.

In the December 2019 UK General Election radical media were a key component within a social democratic electoral campaign. Radical publications and platforms, using their own websites and distributing their content across social media, reaching millions, argued for and supported the progressive policies of the Labour Party, encouraged mobilisations, canvassing and other electoral campaign work. In addition, they challenged the PR of the Conservative Party and attempted to counteract the consistent negative coverage of the British Labour party by the mainstream media (Deacon et al. 2019). Radical media, as a mass force, were more deeply than ever entwined in the mainstream of political life. Despite this the

British Labour Party lost. The radical media were not enough. As one Momentum (the left-wing pressure group within the British Labour Party) activist wrote,

> the circulatory networks of power and privilege that exist between media, politics and big business mutually reinforce one another. In the face of a socialist politician with a chance at office, instincts and interests set into motion a process of absolute strangulation and disorganisation that is difficult for any Left to face down.
>
> *Proletariato_Papi 2019*

To an extent the Bernie Sanders campaign in 2020 was a rerun of this defeat: a bold and bashful radical media ecosystem saw itself as ideological coordinator of a social democratic electoral campaign, its content reaching wider and wider audiences, as well as its personalities intervening in the media mainstream as radical voices. Various radical media publications analysed this defeat as one of the overriding power of corporate money and media (Marcetic 2020), the war by the Democratic Party to defeat him (Allen and Parnes 2021) or the analysis that Bernie Sanders lost the election but it was a victory for the establishment of mass socialism in the USA (Ackerman 2020).

In Ireland, the social democratic wave did not end in defeat, or at least end. Sinn Fein went from a breakthrough electoral force in 2016 to the largest political organisation on the Island of Ireland in 2020 on a social democratic and left programme (Coulter and Reynolds 2020). It can be difficult to account for this contrasting success of Sinn Fein if one is to consider these results in turns of radical media publishing and content. Ireland has had the least advances in radical publishing in the period of the three countries, when taking into account the differences of size and scale. Why then has there been a different result in Ireland?

Ireland remains to a degree on a periphery of the Anglosphere, without centres of capital, or social democratic urban centres such as London or New York. The lack of a concentration of capital is two-sided: the forces of big business are weaker and the layers of social liberal power which contain and co-opt independence struggles are less prominent on the periphery. This can create more political room, particularly with a loss of legitimacy of the ruling class and the state (organic crisis of hegemony), which Ireland has experienced since 2008; and with consideration that Sinn Fein emerged from a context of colonialism and military conflict, this creates a long memory of struggle, organisation and advancement in the face of more powerful forces. In addition, in Ireland, vibrant mass social movements have defended communities and have important wins, as well as had near victories from Water Charges, Repeal of the 8th Amendment and Housing Action in Ireland, Sinn Fein to an extent 'borrowed' this social movement power. This social movement sphere sees a circulation of radical media content without sustained publication, a wider counter-hegemonic public discourse, without major radical media organisation.

Conclusion: Prospects for Anglosphere Radical Media in the 2020s

The 2020s began, haunted by the recent experiences of financial crisis, racial injustice, social reproductive crisis and present, future prospects of ecological destruction. The Covid-19 pandemic entered stage left, compounding the existing crises and introducing healthcare and the social control of disease as a central determinant of everyday life, across the entire globe. In this context, street politics while restricted has surfaced, particularly in a new wave of Black Lives Matter in response to police racial murders, feminist street protest in response to the murder of women and housing and tenants unions and organisation in response to the commodification of housing, rising rents and the closing of public amenities. Ireland, the country most on the periphery of the Anglosphere, retains a strong radical politics, without the emergence of new radical media. In the USA and UK, a plethora of social movements forms, ideas and expression seem to be occurring once again on the margins and on the ground, deeply rooted in the day-to-day struggles of the ordinary people, while the mainstream of electoral political life is stagnant, and the ominous possibility of further crisis and instability looms. What then can be learnt from Anglosphere radical media during this period and what potential forms can emerge?

Here it is worth moving from an analysis of the concepts, theories, histories and changing forms of radical media organisation and politics to a contribution on what could help strengthen and expand the radical media sphere, based on its concrete existing form, and potential advances. The interwoven crises we face seem to grow larger every day, not only strengthening the need for radical political, economic and social change but also making the obstacles we face feel more and more insurmountable. The post-financial crisis and post-Occupy period opened up some similar dynamics (crisis, resistance, defeat, economic recovery and continued state violence), and learning from the successes and limits of this period of radical media development can help chart the 2020s.

The 2010s have established and re-energised a range of professional Marxist, democratic socialists and social democratic media platforms and publications. The sustainable organisational form, sustainable funding models, expansion and institutional building dynamics particularly in the USA are something that can be more generally learned from across radical media and in radical politics in the 2020s. The establishment and reinvigoration of these publications in the early 2010s was part of a process of reorganisation. This was quite an open minded, multi-tendency phase, in which different bodies of radical thought were engaged: movements and elections, identity and class, insurrection and reform, local and national and international. This openness of content can be renewed and supported by orientation towards radical media as radical education instead of political demarcation. *Jacobin* reading groups were just one example of this form of radical media as radical education, as were radical media forums as part of The World Transformed. Such radical media publications and platforms can also serve a resource redistributive function, distributing organisational development knowledge, journalist skills and money to new and smaller radical media and movements themselves.

Radical media from below, the media of activism, community organising, rank and file workers, of social movements and subcultures, of rooted communities, experiences and actions have incredible potential to grow. The majority of radical content in the digital era in circulation still comes from these sources, from the 'publics', 'audiences' and movements themselves, but is largely circulated on digital corporate media sites. The first key lesson from the 2010 period for social movement radical media and radical media from below is to break from the circulation dynamics of digital corporate media, and establish its own sites and infrastructure. For example there have been hundreds of Black power and feminist groups across the Anglosphere and hundreds of thousands of participants, but only dozens of (or less) publications. There are two potential pathways to such radical media organisations from below. Creating and consolidating movement, grassroots union and other organising and activist media into aggregator sites, which can in turn facilitate coordination of platforms, sites and content (bring together what already exists) would be a major step forward. There is also room to adopt funding and ownership models, subscription and membership like *Jacobin and* the *Bristol Cable,* a strategy also adapted by 'base building' tenants, community and grassroots worker unions. This could be used to expand and formalise grassroots radical media. In both cases radical media which roots itself in everyday life and which facilitates radical imagination and emancipatory ideas will play an important role in a wider counter-hegemonic struggle.

Bibliography

Ackerman, S. (2020). The cosmic irony of Bernie Sanders's rise. *Jacobin*. Retrieved 17/2/2020 from www.jacobinmag.com/2020/02/democratic-primary-electability-bernie-sanders.

Allen, J., & Parnes, A. (2021). *Lucky: How Joe Biden barely won the presidency*. New York: Crown Publishing Group.

Arrighi, G. (1994). *The long twentieth century: Money, power, and the origins of our times*. London: Verso.

Atton, C. (2002). *Alternative media*. London: Sage.

Baker, J., Lynch, K., Cantillon, S., & Walsh, J. (2016). *Equality: From theory to action*. New York & London: Palgrave Macmillan.

Bernstein, E. (1993). *Bernstein: The preconditions of socialism*. Cambridge: Cambridge University Press.

Cammaerts, B. (2013). The mediation of insurrectionary symbolic damage: The 2010 UK student protests. *International Journal of Press/Politics, 18*(4), 525–548.

Costanza-Chock, S. (2012). Mic check! Media cultures and the Occupy movement. *Social Movement Studies, 11*(3–4), 375–385.

Coulter, C., & Reynolds, J. (2020). Good times for a change? Ireland since the general election. *Soundings, 75*(75), 66–81.

Cox, L. (2017). The Irish water charges movement: Theorising "the social movement in general". *Interface: A Journal for and About Social Movements, 9*(1), 161–203.

Cox, M. (2002). September 11th and US hegemony—or will the 21st century be American too? *International Studies Perspectives*, *3*(1), 53–70.

Curran, J. (2002). *Media and power*. New York & London: Routledge.

Davis, A. Y. (1990). *Women, culture & politics*. New York: Vintage Books.

Deacon, D., Goode, J., Smith, D., Wring, D., Downey, J., & Vaccari, C. (2019). General election report 1. Centre for Research in Communication and Culture, Loughborough University. www.lboro.ac.uk/news-events/general-election/report-1/

Dorrien, G. (2019). *Social democracy in the making*. Yale: Yale University Press.

Downing, J. D. (2000). *Radical media: Rebellious communication and social movements*. London: Sage.

Dublin Community Television. (2010). *Looking Left Series*. Dublin, Ireland. https://www.dctv.ie/

Enli, G. S. (2008). Redefining public service broadcasting: Multi-platform participation. *Convergence*, *14*(1), 105–120. https://doi.org/10.1177/135485650708442

Evans, S. M. (1980). *Personal politics: The roots of women's liberation in the Civil Rights Movement and the New Left*. New York: Vintage.

Fanon, F. (2007). *The wretched of the earth*. Grove/Atlantic, Inc.

Farrell, S. (2020). *A political economy of radical media* (Doctoral dissertation, Dublin City University).

Fitzgerald, K. J., & Rodgers, D. M. (2000). Radical social movement organizations: A theoretical model. *Sociological Quarterly*, *41*(4), 573–592.

Fenton. (2016). *Digital, political, radical*. Cambridge: Polity Press.

Foley, M. (2004). Colonialism and journalism in Ireland. *Journalism Studies*, *5*(3), 373–385.

Fraser, N., Arruzza, C., & Bhattacharya, T. (2019). *Feminism for the 99%*. London: Verso.

Freeman, J. (1973). The origins of the women's liberation movement. *American Journal of Sociology*, *78*(4), 792–811.

Freire, P. (1971). *Pedagogy of the oppressed* (30th anniversary edition). London: Continuum.

Freire, P. (1996). *Pedagogy of the oppressed* (revised). New York: Continuum.

Fuchs, C. (2012). Some Reflections on Manuel Castells' Book "Networks of Outrage and Hope. Social Movements in the Internet Age". *tripleC: Communication, Capitalism & Critique. Open Access Journal for a Global Sustainable Information Society*, *10*(2), 775–797. DOI: https://doi.org/10.31269/triplec.v10i2.459

Fuchs, C. (2014). *OccupyMedia!: The Occupy Movement and social media in crisis capitalism*. London: John Hunt Publishing.

Fuchs, C., & Sandoval, M. (2015). The political economy of capitalist and alternative social media. In C. Atton (Ed.), *The Routledge companion to alternative and community media* (pp. 165–175). London: Routledge.

Fürsich, E. (2010). Media and the representation of others. *International Social Science Journal*, *61*(199), 113–130.

Goodman, A. (2016). *Democracy now!: Twenty years covering the movements changing America*. New York: Simon & Schuster.

Gramsci, A. (1971). *Selections from the prison notebooks*. London: Lawrence Wishart.

Gray, N. (Ed.). (2018). *Rent and its discontents: A century of housing struggle*. London: Rowman & Littlefield.

Haider, A. (2018). *Mistaken identity: Race and class in the age of Trump*. Verso Books.

Hall, S. (2005). The rediscovery of 'ideology': Return of the repressed in media studies. In *Culture, society and the media* (pp. 61–95). London: Routledge.

Hall, S., & Jefferson, T. (Eds.). (1993). *Resistance through rituals: Youth subcultures in post-war Britain*. London: Routledge.

Hall, S., & Whannel, P. (2018). *The popular arts*. Durham: Duke University Press.

Hallin, D. C., & Mancini, P. (Eds.). (2011). *Comparing media systems beyond the Western world.* Cambridge: Cambridge University Press.

Harrison, S. (1974). *Poor men's guardians: A record of the struggles for a democratic newspaper press, 1763–1973.* London: Lawrence Wishart.

Harvey, D. (2014). *Seventeen contradictions and the end of capitalism.* Oxford: Oxford University Press.

Hearne, R., O'Callaghan, C., Kitchin, R., & Feliciantonio, C. D. (2018). The relational articulation of housing crisis and activism in post-crash Dublin, Ireland. In N. Gray (Eds.), *Rent and Its Discontents: A Century of Housing Struggle* (pp. 153–167). London: Rowman & Littlefield.

Howley, K. (Ed.). (2009). *Understanding community media.* London: Sage.

Ishkanian, A., & Peña Saavedra, A. (2019). The politics and practices of intersectional prefiguration in social movements: The case of Sisters Uncut. *The Sociological Review, 67*(5), 985–1001.

Jeppesen, S. (2016). Understanding alternative media power: Mapping content & practice to theory, ideology, and political action. *Democratic Communiqué, 27*(1), 54–54.

Juris, J. S. (2016). Reflections on# Occupy Everywhere: Social media, public space, and emerging logics of aggregation. *American Ethnologist, 2*(39), 259–279.

Kampf-Lassin, M. (2011, December 8). The Occupied Chicago Tribune: Chicago's voice for a global opening. *In These Times.*

Kauffman, L. A. (2017). *Direct action: Protest and the reinvention of American radicalism.* London: Verso Books.

Kavada, A. (2020). Creating the collective: Social media, the Occupy Movement and its constitution as a collective actor. In *Protest technologies and media revolutions.* Bingley: Emerald Publishing.

Kidd, D. (2013). Indymedia.org: A new communications commons. In M. MacCaughy & M. Ayers (Eds.), *Cyberactivism* (pp. 57–80). London: Routledge.

Kioupkiolis, A., & Katsambekis, G. (2018). Radical left populism from the margins to the mainstream: A comparison of Syriza and Podemos. In *Podemos and the new political cycle* (pp. 201–226). Cham: Palgrave Macmillan.

Lane, F. (1997). *The origins of modern Irish socialism, 1881–1896.* Cork: Cork University Press.

Leach, D. K. (2013). Prefigurative politics. In D. Snow, D. Porta, P. Klandermans, & D. McAdam (Eds.), *The Wiley-Blackwell encyclopedia of social and political movements.* DOI: 10.1002/9780470674871

Lima, V. (2021). Urban austerity and activism: Direct action against neoliberal housing policies. *Housing Studies, 36*(2), 258–277.

Lloyd, D. (2001). Regarding Ireland in a post-colonial frame. *Cultural Studies, 15*(1), 12–32.

Luxemburg, R. (2007). *The essential Rosa Luxemburg: Reform or revolution and the mass strike.* Chicago: Haymarket Books.

Lynch, P. (2015). Bottom-up versus top-down campaigning at the Scottish Independence Referendum 2014. Revue Française de Civilisation Britannique. *French Journal of British Studies, 20*(XX–2), 1–12.

Marcetic. (2020). The corporate media convinced millions that Bernie was "Unelectable". *Jacobin Magazine.* www.jacobinmag.com/2020/07/bernie-sanders-joe-biden-democratic-primary

Marx, K. (1972). *The Marx-Engels Reader* (Vol. 4). New York: Norton.

Marx, K., & Engels, F. (1965). *The German ideology.* London: Wiley.

McVeigh, R., & Rolston, B. (2021). *Ireland, colonialism and the unfinished revolution.* Belfast: Beyond the Pale Publishing.

Meyer, M. (2009). *Word & image in colonial and postcolonial literatures and cultures.* London: BRILL.

Mullally, U. (Ed.). (2018). *Repeal the 8th.* Dublin, Ireland: Unbound Publishing.

Mosco, V. (2009). *The political economy of communication* (2nd ed). London: Sage. DOI:10.4135/9781446279946.

Proletariato_Papi. (2019). Wading through the Mud. *Blog Post.* Retrieved 23/12/2019 from https://medium.com/@jonashombres/wading-through-themud-8809f25d5618

Randell-Moon, H. (2017). Thieves like us: The British monarchy, celebrity, and settler colonialism. *Celebrity Studies, 8*(3), 393–408.

Reinecke, J. (2018). Social movements and prefigurative organizing: Confronting entrenched inequalities in Occupy London. *Organization Studies, 39*(9), 1299–1321.

Schulman, J. (2016). Bernie Sanders and the dilemma of the Democratic "Party". *New Politics, 15*(4), 7.

Scott, C. (2015). How news outlet The Canary aims to 'diversify media'. *Journalism.co.uk.* Retrieved 12/12/2019 from www.journalism.co.uk/news/how-news-outlet-the-canary-aims-todiversify-media-/s2/a576960/

Seymour, R. (2017). *Corbyn: The strange rebirth of radical politics.* London: Verso Books.

Söderberg, J. (2015). *Hacking capitalism: The free and open source software movement (Vol. 9).* New York & London: Routledge.

Streitmatter, R. (2001). *Voices of revolution: The dissident press in America.* Columbia: Columbia University Press.

Sunkara, B. (2014, November ND). Project Jacobin. *New Left Review.* Retrieved 21/11/2019 from https://newleftreview.org/issues/II90/articles/bhaskar-sunkara-project-jacobin

Taylor, K. Y. (2016). *From# BlackLivesMatter to black liberation.* Chicago: Haymarket Books.

Vucetic, S. (2020). *The anglosphere.* Stanford: Stanford University Press.

Wellings, B., & Mycock, A. (2019). *The anglosphere: Continuity, dissonance and location.* Oxford: Oxford University Press.

Whelan, K. (2004). The Green Atlantic: Radical reciprocities between Ireland and America in the long eighteenth century. In *A new imperial History: Culture. identity, and modernity in Britain and the Empire, 1660–1840,* 216–238. Cambridge: Cambridge: Cambridge University Press.

Williams, J. J. (2017). Planting a flag for socialism: An interview with Bhaskar Sunkara. *Symplokē, 26*(1–2), 507–527. Retrieved from muse.jhu.edu/article/710040

Williams, R. (2013). *Keywords (Routledge revivals): A vocabulary of culture and society.* London: Routledge. DOI: 10.4324/9780203124949

Wolfson, T. (2012). From the Zapatistas to Indymedia: Dialectics and orthodoxy in contemporary social movements. *Communication, Culture & Critique, 5*(2), 149–170. https://doi.org/10.1111/j.1753-9137.2012.01131.x

Wood, E. M. (2002). *The origin of capitalism: A longer view.* London: Verso.

5

RADICAL JOURNALISM À LA FRANÇAISE

Between Differentiation and Stigma

Laurent Thiong-Kay and Nikos Smyrnaios

In France, the dominant pole of the journalistic field (Bourdieu, 1994) has been strongly impacted by neoliberal governmentality (Foucault, 2004). Indeed, from the 1980s onwards, the major newspapers, such as Le Monde and Libération, underwent a process of depoliticization (Juhem, 2001). Neutrality became the normative horizon of the profession, in a country where journalism was historically engaged and politicized (Neveu, 2001). At the same time, journalists became increasingly precarious and were subjected to intense competition for material but also symbolic resources such as the 'press card'.[1] The attribution of this card is supposed to distinguish professional journalists, who are meant to respect deontological norms such as rigor, accuracy, integrity, fairness, impartiality and objectivity, from other media workers, outsiders, radicals or militants. Thus, the press card functions as a mechanism of symbolic recognition of the profession – and therefore exclusion of media perceived as non-mainstream.

It was not until the end of the 1990s and the anti-globalization movement that this trend was strongly and concretely challenged. These mobilizations sought to find margins of autonomy vis-à-vis mainstream media. Based on the Indymedia model, a wave of "mediactivism" (Cardon & Granjon, 2010) developed in France. Symmetrically, the criticism of mainstream media spread to professional journalism itself: numerous outlets that carry out an endogenous critique of the media industry were created. The development of online news from the early 2000s onwards has allowed the rise of alternative and participatory media that could reach a wider public with relatively low costs (Marty et al., 2012; Smyrnaios, 2013). Since that period, many original editorial projects have developed, engaging themselves in promoting solidarity, ecology and progressive politics (Lévêque & Ruellan, 2010).

Our research aims to understand the sociopolitical logics behind the emergence of this alternative and sometimes-radical journalism. More precisely, we want to question the identity of politically committed journalists and their relationship to

DOI: 10.4324/9781003221784-5

the norms of their profession. Our objective is to examine the conditions that make the advent of this new professional identity possible. In order to do so, we composed a sample of six journalists who are freelance or have worked as permanent staff for five independent professional online media with a large audience: Grégoire Souchay, who works for Reporterre, a news website sympathetic to ecologist and alternative movements founded by a former journalist of Le Monde; Camille Polloni, who worked for Basta!, an online media with a team of journalists and civil society activists and Les Jours, an independent subscription-based news website founded by former journalists of Libération; Louise Fessard and Jade Lindgaard, who work for Mediapart, a progressive subscription-based investigative journalism website founded by a former director of Le Monde; Gaspard Glanz founder of the press agency Taranis News, which documents social conflict from the inside; and Frédéric Scheiber, a freelance photographer who has worked for several independent outlets covering particularly social movements.

Through lengthy semi-structured interviews with these journalists and content analysis, we studied their productions, their trajectories and their representations in the context of a qualitative study on the media coverage of the movement against the Sivens dam (Thiong-Kay, 2020a,). This mobilization is part of the struggles against what is called in France 'Grands Projets Inutiles et Imposés', a designation that groups together massive construction projects that are considered anti-ecological, inefficient and useless such as the Notre-Dame-des-Landes airport in the region of Nantes, the Center Parks in Roybon or the Bure radioactive waste burial project.

The Sivens dam (Barrage de Sivens) was a dam which was planned for construction across the Tescou, a tributary of the Tarn River in southwest France, near Toulouse, that aimed to support intensive agriculture. Supported by local authorities such as the Department of Tarn, the dam was to be built in the Testet wetland which includes an extremely rich ecosystem, in the heart of a forest that is the "subject of attachment" (Latour, 2017), in the region. In 2011, a collective called "Tant qu'il y aura des bouilles" was created to fight against this project. Later, hundreds of people came to protect the biodiversity of the wetlands and to prevent the construction of the dam, creating a permanent protest camp in 2013 the Testet ZAD (Zone à défendre or 'Zone to Defend'). The Testet ZAD was inspired by one of Notre-Dame-des-Landes, the most well-known 'Zone to Defend' in France that resisted several concerted attempts by the French state to evict it in order to construct a new airport.

The sociological composition, ideological background and repertoires of collective action (Tilly, 1995) of the two groups opposing the Sivens dam differed: the first one was composed mainly by ecologist militants and was legalistic (Ollitrault & Villalba, 2014); the second one included anarchists and radical ecology activists and favored direct and sometimes illegal action. Construction work began in 2014 and was then halted after Rémi Fraisse, a 21-year-old man protesting against the construction project, was killed by a stun grenade fired by police. His death sparked further protests across France, some of which were violent. The project was then abandoned in 2015. This movement was covered by the journalists who we interviewed for this research.

Informational Activism and Fragmentation of the Journalistic Field

At the heart of the rise of radical journalism in France, we find journalists with a political trajectory and socialization that predispose them to forms of, if not commitment, at least critical reflexivity. Most of the respondents have a university education in social sciences (sociology, political science) which gives them the ability to question the characteristics of their profession and their own relationship to it. On the other hand, the creation of left-wing media, in the context of the restructuring of the journalistic field (Demers, 2007), allows political radicalism to flourish in the media. Our respondents have an activist experience that gives a specific meaning to their journalistic practice. But it is necessary to work for certain media so that this politicization can be fully combined with journalism.

For example, Jade Lindgaard graduated from Sciences Po Paris and the Centre de Formation des Journalistes in 1997. She started working for AFP, the French public press agency, in the economics department, which she then left for the cultural magazine Les Inrockuptibles, where she worked on contemporary art until 2007. But Jade Lindgaard then experienced personal activism in the anti-globalization movement through the climate action camps. She recalls:

> [...] A revelation about the importance of the climate issue and the richness of the climate justice movement. I see this thing, both the radicalness of the proposal, the creativity of the mode of mobilization, the intellectual richness of the exchanges, how the very sharp expertise on energy transition plans.
>
> *Jade Lindgaard, Mediapart*

Back in France, she set out to cover the climate issue. This objective coincided with her recruitment at Mediapart, an online investigative media explicitly positioned on the left of the political spectrum:

> I was offered] a position in higher education and research, and I told him [Mediapart's editorial director] that I was really interested, but I asked him what he had planned for ecology [...]. He looked at me and replied: "Nothing, for me ecology means turning off the tap water when we brush our teeth, that's fine.]" [It was] completely anecdotal in his eyes. I was very upset when he said that. And then I remember well, he looked at me and said: "If you also want to do articles on ecology, of course it will be possible". And so, it started like that. To answer your question, it was also, at the beginning, a fight within Mediapart to impose ecology as a subject in its own right. [...] Today it would never occur to anyone in the editorial staff to question the legitimacy of having a full-time person on ecology.
>
> *Jade Lindgaard, Mediapart*

The case of Gaspard Glanz (Taranis News) is also enlightening. Socialized in participatory democracy within the Strasbourg youth council, he is strongly committed during his university years against the two neoliberal laws promoted by right-wing Presidents Jacques Chirac, in 2006, and Nicolas Sarkozy, in 2009: respectively, the "first employment contract" and the law on the "freedom and responsibilities of universities". There he rubbed shoulders with the fringes of autonomous university activism, and quickly experienced clashes with the police. At the heart of the confrontations, he became familiar with filming from a first-person point of view (Thiong-Kay, 2020b), which was part of a more general trend of internet activists (Blondeau & Allard, 2007). At that point, for Gaspard Glanz, the objective was less to publicize the conflict than to build up a corpus of images that can defend the activists in case of a trial (Nez, 2015). He once again indulged in the practice at the NATO summit in Strasbourg in 2009, marked by the first appearance in France of the "black bloc", a tactic used by protesters who wear black clothing and other face-concealing and face-protecting items associated with anarchism. At the heart of the protest, the then activist understood that there were no journalists to film these demonstrations from the inside. He then saw the potential of such a practice as a professional journalist:

> And it's also the first time I'm in a place where there are no journalists. I'm in my city, I'm at the heart of the demonstration, of the "bloc" as it could exist at the time, without a banner, without anything, but I'm embedded in the middle of the demonstrators, and while demonstrating, I don't have a TV headset, I just have a camera. [...] It was the real turning point, April 2009, when I was no longer an activist in the sense of being active on the ground.
>
> *Gaspard Glanz, Taranis News*

It is therefore in his activist commitments that Gaspard Glanz draws the specificity of his journalistic activity. He finished his studies in sociology and created his company in Rennes in 2011. Initially planned to be a subsidiary of Rue89's network of local news websites, the project was abandoned and then transformed to a TV agency and renamed Taranis News. The agency's journalist started working on the subjects of Notre-Dame-des-Landes and Sivens Zones to defend, the situation of migrants in Calais, and then the Yellow Vests movement, a series of grassroots weekly protests for economic justice and institutional political reforms that began in France in November 2018. Of course, the subversive and sometimes ambiguous nature of Taranis News' reports and publications earned our interviewee hostility. This hostility comes not only from the political field, but also from his fellow journalists, as we will see later.

The French journalistic field is indeed characterized by fragmentation, power struggles and legitimacy disputes that are exacerbated by its depoliticization. Thus, committed journalists have to work in independent radical media in order to fight for the recognition of certain issues they care about because politically controversial topics are often neutralized by the mainstream press. This is particularly true of climate change. As Jean-Baptiste Comby (2015) has shown, the dominant, generalist national media do not offer regular forums to social actors criticizing the ecological damage provoked by capitalism. This situation is considered structurally unfavorable by our respondents, which leads them to invest themselves in the margins of the journalistic field. However, this "migration" is not an exit, but on the contrary a will to influence the profession and push the media to participate in the emergence of public problems and their inclusion in the political agenda (Hassenteufel, 2010). For our interviewees, this requires the consolidation of their media ventures. It is therefore a question of fighting not only 'through' the media but also 'in' the media.

> My activism includes politics, ecological and social commitment, but it is above all how to allow other media to exist in the journalistic universe. So that we can get out of the niche. As François Ruffin (French journalist who is now deputy of the Left) says: "alternative media are not an alternative".
>
> *Grégoire Souchay, Reporterre*

Committed journalists thus assert their desire to treat information differently. By seeking to change their 'framing' or 'angle', they have a twofold objective: to offer original coverage in order to establish the specificity of their media, but also to deploy a counter-framing to the representations of the social world in force within the dominant media space formed by the national and regional press, as well as political communication. During the latest social movements in France, stereotypes were aimed at the subaltern counter-publics (Fraser, 2003), such as the 'zadists', the 'black blocs' or the 'Yellow Vests':

> [On the subject of the environmentalist mobilization against the Sivens dam] We also had this concern at Rue 89 to shift the gaze a little in relation to what could be done in the daily press [...] We agreed on the fact that it was more interesting to tell where the people who were demonstrating there came from, what their intellectual influences were, their militant backgrounds, and what they came to find on the ZAD.
>
> *Camille Polloni, Les Jours*

Finally, radical journalism also comes about as a reaction to what the actors perceive as the dysfunctions of the mainstream media. These dysfunctions have prompted them to join the politicized margins of the field, which carry out a critique in action of the latter. Thus, the strong dependence of the regional daily press on local political actors (Bousquet, 2014) and institutional sources is pointed out:

> I had done a month's internship at La Dépêche du Midi[2] in Toulouse, I didn't like it [...] As a local intern during the summer, it was really disgusting and the little I had done (he blows his nose), it had been rewritten, you could feel the weight (he insists on this word) of routines and heaviness that there was to write [...] and then ... the self-censorship, even direct censorship.

There was really this thing where you said wow [...]. I really don't want to be there.

Grégoire Souchay, Reporterre

The facts that are reported by the regional press, generally we see quite quickly that it is told through the police version, and there is very little room for another version because it is told the very next day, [...] I understand, I don't necessarily know how to meet the family, etc. [...] I understand, I know a lot of journalists from La Provence (main newspaper in the region of Marseille), for example, there's an emergency, they have to fill in the paper for the next day, etc. [...] They're the ones who have to do it. [...] These are journalists who will enter the police station much more easily. They have a relationship of trust with the police officers, who are also their suppliers of ... of news in fact.

Louise Fessard, Mediapart

The same applies to the media's submission to the political and media agenda, which generally forces journalists to cover the hottest news. However, our respondents consider that it is sometimes necessary – and rewarding – to work on events that are not in the main agenda. For them, it is therefore a question of breaking with the injunction to instantaneity:

[Working for Les Jours] I was really interested in this multi-article format. To be able to dig into issues over several weeks, several months, and I function a bit like that, I have obsessions. I'm interested in all police issues. [...] Since I've been here, almost two years, I've worked on four or five subjects, no more. It allows you to do the preliminary documentation, you're not a researcher but you can take the time to read books, to read the press that has already appeared to try to get up to speed on the subject, to go and see people with not just three specific questions to ask them but a discussion to have with them on what would be interesting to do journalistically, What do they think of the way the media report their activity, are there possible improvements in the journalistic treatment of an issue, because there are subjects that have been little or badly treated and that deserve to be revisited. [...] It is quite satisfying intellectually.

Camille Polloni, Les Jours

Autonomy, Subjectivation, Proximity

To attract competent journalists, media companies that invest in the margins of the field also understand that they have to rethink their internal organization. For committed journalists, it is not so much a question of joining a politicized media as of working in conditions that suit them. These conditions are often thought in opposition to the model of management and the editorial strategies in force within the mainstream media:

On the web, there is Rue89, which is in the process of collapsing, there
is Mediapart, which is doing very, very well, there is Les Jours, which is
also starting to do well after a year, and Basta! [...] In a few years, openings
have been created everywhere. With organizations that are also flexible and
interesting. Here, in the way we work, we are 26 employees, but not like in a
very hierarchical daily newspaper with a head of department on every floor.
I have two editors-in-chief, and it's one or the other who proofreads my
papers, who gives me indications on what I could do, who suggests things. It's
also a more pleasant way of organizing work.

Camille Polloni, Les Jours

We send the articles in the evening, in the morning Hervé Kempf reads them,
he calls between 7 and 8 am for the last modifications and at 8 or 9 am they
are published. Hervé Kempf is editor-in-chief and director of the publication.
In 2014, there were four journalists in Paris, and about twenty freelancers.
[...] I was free in Reporterre to write as I wanted. I was never rewritten. And
therefore, I had total freedom to explain my perception of things.

Grégoire Souchay, Reporterre

In the choice of their subjects, sources and treatment, we therefore find among
our interviewees an aspiration to autonomy that resonates strongly with that of
the activists of the new social movements (Ion, 1994; Dupuis-Déri, 2005). As a
result, journalists and their sources are connected by 'elective affinities' (Löwy,
2004): autonomy as a political value resonates with the radical media's desire to
free journalism of the straitjacket of the dominant press. Our journalists, driven by
autonomy, do not fetishize objectivity and instead leave more room for their subjectivity (Lemieux et al., 2010). The following passages attest of a desire to work on
subjects that affect them personally. But also, to 'change the order of things':

Basically, there are things that interest me, a ZAD is opening up not far away,
I'm interested in anti-capitalists, I want to know. For me it's part of history!
It's important, there are things that are created, even if they are epiphenomena
on the scale of humanity, but it's my own history. I won't live long but on my
scale it's interesting. [...] In fact, it's super egotistical, because I do things that
interest me. And I'm not good at it because I don't think about the subjects
that interest "them", the press. I do things that interest me. I do my own journalism, in fact.

Frédéric Scheiber, freelance photojournalist

I insist on this: posing as a journalist on ecology means that yes, it is a
commitment [... I insist on this: posing as a journalist on ecology means that
yes, it's a commitment [...] i.e. the Notre-Dame-des-Landes airport must not
be built, Europacity if it is built, it's really a problem and well 1), Mediapart

allowed me to do it, 2) it allowed me to do articles that were different from the articles published by the newspapers or media with which we compare ourselves, so that means the mainstream media Le Monde, Les Echos, Le Figaro for example, and 3) it allowed me to, how shall I put it, to gain a particular audience who came to read it.

Jade Lindgaard, Mediapart

Journalism […] I have the impression that it is the means by which I am most useful for advancing "The Cause", that is to say that it is my lever. Some people are going to be trade unionists in their company, some are going to write revolutionary pamphlets like the Invisible Committee, some are going to be involved in a party or take up positions of power. […] Where I am effective and useful is here. […] I didn't write an article on Sivens to attract militants, but if it did, then it was useful. You see, it's this relationship that's a bit difficult, because an ordinary journalist doesn't have to have an impact somewhere. You make the news, and it's pure news. And if it has an impact, it's almost suspect. So there is this thing, this positioning that is a bit complicated.

Grégoire Souchay, Reporterre

This logic of subjectivity is embodied in the proximity between our interviewees and their activist sources. As for local press correspondents, committed journalists' identity is constructed in the opposite way to the discourse founding the professional autonomy of journalists. It is through the search for social proximity and not through the distance established between the editor, the sources and the readers that belonging to the profession is forged (Bouron, 2015, p. 96). Thus, our journalist respondents seek to build relationships of trust with activists (Thiong-Kay, 2021). This is a way for them to neutralize the 'substantialist' critique that considers journalism as an entity governed by universal rules and logics, despite the diversity of media (Nollet, 2009). Similarly, they rely heavily on counter-expertise, 'fact checking' and material such as amateur video content that activists post on their websites and social media profiles. Finally, through the participatory dimension of their media, committed journalists fully involve activists and militants in their production process.

Toward a New Mythology of Professional Excellence?

Journalists deploy this range of practices for different reasons. First, they are generally more in tune with the activist perception of the issues they are working on. Second, they know that their first readers will be activists or sympathetic audiences. Third, unlike their mainstream counterparts, they have little access to institutional sources. Fourth, they want to show, on the ground, that 'another journalism' is possible. This 'other journalism' is not just a question of investigative subjects or ways of handling information. It is claimed as a reaction to the coverage by mainstream media, and to the way the latter manage the social distance separating them from their interviewees. Journalists want to *distinguish* themselves from their colleagues, in the sense of Bourdieu (1979):

> There's a colleague and friend who's not super flexible we'll say, who's a bit more into the salons. Well, he's got a good background, but he's not always prepared to go and see people with dreadlocks and dogs, things like that, whereas I don't have any worries. Anyway, I don't have any problems with anyone, really: suits and ties, djellabas, I talk to everyone.
>
> *Frédéric Scheiber, freelance photojournalist*

This logic of distinction of 'another journalism' promoted by our interviewees aims also in occupying a better position in the journalistic field. As we wrote above, journalists as a social group are characterized by strong internal competition. This competitive dimension produces orders of magnitude by valuing specific trajectories, social capital and professional practices. As we have said earlier, through the press card allocation commission, the field of journalism in France provides itself with a validation mechanism (symbolic and effective) that institutes certain actors and marginalizes others. This exacerbated competition between members of the journalistic field may lead some of them to assume an explicitly 'rebellious' position with regard to these legitimacy grids. It may be a question of making the non-respect of the journalistic *cursus honorum* a reason for audacity, and therefore excellence, which turns the stigma of illegitimacy to an advantage. The case of Gaspard Glanz is particularly enlightening here as he encounters the beginning of his career:

> I arrive at the first municipal council of the city of Rennes, the boss of Ouest France *(the main local newspaper in northwest France)* arrives, he does not shake my hand. He looked at me with contempt, like you don't exist. It took him three years to shake my hand, I think ...] So disdainful as if we were a danger for Ouest France, with a turnover of 25 million euros. Why this contempt? [...] And so, at some point, having to make our own way without having to rely on the others, well, I understood that straight away. They didn't want us because we hadn't followed the normal route, because we hadn't done the training courses, because we hadn't said 'yes' to serving coffee. Because we hadn't been 'stamped' correctly, because we didn't correspond to the social norm of the young journalist.
>
> *Gaspard Glanz, Taranis News*

This criticism of the journalistic *cursus honorum* is not without consequences for the autonomy to which the activists aspire or which they claim, and which we have described above. For Gaspard Glanz, it becomes 'critique in action' through the creation of a media centered on social conflict. It is expressed in the strengthening of a do-it-yourself journalistic identity, of the reporter as an entrepreneur of himself in reaction to a highly competitive field. He continues:

> And still today it remains, you see. When people tell me: the 'alternative' media, the 'militant journalist', the 'journalist but not a journalist because he doesn't have a press card', it's always the same story. Being the black sheep has never bothered me, but if you want the press, [...] functions in cannibalism. I'm not from Paris, I didn't go to journalism school and I don't have a press card. And on top of that I have a big mouth, I don't like to be told what to do. [...] We came in saying: 'no, no, we're opening our business, we're journalists now, we're doing it by the book, the way we want to, if we don't make any money, too bad, if we do, screw you'.
>
> *Gaspard Glanz, Taranis News*

Thus, a more autonomous and subjective journalistic counter-ideal is emerging. The latter is a reaction to the structural transformation of the journalistic field. Indeed, in France, certain specialties are constantly at the center of newsrooms. This is notably the case of economic journalism. Other specialties are increasingly successful. This is particularly true of pundits and commentators who in France are called "editorialists". Generally ideologically conservative, editorialists are reactivating a French-style model of journalism, whose emphasis on commentary, as opposed to reporting, reflects the weight of meta-discourse on current events transforming the news into pretexts for the expression of opinions (Neveu, 2001, p. 14). Editorialists who are very present and influential in French newsrooms repel our respondents, who are attached to the legitimacy of investigative journalism and fieldwork. And it is often in opposition to the editorialist model that our journalists position themselves, drawing the contours of their ideal vision of the profession. Jade Lindgaard, for example, talks about the lasting influence on her of the "muckracker" type of journalist, who, at the beginning of the 20th century in the United States, worked as close as possible to the working conditions in the abattoirs and slums of Manhattan:

> It is much more prestigious and valuable as a position than to tell stories from an overhang, or whatever. You have to go for it. On the contrary, you have to go all the way. That's the only way to scratch, how can I put it, this straitjacket of discourse, of dominant representations.
>
> *Jade Lindgaard, Mediapart*

Gaspard Glanz, for his part, calls for a certain fairness of treatment. He considers that the actors of the political and social world do not question the political and ideological attachments of editorialists, unlike those who are designated as committed journalists:

> I'm a bit tired of answering this question, but today when Jean-Pierre Raffarin,[3] Aurélie Filippetti,[4] Gaspard Gantzer,[5] are judged as journalists when they are people who have just finished a forty-year career in politics without ever having done anything else, [...] hardcore politicians, these

people are journalists from one day to the next and they are not considered to be activists? Well, in that case I don't think I am either. [...] The more time goes by, the more journalism and politics become intertwined, journalists become politicians, politicians become journalists, and the less sense this question of militancy has. Today you have raw reporting, which is what I try to do, and you have analysts, commentators, they are two different jobs.

Gaspard Glanz, Taranis News

In return, French editorialists regularly target committed journalists as their adversaries. A tweet from editorialist Brice Couturier, which reads "I had the opportunity to denounce this Gaspard Glanz in 'Les Matins de France Culture' as an extreme left activist disguised as a journalist", is a case in point.

"Radical Journalist": A Label to be Neutralized

We understand that the committed or radical journalist is not just an identity assumed by our respondents. It is also a label or a stigma (Becker, 1963) attached by some of their resolutely hostile colleagues. In reality, left-wing radicalism remains marginal within the French journalistic field. The reasons for this are of different kinds. First of all, although they are committed, the journalists studied remain attached to what generally founds the legitimacy of their activity. As Jocelyne Arquembourg (2011) explains, journalists "stabilize readings of the facts, of a temporal structure, distribute roles between protagonists to whom they attribute responsibilities" (p. 34). Their activity "implies homogenizing, organizing, articulating and confronting a quantity of heterogeneous information" (Arquembourg, 2011, p. 25). Thus " media objectivity [is] the basis of their legitimacy in a democratic regime" (2011, p. 2). Our journalists, however politicized or critical, still adhere to this definition of the role of journalists. They deploy an arsenal of techniques that constitute a particular "reading contract" (Véron, 1985): contextualization of events, factual narration, gathering of all points of view, use of quotation as a way of distancing themselves from the object of investigation, explication of external resources (such as militant websites), etc. The use of these techniques is a necessary condition for the expression of subjectivity. The deployment of the former allows for the acceptance of the latter. As Jade Lindgaard explains:

I worked for the first time on the Sivens dossier, saying to myself, we have to do something, but that's always the problem when you've missed the beginning of a story, as they say in journalism, when you haven't been on the subject since the beginning, you have to get back up to speed: often these are technical and complex dossiers. [...] for me, our role as journalists is to be in a kind of accelerated research compared to the time of the research, but a research [all the same], and therefore a documentary work, of factualisation of the problem, that seems important to me.

Jade Lindgaard, Mediapart

Grégoire Souchay offers a more consistent analysis. He theorizes the complexity of the position he tries to hold between demanding external and internal constraints. Thus, he combines the respect of a certain journalistic deontology with a personal aspiration for political change:

> There is an expression I use to sum up my position, it is "the ass between two chairs" and it is the position I have always adopted and that I have chosen to take because I am not comfortable in the posture of the activist and I am not comfortable in the posture of journalism alone. I need to combine commitment with professional work, without being militant, but without being neutral. This is my position. But I am not an activist in the sense that when I work, it is a profession. And I apply professional techniques.
>
> *Grégoire Souchay, Reporterre*

Criticized for belonging to radical media, and sometimes for their activism supposedly disguised as journalism, our respondents adjust their discourse. This adjustment is designed to ward off criticism from their opponents in the media. But it is also formulated to resist other transformations of the media sphere. In this respect, we have already mentioned the presence in social movements of a type of media activism who sometimes defines itself as 'self-media' (*automedia*). This kind of political and communicational activism (Thiong-Kay, 2020a) also contributes to widening the borders and modifying the structure of the journalistic field. If we consider the mediatization of certain struggles, a range of statuses and identities coexist: self-media, citizen reporters, independent journalists without a press card, committed journalists with a press card, amateur contributors to participatory media, etc. However, when compared to these "associate-rivals" (Neveu, 1999), our respondents wish to differentiate themselves:

> I always had this thing about not becoming self-media, [...] I didn't want to become an embedded journalist on the ZAD. If you do that, then you're affiliated with the zadists: they had their own media, I totally respected them, I was doing my job, we crossed paths, other journalists were doing other types of journalistic work, and we crossed paths and respected each other and it was complementary. It wasn't competition, you see.
>
> *Grégoire Souchay, Reporterre*

In journalism, recourse to ethics functions as a modality of self-institution, because the profession is subject to competition and criticism from the social worlds around it (Ruellan, 2011). For journalists, invoking ethics makes it possible to establish orders of magnitude intended to specify – or even confine – the roles of each person, but above all to justify the relevance of their own work. While Grégoire Souchay recognizes the functional complementarity of committed journalism and activism, such a consideration allows him to reaffirm the specificity and contribution of his own professional activity. According to him, being a professional journalist implies not only reporting what is happening 'on the ground', but also knowing how to use a whole conceptual and analytical panoply to qualify and explain the facts. Such a position relegates the self-media to its primary status of a source or an actor directly implicated in the events. But it can also consist in down-grading it symbolically, by reducing it to a militant ersatz of the editorialists who dominate large news television channels. Thus, the function of journalism, even if it is committed, consists in reporting the facts, but above all in contributing to their deciphering, qualification and reinsertion in a given context.

To conclude, we must specify that the register of committed journalism some-times turns against the interviewees themselves. This is a backlash against the current structure of the journalistic field and its strong polarization, as mentioned above. Thus, several of our interviewees mentioned the difficulty of accessing offi-cial sources. They also testify to an inability to access certain demonstrations and thus do their job, because they are blocked by police. The Yellow Vests movement and a recent draft law in France have shed a harsh light on these practices, which even committed journalists find very difficult to cope with.

> Clearly, they were the ones who had the first information. [...] The journalists from La Dépêche, [...] they had a greater capacity to access official sources, so we heard them more. So, you could hear the prefect, you couldn hear the pro-dam farmers, the FNSEA[6]. I didn't have access to these sources. [...] For the zadists I was Reporterre, whereas I saw myself as a journalist and that's why at the beginning of September when there were police blockades, the head of the gendarmerie told me after passing a first blockade: "I said that Reporterre didn't pass" [...] The big problem I had with the cops was the blockades. According to them, I wasn't a journalist, so I didn't go through the roadblocks.
>
> *Grégoire Souchay, Reporterre*

These practices of the public authorities and the police forces prevent journalists from collecting all points of view. They are the translation of two public representations. Firstly, they inform us about a 'functionalist' reading of the journalistic field, which would thus be a simple copy of the political field. Secondly, these practices corres-pond to a 'deterministic' reading of the journalist with whom the official source or the representative of the police forces is confronted. The journalist is thus assigned to his press card, his specialization, his supposed political convictions and the media to which he belongs, as if he were a prisoner. In both cases, these representations favor a mechanical identification of committed journalists to militant sources. This can be observed empirically in the field.

Indeed, Grégoire Souchay has to find a way into his field of investigation in Sivens. He then takes the same route as the activists to bypass the police blockade and reach the ZAD. Consequently, the forced division of journalistic labor also has very physical causes in the media coverage of a controversy. It reinforces the rou-tinization of relations between journalists and a certain type of source, sometimes confronted with the same adversity. In this sense, the question of journalistic access to the plurality of actors in a conflict has a performative dimension. It establishes entry rights and refusals that influence not only the media's treatment of the conflict on D-day, but also affects that of the following day and the day after. The problem of access to the field, which is closely linked to the polarization of the journalistic field, has a major impact on interactions on the ground. It therefore conditions the content of the journalistic production.

> So I went through the forest and I made the same journeys as the zadists. And so I reinforced the image that I was a zadist. It's like in demonstrations, there are guys wearing balaclavas who attack the cops, so there are people who wear scarves to protect themselves, so they are seen as balaclavas. [] Basically, you are just an enemy. On the day of the burials (protestors burying themselves in the Sivens forest), I found myself stuck with the buried guys, surrounded by cordons of cops for three hours.
>
> *Grégoire Souchay, Reporterre*

In order to do their work in decent conditions, professionals need to neutralize, at least in part, the label of 'committed journalism', which would imply a bias. In these conditions, loyalty to journalistic ethics is a reason for resilience in the minds of our journalists. This allows them to maintain intellectual rigor and professional justification, which are expressed through their attachment to investigation, to the description of public policies or to the study of local configurations. For example, when asked about her view of the 'Grands Projets Inutiles et Imposés', in general, Camille Polloni refuses to pass judgment from above without having access to the data on each of the projects fought by the militants:

> I'm not necessarily comfortable answering that, actually. I don't always know the details of the project and I don't always have the tools to judge their relevance. I read the arguments on both sides. What interests me more is the mobilizations against and the way they are structured, the journey of the people who come to join the ZADs, more than the project itself. But the project itself I have never been led to analyze it in detail to form an absolutely definitive opinion on it.
>
> *Camille Polloni, Les Jours*

Conclusion

In this chapter, we have examined left-wing radical journalism in France. The commitment of journalists can consist in consciously participating in the construction of public problems. From an oppositional perspective (Negt, 2007), this commitment aims to fight against the pejorative stereotypes that target activists. It helps overcome the perceived dysfunctions of the journalistic field. In this sense, the commitment of our respondents seeks to bring about a journalistic counter-field, in which professionals would accept their share of subjectivity and construct new motives for journalistic excellence. However, it should be pointed out that for the actors, this perspective must be carried out in permanent tension with different elements: the normative framework of the profession, the competition of new information producers and the adversity of the political context. The notion of the 'committed' or 'radical' journalist is therefore operative from an empirical – analytical – point of view. However, its social and scientific use must be rigorously apprehended.

Notes

1 The professional card of journalists in France is issued by the *Commission de la carte d'identité des journalistes professionnels* (CCIJP), composed by union representatives and employers. Evidence of full-time work for three consecutive months in a professional media must be presented. However, legally, in France, the press card does not make the journalist: many journalists live from this activity without holding it.
2 Main daily regional press in the Occitanie region.
3 Former Prime Minister.
4 Former Minister of Culture.
5 Former adviser to the President of the Republic François Hollande.
6 Majority union of the agricultural profession in France.

References

Arquembourg, J. (2011). *L'événement et les médias. Les récits médiatiques des tsunamis et les débats publics (1755–2004)*. Paris, Éd. des Archives contemporaines.

Becker, H.S. (1963). *Outsiders: Studies in the Sociology of Deviance*, New York, Free Press (trad. fr., *Outsiders: études de sociologie de la déviance*, Paris, Métailié, 1985).

Blondeau O., & Allard L. (2007). *Devenir Média. L'activisme sur Internet, entre défection et expérimentation*, Amsterdam: Amsterdam Editions.

Bourdieu, P. (1979). *La distinction: Critique sociale du jugement*, Paris: Éditions de Minuit.

Bourdieu, P. (1994). L'emprise du journalisme. *Actes de la recherche en sciences sociales*, Vol. 101–102, pp. 3–9.

Bouron, S. (2015). Un journalisme en mode mineur: compétences d'amateurs et trajectoires de professionnalisation de la presse locale. In Ferron, B., Harvey, N., & Olivier, Tredan O. (dir.) *Des amateurs dans les médias*, Paris, Presses des Mines, Collection Sciences sociales.

Bousquet, F. (2014). Pour une approche globale de l'information infranationale, Habilitation a Diriger des Recherches en Sciences de l'Information et de la Communication. Université Toulouse 3 Paul Sabatier.

Cardon, D., & Granjon F. (2010). *Médiactivistes*, Paris, Presses de Sciences Po.

Comby, J.B. (2015). *La question climatique. Genèse et dépolitisation d'un problème public*, Raisons d'Agir, 256 p.

Demers, F. (2007). Déstructuration et restructuration du journalisme, *tic&société* [En ligne], Vol. 1, n°1 |, mis en ligne le 20 mai 2019, consulté le 11 octobre 2019. URL: http://journals.openedition.org/ticetsociete/298

Dupuis-Déri, F. (2005). L'altermondialisme à l'ombre du drapeau noir. L'anarchie en heritage. In Agrikoliansky, E., Fillieule O., & Mayer N., (dir.), *L'altermondialisme en France. La longue histoire d'une nouvelle cause*. Paris, Flammarion, pp. 199–231.

Foucault, M. (2004). Naissance de la biopolitique, Cours au Collège de France. 1978–1979, éd. par Michel Senellart, sous la dir. de François Ewald et Alessandro Fontana, Paris, Gallimard-Seuil,, coll. «Hautes Études».

Fraser, N. (2003). Repenser l'espace public: une contribution a la critique de la démocratie réellement existante. In Renault E., & Sintomer, U. (dir.), *Ou en est la théorie critique?*, Paris, La Découverte, pp. 103–134.

Hassenteufel, P. (2010). Les processus de mise sur agenda: sélection et construction des problèmes publics, *Informations sociales* n° 157, pp. 50–58.

Ion, J. (1994). L'évolution des formes de l'engagement. In Perrineau P. (dir.), *L'Engagement politique. Déclin ou mutation?* Paris, Presses de la FNSP, pp. 23–41.

Juhem, P. (2001). Alternances politiques et transformations du champ de l'information en France après 1981. In: *Politix*, vol. 14, n° 56, Inconstances politiques, sous la direction de Gaïti B., et Serna P., pp. 185–208.

Latour, B. (2017). *Où atterrir? Comment s'orienter en politique*, Paris, La Découverte.

Lemieux, C. (dir.). (2010). *La subjectivité journalistique*, Paris, Éd. de l'EHESS coll. Cas de figure.

Lévêque, S., & Ruellan D. (2010). *Journalistes engagés*, Presses universitaires de Rennes, séries «Res Publica».

Löwy, M. (2004). «Le concept d'affinité élective chez Max Weber», *Archives de sciences sociales des religions*, 127, pp. 93–103.

Marty, E., Rebillard, F., Pouchot, S., & Lafouge, T. (2012). Diversité et concentration de l'information sur le web: Une analyse a grande échelle des sites d'actualité français. *Réseaux*, 176(6), pp. 27–72.

Negt, O. (2007). *L'espace public oppositionnel*, Payot, Paris.

Neveu, É. (1999). Médias, mouvements sociaux, espaces publics, Réseaux n° 98 CNET/ Hermès Science Publications, pp. 17–85.

Neveu, É. (2001). *Sociologie du journalisme*, Paris, La Découverte.

Nez, H. (2015). Des informateurs citoyens. Usages des images par les indignés espagnols. In «Médias, engagements, mouvements sociaux», *Sciences de la Société*, Presses Universitaires du Midi n° 94, pp. 139–154.

Nollet, J. (2009). Croiser analyse des politiques publiques et sociologie des médias: genèses et usages des concepts de mise a l'agenda et de construction des problèmes, Congres de l'AFSP: "L'analyse des politiques publiques existe-t-elle encore?".

Ollitrault, S., & Villalba, B. (2014). Sous les pavés, la Terre. Mobilisations environnementales en France (1960–2011), entre contestations et expertises. In Pigenet M. (éd.), *Histoire des mouvements sociaux en France: De 1814 à nos jours,* Paris, La Découverte, pp. 716–723.

Ruellan, D. (2011). *Nous journalistes. Déontologie et identité*, Presses universitaires de Grenoble, coll. Communication, médias et sociétés.

Smyrnaios, N. (2013). Quel avenir pour les pure players journalistiques en France?, https:// larevuedesmedias.ina.fr/quel-avenir-pour-les-pure-players-journalistiques-en-france

Thiong-Kay, L. (2020a). La production médiatique de l'opposition au barrage de Sivens sur Internet, entre reconfigurations info-communicationnelles et repolitisation de l'enjeu local. Thèse de doctorat en Sciences de l'information et de la communication, Université Paul Sabatier, Toulouse.

Thiong-Kay, L. (2020b). L'automédia, objet de luttes symboliques et figure controversée. Le cas de la médiatisation de la lutte contre le barrage de Sivens (2012–2015). *Le Temps des médias*, 35, 105–120.

Thiong-Kay, L. (2021). Divisions du travail médiatique entre journalistes et militants, de l'altermondialisme à Sivens. *Sur Le Journalisme, About Journalism, Sobre Jornalismo*, 10(1), 162–173.

Tilly, C. (1995). Contentious repertoires in Great Britain, 1758–1834. In Traugott, M. (ed.), *Repertoires and Cycles of Collective Action*, Durham, NC, Duke University Press.

Veron, E. (1985). L'analyse du contrat de lecture: une nouvelle méthode pour les études de positionnement des supports presse », in *Les médias: expériences et recherches actuelles*, IREP.

6

THE CASE OF ERT AND THE PROSPECT OF RADICAL MEDIA IN THE ERA OF AUSTERITY

Christos Avramidis and Alexandros Minotakis

It is common ground that media play an increasingly important role in social movements. Generally speaking, mainstream media tend to neglect, downplay, or distort public protest activities (Rucht, 2003). Therefore, an integral part of the development of social movements involves an "uphill battle" to transmit their message. Social movements employ different strategies such as abstaining from interacting with media, "attacking" via explicit critique, developing their own alternative media, or adapting by accepting and engaging with the rules of the media (Rucht, 2004). However, radical media possess insufficient resources, and they face significant difficulties in their media strategy. Therefore, whenever a radical medium overcomes these barriers, it is considered an exemplary case. Within this chapter, it will be argued that ERT, the main public broadcaster in Greece, emerged as a radical medium, after its attempted closure by the Greek government, and this provides an important insight into the prospect of radical media in the era of austerity.

The Greek protest cycle during 2010–2015 involved a significant number of protests against austerity measures. One of the most dramatic moments in Greek media history was the overnight closure of the public service broadcaster Hellenic Broadcasting Corporation (Siapera, 2015) by the government on June 11, 2013. Immediately after the closure, employees occupied the buildings and kept working around the clock; they transformed state media into radical media creating what was termed "ERTOPEN" (Fraszczyk, 2015).

ERTOPEN managed to host various views and voices and finally achieve ratings never previously achieved after the deregulation of the media market in 1989: 2.8 million single users watched its programmes in the first days from the European Broadcasting Union site (Iosifidis & Papathanassopoulos, 2019). The ERTOPEN programme has been characterized as a unique experiment in the history of public service media in Europe (Iosifidis & Katsirea, 2014). The post-closure ERT was a wholly original experiment on the transformation, under the

DOI: 10.4324/9781003221784-6

influence of anti-austerity protests, of a state-controlled medium into a radical one that provided opportunities for activists and social movements. The case of ERT's transformation provides crucial insights that clarify issues arising both within alternative media themselves and within media theory debates.

This chapter is structured as follows. The second section engages in a brief literature review, focusing on the distinction between process- and content-oriented approaches to alternative media as well as the history of ERT as a medium tightly controlled by the Greek governments. The third section presents the different research methodologies employed. The fourth section entails a chronicle of events that defined the emergence of "ERTOPEN" while the fifth section presents the results of the qualitative and quantitative analysis. Finally, the sixth section links them to the existing bibliography, concludes this chapter, and points to further research on this field.

Approaching the Radical/Alternative Media

There is no clear consensus on the definition of radical/alternative media as different approaches have been developed, emphasizing different aspects of what renders a medium "alternative" and/or "radical". However, as this section will argue, a common set of issues unify the field.

Downing refers to "media, generally small-scale and in many different forms, that express an alternative vision to hegemonic policies, priorities, and perspectives" (2001, pp. v). This definition is intentionally abstract as Downing (2001, pp. x) emphasizes the contextual nature of being radical – depending on the political circumstances, radical media may be defined differently.

Downing (2001) notes that the small-scale character of radical media implies that they are insignificant. On the contrary, what makes them noteworthy is their ability to influence the public sphere and mainstream political debates despite them being indeed small scale.

Following a different approach, Bailey, Cammaerts and Carpentier (2008) attempt to map the field of alternative media studies and develop a typology of approaches:

a.   community media approach where media are considered alternative as they serve the community and foster participatory practices
b.   alternative media as an alternative to mainstream, where the dialectical relation between mainstream and alternative, hegemonic and counter hegemonic is emphasized
c.   alternative media as part of civil society where a dual dimension of democratization comes to the fore: democratization of the media and democratization through the media

d.   alternative media as rhizome, where the decisive aspect is the role of alternative media as the connective tissue that binds different types of social movements (For a synopsis of this typology, see Bailey et al., 2008, p. 31).

While this formulation is helpful, a more systematic approach is necessary in order to clarify the decisive factors that divide scholars of alternative media. In an attempt to offer a coherent categorization, Fuchs distinguishes between "process- and content-oriented approaches in alternative media theory" (2010, p. 177). This distinction is concrete without becoming rigid and can function as a guide through the field of alternative media theories. Alternative and radical media should be examined regarding both their structure and process of producing and distributing content and their media content per se. However, in this dialectic relationship between structure and content, scholars and radical media themselves place emphasis on different aspects.

Process-oriented approaches emphasize the ways alternative media foster participatory practices and mitigate the dichotomy between transmitter/receiver, producer/consumer of media content. Couldry and Curran (2003, p. 42) refer to media power as the concentration of symbolic resources built on a division of labour "between those who make stories and those who consume them". Therefore, democratization of the media consists in developing open, participatory media where these roles are interchangeable, and no barriers prevent the audience from participating in the production process. In a similar vein, Carroll and Hackett (2006, p. 99) conceptualize media activism (the process of building alternative media) as "a challenge to the system of symbolic production — a critique of the political economy of mass communication and an effort to build democratic alternatives". Moreover, process-oriented approaches are often inscribed within alternative and radical media. The Global Network of Independent Media Centers (known as Indymedia) follows an anti-hierarchical, open publishing policy, inviting its audience to contribute to a radical democratic news organization (Kidd, 2009; Pickard, 2006).

On the other hand, content-oriented approaches maintain that radical content is the defining characteristic of alternative media. Sandoval and Fuchs (2010, pp. 143–145) criticize the approaches that equate alternative media with participatory media noting that small-scale participatory media risk limiting their influence within a cultural "alternative ghetto". Additionally, participation in itself can be utilized by commercial digital media that exploit the labour of their audience for capital accumulation (Fuchs, 2014). Also, employing journalists who operate within professional organization structures may prove to be useful in producing radical content, while media that are organized in this manner should not be excluded from the category of alternative media (Sandoval & Fuchs, 2010, p. 145). Bendon (2003), in his study of California's weekly newspapers, notes that dependence on advertising revenue does not necessarily lead to a nonpolitical or conservative news content. Moreover, while the newspapers in question are produced by professional journalists who operate within hierarchically structured newsrooms, they encourage their audience to participate in social activism. Ideally, alternative media should combine radical content with a process of production entirely separated from the process of capital accumulation and, therefore, from commercial advertising (Sandoval & Fuchs, 2010). However, as this is often not attainable, critical content should be considered the "minimum requirement" (Fuchs, 2010, p. 180) for an "alternative/radical" medium.

However valuable the aforementioned distinction is, it is not possible to understand the notion of alternative media solely based on the debate between process and content. Alternative media are not created ex nihilo; specific socio-political circumstances favour or impede their development. The political upheaval in the 1960s and 1970s resulted, among others, in the creation of underground, self-managed media as well as critical commercial media (Bendon, 2003). The anti-globalization protests in the late 1990s, which culminated in the 1999 protests during the World Trade Organization conference in Seattle, provided the breeding ground for the development of alternative media (Carroll, 2015) and the creation of the Independent Media Centers (Kidd, 2009; Pickard, 2006). After the economic crisis of 2008 and the emergence of the Occupy Movement in the USA, media activists that had contributed to the development of the Indymedia network assisted a younger generation of activists in creating and sustaining alternative media (Costanza-Chock, 2012). Evidently, an organic link exists between social movements and radical media. Through social movements, oppressed social groups and minorities express their grievances and demands and often face exclusion from the public sphere as mainstream media are geared towards elite political institutions (Tuchman, 1980). In addition, while mainstream media misrepresent the participants in social movements, alternative media are often willing to assist them in an effort to represent themselves in the public sphere (Bailey et al., 2008, p. 16). This means that social movements often struggle simultaneously for visibility in mainstream media and create their own media organizations (Carroll, 2015) and inspire journalists to break from commercial mainstream media.

Therefore, the continuing existence and development of social movements should be understood as a necessary precondition for the flourishing of alternative media. Thusly, a new set of challenges arises. When social movements retreat, alternative media may face problems in operating and may end up losing their radical character (Jauert, 2015). Generally speaking, the issue of sustainability is a constant threat for alternative media and there is no guarantee that radical media will gain more visibility on the internet (Downing, 2001, p. 210). Small-scale media organizations, built around social movements and media activists, may find themselves content with "creating their own media space" (Carroll & Hackett, 2006, p. 98), which coexists with mainstream media without challenging them. In that case, what ensues is further fragmentation of the public sphere (Sandoval & Fuchs, 2010) instead of a large-scale social transformation process. Nonetheless, the importance of social media and online networks should not be underestimated. As internet usage proliferates, social movements find it favourable to utilize low-cost media platforms to increase their audience. While avoiding any notions of techno-optimism, Kidd and McIntosh (2016) correctly note that large-scale social transformation will necessarily include social media but "will also need much more than that".

Public Broadcasting Service in Greece

The ERT is the public radio-television broadcaster in Greece, which was founded in 1975. ERT operates three television channels (two are stationed in Athens and one in Thessaloniki) and 28 radio stations.

The development of ERT was significantly influenced by the dominant role of the state in the media sector in the post-dictatorship period and subsequent clientelist relationships that shaped public broadcasting (Papathanassopoulos, 2001). As Hallin and Mancini (2004, p. 125) point out, in the Greek media system "public broadcasting … always lacked independence from the state". In that sense, public broadcasting functioned as a "trophy" awarded to the party that secures a parliamentary majority. Newly elected governments reconfigure public broadcasting services (PBS), and appoint new executives and editors-in-chief in order to ensure that television and radio news adapt to their priorities (Papathanassopoulos, 1997, p. 354).

After a period of rapid deregulation and the creation of private television channels in the late 80s (Hallin & Mancini (2004, p. 44) prefer the term "savage deregulation"), public broadcasting suffered tremendous losses in audience rating, losing 86% of their viewership (Papathanassopoulos, 1997, p. 358). Private media dominated the broadcasting sector and public television was negatively affected, facing economic problems as debt began to accumulate (Papathanassopoulos, 2001, p. 509). However, this process of rapid commercialization did not result in a renewed independence of public broadcasting from the state.

Therefore, news bulletins continued to be oriented towards government and state officials, and until 2013, social movements had a marginal (at best) presence in public broadcasting.

A few months later, under no circumstances could post-closure ERT (ERTOPEN) be considered as an alternative/radical medium or as an advocate of social movements based on critical and creative programming and worker's self-management (Sheehan, 2017) engaged against government of New Democracy and austerity policies imposed on Greece (Smyrnaios & Karatzogianni, 2020). Summarily, prior to the closure, ERT could be characterized as a –delegitimized– voice of the status quo. What changed then after that night of June 11, 2013?

Based on the abovementioned, the following questions will be examined regarding ERT:

a. Why is post-closure ERT characterized as an alternative medium, in regard to both media content and production process?
b. In what ways may ERT transform the debate of "process versus content" in the alternative media literature?
c. What rendered ERTOPEN sustainable for more than two years after the closure?

The Crisis Years

Since 2010, Greece has suffered a significant and catastrophic recession. The Memorandum between the Greek state, the European Union, and the International Monetary Fund forced Greece to implement measures of fiscal adjustment, which in practice meant massive disinvestment from the public sector and the sale of public assets. Demonstrations and a multitude of social movements against austerity (Kousi & Kanellopoulos, 2014) coalesced into a protest cycle (Serdedakis & Tompazos, 2018). As Tarrow (1989, pp. 14–15), notes "Protest becomes a protest cycle when it is diffused to several sectors of the population, is highly organized, and is widely used as the instrument to put forward demands".

On June 11, 2013, the tripartite government of New Democracy – Panhellenic Socialist Movement – Democratic Left led by Prime Minister Antonis Samaras decided to shut ERT down and fire its 2,650 employees. In the next days, ERT employees alongside thousands of citizens took to the streets and occupied the public corporation's TV stations in Athens and Thessaloniki, as well as radio stations throughout Greece, airing their own programme in a struggle that is considered as one of the most significant during 2012–2015 (Rogas & Papanikolopoulos, 2018).

Daily demonstrations were held outside ERT buildings in several Greek cities, often followed by solidarity concerts. In this sense, ERT played an important role in the protest cycle. What began as employees' struggle culminated in the occupation of state buildings along with broadcasting equipment, while at the same time maintaining the demand for the reinstatement of all employees. Thus, ERT transformed into a mass medium that enabled the expression of social movements and relied on them for legitimacy. At the same time, the government established an official public broadcast service firstly known as DT and then as NERIT. Those were two PBS considered as controlled by the government (Iosifidis & Katsirea, 2014).

Major European newspapers published headlines critical of the Greek government. The intensity of the demonstrations caused a rupture in the government, as the party of the Democratic Left withdrew its support to the government.

In November 2013, police forces evicted the central building of ERT in Athens. The newscast was broadcasted in front of the central building's locked gates with armed police squads in the background. This image quickly gained international appeal and the broadcast report reached more than 1 million online views ("The Entire Newscast," 2013). Even after this evacuation and the formation of the New Hellenic Radio, Internet, and Television (NERIT), 19 buildings remained under the management of the former employees. They continued to broadcast through radio, television, and the web.

In January 2015, the party of SYRIZA won the elections and formed a government with the party of ANEL. The new government opened ERT and the 2,650 employees got their jobs back so ERT became the official state-controlled media again.

ERTOPEN has been a notable case because it was not just another alternative medium preaching the converted since it had a significant engagement. In most major Greek cities, ERTopen's TV channels had been broadcasting simultaneously with NERIT. In a few big cities, NERIT wasn't even broadcasting, and the audience was receiving only the programme of ERTOPEN.

ERT utilized new technologies by sending its signal via hundreds of internet sites and social media. After all, ERTOPEN achieved ratings never previously achieved in ERT's history (Iosifidis & Papathanasopoulos, 2019). Eleven days after the closure, ERTOPEN's stations had more than 4,500,000 views in 77 different countries ("Let's count: We are 4,500,000", 2013)

According to the official analytics, ERT had more than 5,000,000 views in the website of YouTube until the reopening (YouTube, 2021). The magnitude of the engagement is also substantiated via the interviews given. One journalist of ERT Open mentioned:

> There was a 80-year-old conservative neighbor who had been listening to ERT since he was a kid. The programme of ERTOPEN was transmitted in the same frequency so he had not realized that the radio station he was listening to was not the official state radio. So he started questioning "how is it possible not to be informed for all those redundancies".
>
> *P.K., personal communication, July, 22, 2021*

So this range gave the opportunity to the social movements to approach people neutral or hostile to social movements.

Research Methodology

A multifaceted research methodology was necessary in order to examine the content, the production process, as well as the resources of ERTOPEN.

Content analysis was employed in order to examine the agenda-setting of pro- and post-closure ERT. McCombs and Shaw (1972) have theorized that media influence public perception by organizing news stories hierarchically, distinguishing what they consider newsworthy. The methodology of this research is based on the quantitative analysis of media content (Riffe et al., 2019).

Firstly, a content analysis was conducted examining the news bulletins. The sample entailed 141 news bulletins between 9/11/2012 and 1/9/2015. This period was selected in order to contrast ERT's programme while it was under state management with the programme that was developed while ERTOPEN was under employees' control. We chose to analyse the newscasts that were broadcasted every Tuesday. The first point of research focused on the percentage of stories aired on social movements in relation to stories on other topics. The second point engaged with the number of activists' statements aired in each bulletin, while the third one involved the number of news stories containing references to social movements presented in the first five stories of each newscast.

We also combined qualitative tools with quantitative ones, so we conducted 15 interviews with journalists and activists participating in ERTOPEN. Specifically, in-depth interviews with activists participating in five grassroots collectives were employed, following Della Porta's (2014) argument that in-depth interviews help researchers pay more attention to people's interpretations of reality, and in this sense, they have contributed not only to theory building, but also to theory testing.

The selection of the interviewees was based on two main criteria: their seniority in the grassroots collectives and their role in them. We specifically contacted founding members as well as key members so that they could offer a deep insight into the issues of our study. These interviews were analysed through thematic analysis, which is one of the most common forms of analysis in qualitative research and a theoretically flexible method that organizes, describes, and interprets qualitative data (Braun & Clarke, 2006).

The main topic of the questions was about the production process and the content produced. Furthermore, the interviews shed light on the various ways in which material and immaterial resources were collected and managed, rendering ERTOPEN a viable alternative medium. Complementary to the interviews was the examination of the new, post-closure mission statement of ERT. This document, combined with the interviews, improved our understanding of the daily activities that defined ERTOPEN.

Secondary data on viewership rates were utilized in order to demonstrate the widespread diffusion of the ERTOPEN's news content. In that sense, it will be shown that ERTOPEN, unlike what is often the case on alternative media, had an impact on a national scale.

Findings

The Radical Content of ERTOPEN

The direction of ERTOPEN, regarding media contents, was crystallized in the new mission statement published by the journalists and activists of ERTOPEN after general assemblies. This document was named "Which ERT do we want?" (2014). They describe the production process in post-closure ERT and highlight the characteristics of new ERT and main principles, acquisition of funding, labour relations, societal participation, and process of "administration" in this new period. Concerning the content, the maintaining of a radical direction is outlined:

"ERT denounces any instances of racism, bigotry, sexism, nationalism, state authoritarianism or any kind of discrimination against people or groups of people who are targeted for their political/social/unionised action". It is also noted that "ERT serves society and its needs", while it is also explicitly mentioned that it "scrutinizes power and it does not relate to it, nor does it constitute an instrument in the hands of the government and its apparatus." Therefore, a radically new concept of "public service emerges" … content is not dictated by the officials who were appointed by the government. ("Which ERT do we want?", 2014).

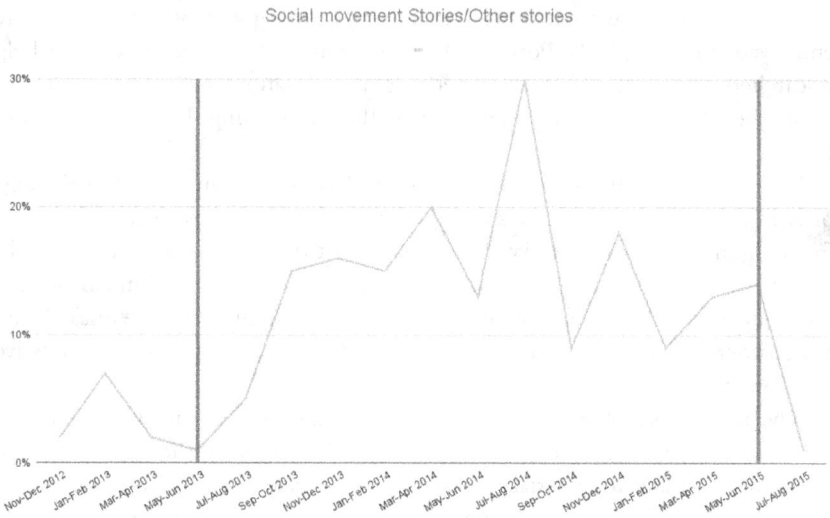

Social movement Stories/Other stories

FIGURE 6.1 The percentage of time devoted to news stories referring to social movements' actions

An activist of the environmental movement mentioned that "no media covered the demonstrations however, it's okay, ERT came" (D.S., personal communication, June 14, 2021).

The "fired cleaning ladies" has been one of the most notable cases. Their repetitive beating by the police appeared on the front page of *The New York Times*. NERIT presented the story as "cleaning ladies attacking the police", thus portraying middle-age women as the violent attackers. ERTOPEN invited the cleaning ladies in the studio. One of them mentioned "I want to say, let this voice never silence. It is the voice of every activist" (EPT AE, 2014a).

An important criterion according to the content is the agenda-setting function of news organizations: what is considered newsworthy. Our content analysis has produced the following three figures. Figure 6.1 indicates the percentage of time devoted to news stories referring to social movements' actions. Figure 6.2 shows the number of news stories featuring social movements broadcast among the first five of each bulletin. Finally, Figure 6.3 indicates the number of statements by activists or social movement organizations being broadcasted. The time frame for ERTOPEN is located between the vertical red lines.

As it is evident, social movements were broadcasted by "ERTOPEN" considerably more in comparison to the state ERT both pre-closure and after-opening.

The Radical Production Process of ERTOPEN

In the days following the closure, ERT employees decided through a general assembly to evict senior executives from their offices. A "Programme Committee"

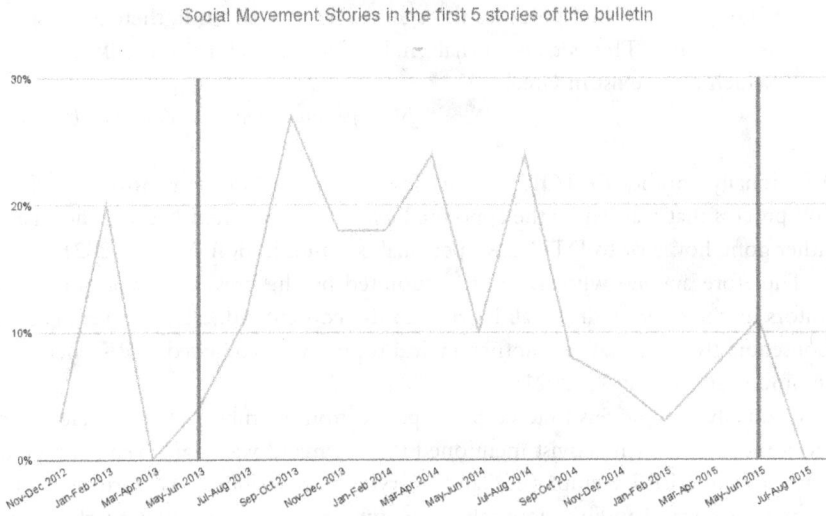

FIGURE 6.2 News stories featuring social movements broadcast among the first five of each bulletin

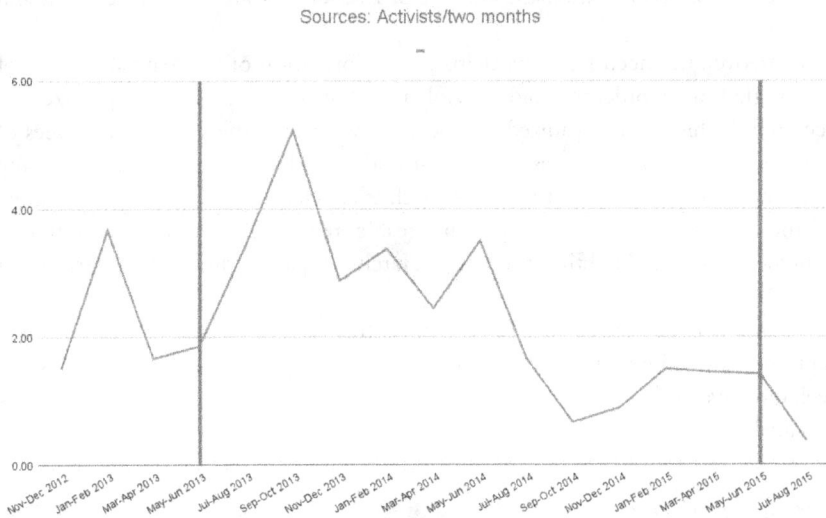

FIGURE 6.3 Statements by activists or social movement organizations

elected by the general assembly was making the decisions about the programme. There seems to be a connection between the procedure of decision-making and the radicalized content. A former ERT journalist, who worked at the newscast of ERTOPEN, mentioned:

> The editor in chief proposes the agenda, we discuss on it, there is no strict guiding line. This is true journalism, less hierarchical. ERT is talking things which don't exist in Greek TV.
>
> *N. T., personal communication, July 19, 2021*

Additionally, another ERTOPEN journalist, noted that "in the radio, the production process that was led by the appointed executives, vanished, because they 'have either gone home or to DT'" (P.K., personal communication, May 27, 2021).

Therefore anyone who had been appointed by the previous managements as editors in chief resigned, and all barriers to the content radicalisation were erased. Consequently, "one way or another, radical topics were approved" (P.K., personal communication, May 27, 2021).

Gradually, this process fostered participation from members of civil society and social movements. An activist mentioned that "demand was high, even for people that were not ERT's employees, and everybody contributed, all sorts of work, cleaning, camera handling, journalism, anywhere they could offer work" (K.S., personal communication, April 2, 2021).

This social participation transformed the programme. The production process was outlined in the statement "Which ERT do we want?" (2014) as it is mentioned that two of the basic features of ERTOPEN are self-management and self-governance.

Moreover, the need for a "participative co-formation of the general strategy of the programme in order to avoid the violation of the people's will" is emphasized. To accomplish this, ERT organized democratically through the general assemblies of employees and civil society as the highest bodies of decision-making. Additionally, "the department editor and the editor-in-chief are elected by the General Assembly of the employees" following interchangeable revocability. A radically different structure arises, highlighting the anti-hierarchical, participatory characteristics of ERTOPEN.

Finally, it is referenced that ERT "conceptualizes quality reporting, news content and entertainment as public goods and not as goods for sale, and does not seek out advertisements". Therefore, the question arises: what rendered ERTOPEN sustainable?

Funding and Resources

In the case of ERTOPEN, 500 people had been working for two years in order to produce a programme in radio televisual stations throughout the country. Consequently, the funding volume needed was significant. Given that ERTOPEN, besides a radical medium, constituted a social movement on its own (Della Porta et al., 2017), it is crucial to examine the ways it collected resources to transfer these to other campaigns. The answer is that the activists made use of the Political Environment and its signals to utilize available resources.

According to Goldstone and Tilly (2001), any changes that shift the balance of economic, political, and/or symbolic resources between authorities and "claimers" in favour of the latter increase political opportunities.

There are five distinct types of resources: moral, cultural, social-organizational, human, and material. Moral resources are legitimacy, integrity, solidarity support, sympathetic support, and celebrity. Cultural resources include artefacts and cultural products such as conceptual tools and specialized knowledge that have become widely, though not necessarily universally, known. Human resources are both more tangible and easier to appreciate than the above resource types. This category includes resources like labour, experience, skills, expertise, and leadership. The category of material resources combines monetary resources, property, office space, equipment, and supplies. (Edwards & McCarthy, 2004).

Regarding material resources, participants drew their resources from the 19 occupied buildings. Through this occupation, means of production worth millions of euros were made available. At the same time, activists had access to free electricity. Whenever problems arose, activists and journalists devised their own solutions. This was the case in Thessaloniki, where the activists were connecting to the internet to broadcast, through bypassing the Wi-Fi firewalls of Aristotle's University (D.M., personal communication, May 16, 2021).

Evidently, the abovementioned depended upon the state's unwillingness to evict the occupied 19 buildings and to abstain from cutting access to electricity. Therefore, one of the factors that contributed to the expansion of political opportunities is the decrease of the repressive ability of the state. Namely, the reluctance of the state to repress plays an important role, as the state's inaction provides an opportunity for activist action. (Goldstone & Tilly, 2001).

Consequently, after the removal of transmitters, and ERTOPEN's inability to nationwide transmit to the televisions through the previous frequencies, the cost of toleration was reduced. With the term "cost of toleration" what is referenced is the cost, paid by the political elites (Dahl, 1971) for concession and social rights. In this case, we have to do with the toleration to the assertions and not with the concession of rights. Concurrently, in the case of ERTOPEN the cost of repression seems to be rather high. By "cost of repression" we refer to how costly it is for the elite to repress assertions (Seferiades, 2008). The immaterial resource of the legitimacy of action is reflected upon the cost of repression. ERTOPEN was significantly legitimized, which is proved by the support it received.

Particularly, all the parties in the parliament, besides New Democracy and Golden Dawn, express their disagreement, namely, even the two parties in coalition [with New Democracy] in the government, which shows that an imminent dissolution of the government was an actual threat. Four out of seven parties in the parliament boycotted the succeeding official state channel DT, as they chose to appear on a radical medium, namely, ERTOPEN.

Moreover, the President of Democracy, the Archbishop, MPs of New democracy, and right-wing Mayors sided against the shutdown (EPT A.E., 2014b). Statements against shutdown were made by European Parliament as well as by European Broadcasting Union, which is the largest entity among the broadcasting companies, with public service. In France, Humanité and Liberation released a black front page in support of ERT. The Belgian channel Télé Bruxelles transmitted the logo of ERT, writing "Solidarité" under it (ERT Solidarite, 2013)

At the same time, the movement of ERT reaps the benefits of great support through demonstrations. The workers' federations call for a general strike, and immediately after the shutdown, 10,000 people rallied at the building of Athens, whereas demonstrations developed across Greece, simultaneously.

In a poll, 68% of the citizens stated that they disagree with the shutdown of ERT, while 29% stated that they agree (The majority of the citizens, 2013). These reactions raised the cost of repression higher than the cost of toleration, because "the government was almost dissolved", as was stated by the MP of New Democracy and its later vice-president, Adonis Georgiadis (2013).

The support given to the employees by trade unions should be undoubtedly added to the material resources. Particularly, POSPERT, second-degree federation of employees, mainly technicians, funded the attempt to cover a part of expenses.

One important aspect of the work is the integrity and solidarity support, which transfigured into the human resource of the offered labour. Highly skilled and experienced labour was a valuable resource. Technicians and journalists, assisted by the solidarity movement, produced and transmitted a new kind of ERT content: radical and politically alternative.

In order to make this happen, the employees should have the material resources to survive. This was achieved in many different ways. Firstly, during the first year after the shutdown, the fired employees received an unemployment benefit, while people and various entities donated money and commodities to help the struggle go on. Additionally, many retired journalists and technicians participated in the production of the programme. Even retired technicians of ERT were used in a series of "ventures" towards the antennas, to newly establish the signal for ERTOPEN (T.K., personal communication, August 30, 2021).

This effort was also supported by many unemployed journalists. This constitutes a tendency also described by Treré, Jeppesen and Mattoni (2017) according to which many major media were shut down in Greece and the now unemployed journalists were moving to help the media of the movement and to demonstrations of movements.

Moreover, many people found another job and consequently work for the production of the programme through part-time voluntary work. Indeed, a technician was working at a radio station full-time, had to raise two children, and despite all these, he was saving a few hours per week to help in the newscast (P.K., personal communication, May 27, 2021). In any case, the resources were considerably limited and employees managed to keep going with great difficulty.

The general mood is described by a director of ERT:

> Every one of the activists had families. They had two kids, rent to pay, expenses as usual. There are people that paid no rent for two years, because the landlord expressed solidarity to ERT and didn't want to take any money. There are

people who left their bills unpaid. There were people that commuted on foot. They didn't have 1€ to take the bus and participate.

D.K., personal communication, June 12, 2021

Consequently, the offered solidarity turned into material funding in various cases, i.e. rent exemption. Additionally, lack of money as a material resource was counteracted by self-exploitation, a trait noted in many radical media (Fuchs, 2010).

While ERTOPEN did not feature any commercial advertisement, an "advertising the movements" campaign was organized. Thus, it contributed resources to the social movements that acted within the protest cycle. Moreover, ERTOPEN produced a special video containing citizens' statements about ERTOPEN as a TV channel without advertisement, which shows the importance of this characteristic ("Which ERT do we want?", 2014).

This way of operation was also pointed out in the mission statement: "ERT, as a public medium that understands quality broadcasting in practice, as well as the productions and the entertainment as public goods and not commodities, remains outside the advertising network" ("Which ERT do we want?", 2014).

Conclusion

Radical media theory is divided along three decisive, intertwined issues: what renders a medium radical, sustainable, and mass in appeal? Theoretical approaches place emphasis on different aspects. However, there seems to be an underlying notion that radical media often have to engage in a compromise, forced to sacrifice the radical nature of their content or their structure to gain audience or resources. While compromises are, undoubtedly, part of the process of building mass radical media, the case of post-closure ERT provides a different example, standing at the crossroads of content- and process-oriented, combining characteristics that both approaches consider important, while also attracting a mass viewership.

In order to come up with our findings, quantitative content analysis and thematic analysis were deployed. Particularly, in order to examine the research question regarding the radical content of ERTOPEN, the presence of social movements on newscasts was examined. Regarding the issues of structure and process of production, the analysis of interviews proved to be useful, combined with the mission statement of ERTOPEN. Analytical tools were drawn from radical media theory and theoretical approaches to social movements. On the question of sustainability, the conceptual framework of political process was utilized in order to examine the material and immaterial resources render the ERTOPEN project viable. Once again, interviews proved valuable in clarifying the multi-faceted strategies employed by ERTOPEN.

The main conclusion that was derived from our research is that ERTOPEN presents a case of a positive feedback loop: open, participatory processes of decision-making foster radicalization of content, while the implementation of "anti-commercial" policy encourages activists and journalists to engage with the needs of civil society and social movements. Being radical in content, bottom-up in structure, and mass in appeal does not have to be mutually exclusive, provided that the link between radical media and social movements is maintained and strengthened. Our research indicates that journalists and activists involved in ERTOPEN struggled daily to nurture this connection.

Through this process, ERTOPEN achieved a significant legitimacy followed by an impaired repressive ability by the government. The cost of repression grew high enough to the point that government could not reclaim expensive buildings and equipment. The rupture within the tripartite ruling coalition was an important moment followed by increasing discontent with the government, expressed in opinion polls in which 81% of respondents expressed dissatisfaction with the government after ERT's closure (VPRC, 2013).

These developments would be inconceivable without the rise of social movements in support of ERTOPEN as well as the decisiveness of journalists and broadcast technicians. Social movement organizations that were disenfranchised with the existing media system conceptualized the rupture between ERT personnel and government as a turning point·— struggles against austerity measures were now given voice on a nationwide scale. What emerged was a favourable structure of political opportunity that significantly shifted the balance of power in favour of radical media and social movements alike.

Evidently, ERTOPEN was situated within a crucial period in contemporary Greek history such as the cycle of content 2010–2015. In that sense, it features certain unique characteristics, most evidently the abrupt radicalization of thousands of employees combined with the overnight "transfer" (via occupation) of building and equipment from the state to the hands of social movements. Having said that, however, we have argued throughout this chapter that ERTOPEN provides valuable lessons for radical media theorists and radical journalists.

Finally, the process of ERTOPEN came to a halt in 2015 as the newly elected coalition government SYRIZA-ANEL (who run on an anti-austerity platform), reestablished ERT as an official public service broadcast. During that crucial point, most of the demands as well as the experience of almost two years of self-management were ignored (Oikonomakis, 2018). Future research on ERT and its transformation from a state-controlled medium to a radical one (and back again) needs to engage with the question of how ERT reopened and what this meant for social movements and journalists and for the legacy of ERTOPEN.

References

Bailey, O., Cammaerts, B., & Carpentier, N. (2008). *Understanding alternative media.* Maidenhead: McGraw-Hill/Open University Press.

Bendon, R. (2003). Commercialism and critique: California's alternative weeklies. In Couldry N., & Curran J. (eds.), *Contesting media power: Alternative media in a networked world* (pp. 111–127). Lanham, MD: Rowman & Littlefield.

Braun, V., & Clarke, V. (2006). Using thematic analysis in psychology. *Qualitative Research in Psychology*, 3(2), 77–101. https://doi.org/10.1191/1478088706qp063oa

Carroll, W. K. (2015). Alter-globalisation and alternative media. In Atton C. (ed.), *The Routledge companion to alternative and community media* (pp. 222–234). London: Routledge.

Carroll, W. K., & Hackett, R. A. (2006). Democratic media activism through the lens of social movement theory. *Media, Culture & Society*, 28(1), 83–104. https://doi.org/10.1177/0163443706059289

Costanza-Chock, S. (2012). Mic check! Media cultures and the Occupy Movement. *Social Movement Studies*, 11(3–4), 375–385. https://doi.org/10.1080/14742837.2012.710746

Couldry, N., & Curran, J. (Eds.). (2003). Beyond the hall of mirrors? Some theoretical reflections on the global contestation of media power. In *Contesting media power: Alternative media in a networked world* (pp. 39–54). Lanham, MD: Rowman & Littlefield.

Dahl, A. D. (1971). *Polyarchy: Participation and opposition.* Yale University Press.

Downing J.H., 2001. *Radical Media: Rebellious Communication and Social Movements.* London: Sage

Della Porta, D. (2014). In-depth interviews. In Della Porta, D. (ed.), *Methodological practices in social movement research* (pp. 228–261). Oxford: Oxford University Press.

Della Porta, D., Fernández, J., Kouki, H., & Mosca, L. (2017). *Movement parties against austerity.* Cambridge: Polity Press.

Διαφωνεί η πλειονότητα των πολιτών με το κλείσιμο της ΕΡΤ [The majority of the citizens disagrees with the shutdown of ERT], (2013, June 13). Retrieved from https://tvxs.gr/news/%CE%B5%CE%BB%CE%BB%CE%AC%CE%B4%CE%B1/%CE%BD%CE%AD%CE%B1-%CE%B4%CE%B7%CE%BC%CE%BF%CF%83%CE%BA%CF%8C%CF%80%CE%B7%CF%83%CE%B7-%CE%BA%CE%B1%CF%84%CE%B1%CE%B3%CF%81%CE%AC%CF%86%CE%B5%CE%B9-%CE%B4%CE%B9%CE%B1%CF%86%CF%89%CE%BD%CE%AF%CE%B1-%CF%84%CF%89%CE%BD-%CF%80%CE%BF%CE%BB%CE%B9%CF%84%CF%8E%CE%BD-%CF%83%CF%84%CE%BF-%CE%BA%CE%BB%CE%B5%CE%AF%CF%83%CE%B9%CE%BC%CE%BF-%CF%84%CE%B7%CF%82-%CE%B5%CF%81%CF%84

Downing, J. H. (2001). *Radical media: Rebellious communication and social movements.* London: Sage.

Edwards, B., & McCarthy, J. D. (2004). Resources and social movement mobilization. In Snow, D., Soule, S., & Kriesi, H. (eds.), *The Blackwell companion to social movements* (pp. 116–152). Malden, MA: Blackwell.

ΕΡΤ Α.Ε. (2013, June 12). Ο Α. Τσίπρας στον Πρόεδρο της Δημοκρατίας [A. Tsipras to the president of democracy]. [Video]. YouTube. www.youtube.com/watch?v=HQk2pBn_jgY.

ΕΡΤ Α.Ε. (2014a). ΔΕΛΤΙΟ ΕΙΔΗΣΕΩΝ 26/03/2014: Άγρια καταστολή στις διαμαρτυρόμενες Καθαρίστριες του Υπ.Οικονομικών [Newscast: 26/03/2014: Brutal suppression against the fired cleaning ladies of the Finance Minister]. [Video]. YouTube https://www.youtube.com/watch?v=_8Vma9XrTUo.

ΕΡΤ Α.Ε. (2014b). Βραδινό Δελτίο Ειδήσεων ΕΡΤ 22-01-2014 [Night newscast ERT: 22/01/2014]. [Video]. YouTube. https://youtu.be/adG5E3sUzuU?t=1778.

Fraszczyk, T. (2015). A structural change in Greek public media: A self-governing media model or another emanation of the Mediterranean model. *Media Studies*, 61(2), 1–13.

Fuchs, C. (2014), *Social Media: A Critical Introduction*, London, Sage.

Fuchs, C. (2010). Alternative media as critical media. *European Journal of Social Theory*, 13(2), 173–192. https://doi.org/10.1177/1368431010362294

Γεωργιάδης: Για την ΕΡΤ πήγε να πέσει η κυβέρνηση - για τον ΕΟΠΥΥ δεν ενδιαφέρθηκε κανείς [Georgiadis: For ERT the government was ready to collapse. No one was interested for EOPYY]. (2013). *SKAI.* www.skai.gr/news/greece/georgiadis-gia-tin-ert-pige-na-pesei-i-kyvernisi-gia-ton-eopyy-den-e

Goldstone, J., & Tilly, C. (2001). Threat (and opportunity): Popular action and state response in the dynamic of contentious action. In Goldstone, J. & McAdam, D. (eds.), *Silence and voice in the study of contentious politics* (pp. 179–194). Aminzade, Cambridge: Cambridge University Press.

Hallin, D., & Mancini P. (2004). *Comparing media systems.* New York: Cambridge University Press.

Iosifidis, P., & Katsirea, I. (2014). Public service broadcasting in Greece in the era of austerity. Robert Schuman Centre for Advanced Studies Research Paper No. RSCAS 2014/42, Available at SSRN: https://ssrn.com/abstract=2459483 or http://dx.doi.org/10.2139/ssrn.2459483

Iosifidis, P., & Papathanassopoulos, S. (2019). Greek ERT: State or public service broadcaster? In Polonska, E. & Beckett, C. (eds.), *Public service broadcasting and media systems in troubled European democracies* (pp. 129–153). London, UK: Palgrave Macmillan.

Kidd, D. (2009). The Global Independent Media Center network. In Mathison, D. (ed.), *Be the media* (pp. 413–422). San Francisco, CA: Natural Creative Group.

Kidd, D., & McIntosh, K. (2016). Social media and social movements. *Sociology Compass*, 10(9), 785–794. https://doi.org/10.1111/soc4.12399

Kousis, M., & Kanellopoulos, K. (2014). Impacts of the Greek crisis on contentious and conventional politics, 2010–2012. In Petropoulos, N. & Tsobanoglou, G. (eds.), *The social impacts of the Eurozone debt crisis* (pp. 443–462). Athens: Gordios Books.

Ελάτε να μετρηθούμε: Εμείς είμαστε 4.500.000! [Let's count: We are 4,500,000!]. (2013). *ThePressProject*. https://thepressproject.gr/elate-na-metrithoume-emeis-eimaste-4500000/

McCombs, M. E., & Shaw, D. L. (1972). The agenda-setting function of mass media. *Public Opinion Quarterly*, 36(2), 176–187. https://doi.org/10.1086/267990

Oikonomakis, L. (2018). Από τη λατινοαμερικανική ροζ παλίρροια μέχρι τη Μεσόγειο [From the Latin American Pink Tide to the Mediterranean]. In Serdedakis, N. & Tombazos, S. (eds.), Όψεις της Ελληνικής Κρίσης: Συγκρουσιακός Κύκλος και θεσμικές εκβάσεις [Aspects of the Greek Crisis: Cycle of Contention and Institutional Outcome] (pp. 249–282). Athens: Gutenberg.

Jauert, P., (2015). Community Media in the Nordic Countries: Between Public Service and private media. In Atton, C. (Ed.) Routledge Companion to Alternative and Community Media (pp. 189–198). London: Routledge.

Papathanassopoulos, S. (1997). The politics and the effects of the deregulation of Greek television. *European Journal of Communication*, 12(3), 351–368. https://doi.org/10.1177/0267323197012003003

Papathanassopoulos, S. (2001). Media commercialization and journalism in Greece. *European Journal of Communication*, 16(4), 505–521. https://doi.org/10.1177/0267323101016004004

Pickard, V.W. (2006). United yet autonomous: Indymedia and the struggle to sustain a radical democratic network. *Media, Culture & Society*, 28(3), 315–336. https://doi.org/10.1177/0163443706061685

Riffe, D., Lacy, S., Watson, B. R., & Fico, F. (2019). *Analyzing media messages: Using quantitative content analysis in research.* London: Routledge.

Rogas, B., & Papanikolopoulos, D. (2018). Οι κινητοποιήσεις των δημοσίων υπαλλήλων, 2009–2014 [The mobilization of civil servants, 2009–2014]. In Serdedakis, N. & Tombazos, S. (eds.), Όψεις της Ελληνικής Κρίσης: Συγκρουσιακός Κύκλος και θεσμικές εκβάσεις *[Aspects of the Greek Crisis: Cycle of Contention and Institutional Outcome]* (pp. 374–402). Athens: Gutenberg.

Rucht, D. (2003). Violence and new social movements. In Heitmeyer, W. & Hagan, J. (eds.), *International handbook of violence research* (pp. 369–382). New York: Springer Link.

Rucht, D. (2004). The quadruple 'A': Media strategies of protest movements since the 1960s. In Van De Donk, W., Loader, B., Nixon, P., & Rucht, D. (eds.), *Cyberprotest: New media, citizens and social movements* (pp. 29–56). London: Routledge.

Sandoval, M., & Fuchs, C. (2010). Towards a critical theory of alternative media. *Telematics and Informatics*, 27(2), 141–150. https://doi.org/10.1016/j.tele.2009.06.011

Seferiades, S. (2008). Κινηματικές συλλογικές δράσεις και δημοκρατία: ένα μακροσκοπικό υπόδειγμα [Social Movements' collective actions and democracy: A macro-level paradigm]. *Diaplous*, 25, 49–52.

Serdedakis, N., & Tombazos, S. (2018). Introduction: Greek crisis and the social protest. In Serdedakis, N. & Tombazos, S., Όψεις της Ελληνικής Κρίσης: Συγκρουσιακός Κύκλος και Θεσμικές εκβάσεις [Aspects of the Greek Crisis: Cycle of Contention and Institutional Outcome] (pp. 11–35). Athens: Gutenberg.

Sheehan, H. (2017). *Syriza wave: Surging and crashing with the Greek Left.* New York: NYU Press.

Siapera, E. (2015). Building a safety net for European journalists. Osservatorio Balcani e Caucaso Transeuropa.

Smyrnaios, N., & Karatzogianni, A. (2020). The rise of SYRIZA in Greece 2009–2015: The digital battlefield. In Veneti, A. & Karantzogianni, A. (eds.), *The Emerald handbook of digital media in Greece* (pp. 289–312). Bingley: Emerald Publishing.

Tarrow, S. (1989). *Democracy and disorder: Protest and politics in Italy, 1965–1975.* Oxford: Oxford University Press.

ERT Solidarite: Αλληλεγγύη στην ΕΡΤ από το βελγικό κανάλι [ERT Solidarite: The Belgian channel in solidarity with ERT]. (2013). TVXS https://tvxs.gr/news/%CE% B5%CE%BB%CE%BB%CE%AC%CE%B4%CE%B1/%CE%B5rt-solidarite- %CE%B1%CE%BB%CE%BB%CE%B7%CE%BB%CE%B5%CE%B3%CE%B3%CF% 8D%CE%B7-%CF%83%CF%84%CE%B7%CE%BD-%CE%B5%CF%81%CF%84- %CE%B1%CF%80%CF%8C-%CF%84%CE%BF-%CE%B2%CE%B5%CE%BB% CE%B3%CE%B9%CE%BA%CF%8C-%CE%BA%CE%B1%CE%BD%CE%AC%CE %BB%CE%B9.

Ολόκληρο το δελτίο ειδήσεων της ΕΡΤ έξω από το Ραδιομέγαρο [The Entire Newscast of ERT Outside the ERT Building]. (2013). Radiofono. www.radiofono.gr/node/3888

Treré, E., Jeppesen, S., & Mattoni, A. (2017). Comparing digital protest media imaginaries: Anti-austerity movements in Greece, Italy & Spain. TripleC: Communication, Capitalism & Critique. *Open Access Journal for a Global Sustainable Information Society*, 15(2), 404–422. https://doi.org/10.31269/triplec.v15i2.772

Tuchman, G. (1980). *Making news.* New York: Free Press. Athens: Gutenberg.

VPRC. (2013). Annual Poll. https://tvxs.gr/news/%CE%B5%CE%BB%CE%BB%CE% AC%CE%B4%CE%B1/vprc-%CE%BC%CE%B5%CE%B3%CE%AC %CE%BB%CE%B7-%CF%80%CF%84%CF%8E%CF%83%CE% B7-%CE%B4%CE%B7%CE%BC%CE%B1%CF%81-%CE%BC%CF%80%CF% 81%CE%BF%CF%83%CF%84%CE%AC-%CE%BF%CF%83%CF%85%CF%81%CE %B9%CE%B6%CE%B1-%CE%BC%CE%B5-05

Ποια ΕΡΤ θέλουμε; [Which ERT do we want?] (2014). Info-war. https://info-war.gr/ %CF%80%CE%BF%CE%B9%CE%B1-%CE%B5%CF%81%CF%84-%CE%B8% CE%AD%CE%BB%CE%BF%CF%85%CE%BC%CE%B5/

YouTube. (2021). Analytics of ERT. Copy in possession of Christos Avramidis.

7

LEFT-WING PUBLIC SPHERES IN POST-SOVIET CONTEXTS

Yiannis Mylonas

This chapter examines left-wing media practices and discourses in today's (January 2022) Russia. The study is based on a theoretical discussion of the context and the challenges that the left and independent media are facing in contemporary Russia. The study draws on relevant literature, as well as on interviews with intellectuals and activists involved in leftist media projects in Russia nowadays, understanding them as pivotal sources of counter-hegemonic politics and communication practices in the Russian society.[1] In that sense, the study draws on critical theories related to the notion of the public sphere, addressing them in relation to the challenges and specificities of the Russian post-socialist context, which is addressed through the examination of studies on contemporary Russian politics, society, and culture.

The post-soviet and contemporary Russian context is primarily unfolded through critical approaches on the ways in which Russia is generally constructed in the West by liberal discourses. This is important to advance a critical understanding of Russia beyond the hegemonic liberal framing of Russia, reproduced by Western intellectuals, politicians, and the media, perceived as a "transitional" country and, a sinister force. Instead, Russia is understood here as a capitalist country caught in imperialist antagonisms, striving to advance its own national and capitalist interests. Simultaneously, the state of the Russian media is also discussed from concerns associated with the framework of the public sphere, drawing on relevant studies on Russian media that address the challenges and the acute problems that the Russian civil society is currently facing.

The study then focuses on different leftist media projects that are currently developing in Russia, such as social media channels, news and analysis websites, and political analysis podcast productions. The association of such media with the Left has to do with their emphasis in intersectional agendas that stress issues and demands associated with class, gender, ethnicity, and ecology, while generally being

DOI: 10.4324/9781003221784-7

orientated toward social equality, democracy, and socialism. In the words of the founders of Zanovo website:

> Project 'Zanovo' [one more time] is a socio-political publication about life, work and struggle. We give the floor to those who are not heard and explain in order to change. Our focus is on labor rights, inequality, ecology, gender, activism. Individual destinies and great social processes. We are interested in new ideas about the future and those who are fighting to implement them. We are engaged in journalism, research, activism. Zanovo means high-quality texts for thinking people interested in change.
>
> *https://zanovo.media/*

Along with interviews (mostly conducted during 2021) with individuals involved in the specific media projects, the study also draws on discussions with academics, as well as with individuals working in cultural institutions (such as Garage, a privately owned, prestigious arts and culture institution that is based in Moscow),[2] who are broadly associated with leftist media practices and leftist discourses in Russia. Additionally, the study is also informed from the researcher's situated position in Russia, and his observation of the field of Russian politics and culture.

Russia beyond Liberal Western-Centrism

Drawing on liberal auspices, mainstream scholarship on post-soviet Russian media and politics developed a narrative based on notions of "totalitarianism", "oriental autocracy", and "transition" toward the Western liberal democratic framework, which is perceived in teleological terms as the most optimal and even "final" (according to Fukuyama's "end-of-history" thesis) sociopolitical system for humanity (Prozorov, 2009; Amin, 2016). The transitionist liberal, Western-centric narrative saw post-socialist Russia, along with other former socialist countries, to be lacking of a vibrant civil society, while lagging of solid liberal democratic foundations and traditions that would enable the establishment of a democratic public sphere and would allow the advance of pluralism in society, ensuring transparency and accountability in political affairs, as well as the effective control of political power. To this regard, the Russian political theorist Sergei Prozorov (2009: 4) defined post-communist studies as a "continuum between transitionalism and traditionalism"; by transitionalism, Prozorov meant the establishing of Western liberalism (in line to Fukuyama's thought) as a cannon and a benchmark to evaluate the reforming of previously socialist states, understanding deviations from such a model as a failure to "develop". By traditionalism, Prozorov perceived the advances of culturalist biases toward Russia and other post socialist states (associated with Samuel Huntington's "class of civilizations" thesis), which formulate fundamentalist notions of identity for those deemed as Western Others; according to such premises, the (essentialist) "traditional" (non-secular) identity of Russia makes it incompatible with Western (secular) liberal democratic values and "culturally" prone to authoritarianism. While transition offers a potential for development (under Western-centric and liberal criteria), tradition makes a pessimistic case of the impossibility of such a leap due to ontological reasons of incompatibility with such standards.

Scholars (Macgilchrist, 2011; McLaughlin, 2020) note the ways in which the Cold War imaginary has shaped the mainstream Western understanding of Russia and the ways in which the Western mass media in particular produce Russia's image in Western public spheres. The coming to power of Vladimir Putin in 2000, and his remaining in power up until now (January 2022), meant the regeneration of the Western, Cold War narrative on Russia. This involves the reproduction of a monolithic understanding of Russia as a somewhat perennial sinister and evil force that constantly threatens the West (Wood, 2018). A binary understanding between the West and Russia is sustained by the mainstream Western media and liberal pundits, with Russia conceptualized to incarnate everything that the West is not; Russia thus emerges as authoritarian, corrupt, conservative, and aggressive, whereas the West as democratic, progressive, open, and righteous. This Cold War perspective largely continues to be reproduced today, despite the demise of the Soviet Union 30 years ago, and Russia's Westernizing directions that took place during the 1990s at least. McLaughlin (2020: 17) traces the emergence of such a Russophobe narrative in 1917, in response to the fears that the Russian revolution sparked to the Western bourgeoisies.

Russian Media, Politics, and the Public Sphere Today

Departing from critical theorizations (Negt & Kluge, 2016), the notion of the public sphere is understood as a contested realm, associated with the sustaining of political hegemony and the reproduction of the capitalist social relations of production, and the potentials of confronting it. In that sense, different civil society agents, such as intellectuals and journalists among other, produce the public, so as to legitimize established power, or to effectively challenge it. While the public sphere is the space where political communication occurs, the notion of the public refers to the people constituting a historical actor, produced by the discourses that circulate in the very public sphere (Coleman & Ross, 2010: 21); thus, the public and the public sphere are dialectically interconnected and historically and structurally defined. The historical rise of the public sphere opened the possibility for civil society to address questions through a publicity that could make political authority accountable for its decisions and policies (Habermas, 1992). Critics, however, have emphasized issues of class, gender, ethnicity, and race as under-theorized in Habermas' notion of the public sphere. As a bourgeois institution, the public sphere has been an exclusive space where only those who hold economic and cultural capital could enter. Maintaining that the public sphere is an indispensable realm for the overall human experience, Negt and Kluge argued that its bourgeois character sustains the advantageous politico-economic and social positions of the upper classes. The divisions between the different spheres of life and practice in bourgeois society make the political expression and organization of the general proletarian experience to be a very difficult task.

Its success is connected to the degree of the development of class struggle at a given historical moment (Negt & Kluge, 2016: 94). The public sphere is therefore a divided, uneven, and potentially antagonistic realm, defined by the time's historical stakes and conflicts in society and the world, where different publics coexist and may potentially compete with each other. While the mainstream public sphere reproduces hegemonic discourses and identities, the potential politicization of different issues by social groups, organizations, and citizens may develop counter-hegemonic public spheres, associated with antagonistic political agents and media producing counter-publics, and advocating contrasting understandings of reality and its stakes.

The discussion of the public sphere in Russia is usually grounded on the earlier mentioned understanding of Russia as a "transitional country", implying a linear historical trajectory that leads from authoritarianism to liberal democracy. The development of a "free market" system here is perceived to be a democratizing force. To this regard, the soviet media's class-orientated and propagandistic role (according to the scientific premises of Marxism-Leninism and the political goals of socialist consolidation and advance, while antagonizing global capitalism) has been analyzed under the vantage point of Western liberal norms of media conduct, associated with notions of pluralism, objectivity, and impartiality (McNair, 1991). The commercial character of mainstream media in bourgeois democracies is also often viewed in positive terms; as far as the soviet media system is concerned, commercialization was understood to bring "democratization". Hence, the "opening" of the soviet media to Western advertising during the era of glasnost and perestroika in the 1980s was viewed as something that potentially advances pluralism and freedom of speech (McNair, 1991: 73), disregarding the propagandist mechanisms and functions of the media in Western capitalist states (Herman & Chomsky, 1988; McChesney, 2009), and the reduced forms that democracy bears under capitalism. To this regard, Susan Buck-Morss (2002: xv) instead argued that socialism in Russia failed because "it mimicked capitalism too faithfully". Additionally, liberal accounts fail to take into account the complexity and the differences of the 74-year-old history of the existence of the Soviet Union. To this regard, scholars (Buck Morss, 2002; Steinberg, 2002) have highlighted the revolutionary and experimental practices that took place across the 1920s in Russia, bringing progressive and emancipatory changes in social life, culture, the arts, and politics. Research has also showed that during the last decades of the USSR, informal cultural spheres and communities widely proliferated across the USSR; far from being marginal, these milieus discussed the problems of the Soviet Union widely and developed new and alternative narratives, aesthetics, and lifestyles, deterritorializing and reinterpreting the Soviet norms and goals (Yurchak, 2005; Budraitskis, 2022). Further, toward the end of the USSR, the Soviet media became more diverse and plural for a variety of reasons, including the advance of media technologies and the rise of media convergence (Chupin & Dauce, 2017a). Moreover, alternative media projects, notably the infamous samizdat publications emerging in the 1960s, also confronted the official Marxist discourse of the USSR as well as the repressive state apparatuses of the time (Filimonov, 2021: 21).

While commercialization has been highly advanced in nearly all spheres of social life in Russia after the collapse of the USSR, democratization has been a more challenging process. According to Filimonov (2021: 18), although the moving toward a market system in Russia was completed during the 1990s, different developments dislocated the transition narrative with emerging ones to stress (under different labels) a neo-authoritarian turn in Russian politics. More nuanced approaches understand the Russian political system as a "hybrid regime"; these imply the coexistence of democratic and authoritative elements, observing a progressive hollowing out of democratic institutions, but without them being fully eliminated. Likewise, Russia's media system is understood as a "hybrid model with strong state intervention, poor professionalization, and fairly strong market influence, characterized as 'statist commercialized' media system" (Chupin & Dauce, 2017a: 7). In this context too, the delimited nature of contemporary Russian public sphere is also stressed, marked by "commercialization, state manipulation and the domination of the political and economic elites in public discourses" (Pape & Smirnova, 2018: 776). The media are under varying degrees of state control in contemporary Russia. Though independent political journalism advanced rapidly during the 1990s and through the use of the Internet, from 2000s onwards, the pluralism initially pursued started to fade. Media control has been accomplished through state media corporations and also through the ownership regimes of private media and the affiliations of media moguls with state authorities (Filimonov, 2021: 22). Persecution is often the case for oppositional journalists, regardless of political affiliation. Laws allegedly targeting "extremism" and "foreign agents" are often flexibly used to persecute civil society agents, journalists, and different media (Filimonov, 2021: 19). Reflecting about the political climate in the country (during the summer of 2021), as one discussant stressed "[at the moment] journalists and experts think about the very basic tasks to maintain their projects (and lives) and are less open to research and reflection". In that sense, self-censorship practices can be common in the Russian media, so as to avoid political controversy and its associated risks (Chupin & Dauce, 2017b: 41). Simultaneously, the need for a proletarian type of journalism was stressed by respondents, along with the problems posed by state repression, discursive-ideological antagonism, and broader issues associated with structural and resource-orientated inequalities between different media practices in the Russian public realm:

> there is now [January 2022] more repression against journalists generally in Russia, but the liberal media have more legal and financial support because they can fall back on a huge variety of business-friendly organizations and institutions, in addition to the media business itself. So defending journalists is a necessary function of the media, but the capabilities of leftwing media are much smaller, whereas the danger is greater. [...] the kind of journalism necessary is the one to bring to the public light things happening. How work is done in the factories, and in plantations; how value is produced. How they, even small producers, besides the big capitalists, prefer to drive 400 km away and bring migrant workers, who are generally hated by Russians, instead of hiring local workers... if liberal journalists report such things, they will do it from a charity-driven

stance; without the necessary analysis of value, maintaining illusions like "there is no slavery today", and "work is provided and these people are lifted out of poverty".

At the same time, nationalist rhetoric is generally high in the public realm, drawing both on peak moments of the Soviet era and on Russia's imperial legacies (Wood, 2018), with conservative values to be highlighted. Nevertheless, the media are not under the state's total subjugation, with liberal and progressive voices to continue to exist online, as well as in the print press and the radio. The advance of the Internet and digital media in particular provided a counter-paradigm to the aforementioned authoritarian and monopolistic trajectories, though the Russian cyberspace remains a site of constant state intervention for control. The cumulating attacks of the state's repressive apparatuses on the media during the recent years have created a sense of political disengagement along with "a permanent condition of fragility" to media activists and practitioners (Filimonov, 2021: 161). Scholars (Bozovic & Djagalov, 2022) also note the presence of artistic and cultural practices (through music, literature, visual arts, and cinema) to be advancing critical views on the contemporary Russian social formation, countering liberal hegemony, nationalism, and post-modern cynicism from leftist perspectives.

Morozov (2015: 135) comprehends Russia's current authoritarianism and conservatism under the lens of the semi-periphery. Russia is understood as economically and military inferior to the West (Wood, 2018), putting her in a defensive position to the West's military, political, and economic interventionism. In Morozov's sense, Russia securitizes itself against Western expansionism, through a variety of practices, including authoritarian governance and an overall conservative ideological consolidation. Authoritarianism is meant to block the potential politicization of the population, while conservatism is meant to contain the cultural realm from Western interventions. From a class perspective on the social composition of the post-Soviet Russia, the process of deindustrialization that advanced after the dissolution of the Soviet Union lowered the living standards of the working people and weakened organized labor power, forcing workers to seek individual solutions usually in the informal economic sector (Morris, 2016). Concurrently, while oppositional politics (through political, parties, protests, and trade union activities) are generally repressed by the state (Morris, 2017: 45), a general sense of atomization and individualism is noted to exist in Russia, which is associated with the ideological disillusion (as well as the impoverished material conditions) commonly noted in the ordinary people's post-socialist experience of living in capitalism (Baysha, 2014; Matza, 2018). Budraitskis (2022: 15) argues that social depoliticization is an enduring feature of Putinism, alongside a regressive turn to nationalism and traditionalism, associated with so-called Russian spiritual values, which presumably stand in sharp contrast toward the values that the West stands for. Conservative ideology is combined with neoliberal practices subordinating social life to market competition "creating a hybrid ideological construct" (Budraitskis, 2022: 46).

Nevertheless, along with the atomization processes advanced by neoliberal restructuring and the conservative state ideology, Morris (2016, 2017) also notes the continuity of the working-class community experience, which entails a sense of political contingency as it is associated with a different identity and life expectation from that of what Fisher (2009) described as "capitalist realism", notably the impossibility of conceiving a post-capitalist society. At the same time, generated after the elections of 2004, the hegemonic character of the Russian political opposition is liberal, cosmopolitan, and market-orientated, with both left-wing and far-right tendencies existing in the broader Russian oppositional realm (Wood, 2018). The course of events has also shown the developing of temporary coalitions between different politico-ideological currents, in futile attempts to create a broad, social counter-hegemonic block. The trajectory of Alexei Navalny, the liberal journalist viewed as the unofficial leader of the Russian opposition, is exemplary to this regard; in the past, Navalny had aligned himself with the far-right, and even engaged himself with racist discourse, to move toward more left-wing populist agendas (during 2020–2021), stressing issues connected with poverty and unequal wealth distribution, as well as supporting the voting of Communist party delegates in the September 2021 Russian national elections, through his "smart voting" system (Budraitskis, 2022: 184).

In such a perplexed context, the post-Soviet Russian left maintains a limited positions, despite the fact that the Communist Party of the Russian Federation (CPRF) has a strong social basis and organizational form, and is still the second biggest party in the Russian parliament. The rather established presence of the CPRF in the Russian political life hardly makes it an oppositional and radical party. Thus movements and parties outside the official CPRF framework formulate the more vital segments of the contemporary Russian leftist realm. According to Budraitskis (2022), what can be described as the "new Russian left" emerged from the early 1980s and took part in a variety of struggles since then. In Budraitskis sense the current Russian left is characterized by a "nostalgic idealization of the USSR and criticism of it from the left".

Non-Public Spheres

The research respondents explained the limited scope of counter-hegemonic political communication in Russia today. On the one hand, a prevailing individualistic ethos, connected to the post-Soviet neoliberal structure of feeling that predominated the post socialist world, and on the other, a mixture of disillusionment for the possibility of change, the effective control of the media, and fear of state repression, seem to be central variants defining the general shrinking of counter-hegemonic political discourse in the Russian public life. Simultaneously, as the collective experience of the socialist past is vividly strong in Russia still, it often mediates the experience of the contemporary context:

> … a main difference (between Russian and European or US public spheres) is the replacement of real political struggles and debates with debates about history, and the great popularity of conspiracy theories in You Tube. There are no real politics in Russia and it is hard to provide interesting analyses of current affairs, because people know how

> *things are, there is nothing new, no big surprises in this political system, and people sublimate this lack of real political life in Russia with some topics outside of this political reality; they can discuss history, or political events in other countries like the USA, Western Europe, with a very little knowledge about these events… depoliticization is a very important foundation of this political system… There is an interest in politics but there is a lack of institutional basis to express political concerns so politics are sublimated in the social media.*

As also suggested, the Soviet past, instrumentalized by the current Russian government in nationalistic ways, is often publicly deployed in a pseudo-political way. For the respondent, this serves as a refuge for the absence of legitimate meaningful politics, and deliberation, demonstrating the low information level of the general public on political events happening elsewhere. Essentially, the specific process is connected with the hegemonic trend of depoliticization, which is supported from both the ideological and the repressive state apparatuses. As scholars have noted too, the depoliticization of public life is "one of the trademarks of the present [Russian] regime and the way in which it exercises power" (Chupin & Dauce, 2017a: 42).

> *Their [social media] popularity is based on the mood of their production. If you want to be popular on You Tube, you should be confrontational and touch upon topics that provoke negative emotions. If you talk about labor rights, it will be a failure. But if you talk about Stalin, it will be a success; if you talk about how great the Soviet Union was, or how under evaluated Stalin is today; the most popular Stalinist-communist You Tubers in Russia today focus on history topics, and on topics that are the most controversial and trigger some emotions… such a history research is a hoax and has nothing to do with actual historical research. You may be a Stalinist and for this reason you find some arguments for Stalin from two-three books that you read supporting your point of view. This is also a popular production in the book market, a kind of fake history, based on historical imagination that is politically engaged… most of these You Tube channels do not involve people in true politics; they induce some kind of consumption of some information and political emotions….*

Social media here seem to reflect the general mood of the political talk-shows and news of the Russian mainstream media, which generally advance a patriotic and confrontational stance toward different and opposing views. Likewise the problems of social media and the "user generated ideology" (Fuchs, 2016) developed by social media users distort historical inquiry and political discussion and, in this sense, reproduce a stagnant and anti-political form of public debate.

Identity, Structure, Antagonisms

The rise of the Internet seems to have created a generational gap in terms of political identification and consciousness in Russia. Technology uses create different forms of experiencing the world to different generations (Bolin, 2017). Social media have been conditionally able to escape different government censorship practices. This gave way to the rise of identity discourses and identity politics, associated with feminism in particular, which have gained popularity among the Russian urban youth. Nevertheless, as empirical studies in social media and politics elsewhere also suggest (Fuchs, 2017), the use of social media does not by default mean political enlightenment of the advance of progressive politics. Nostalgia, pseudo-politics, as well as conspiracy theories and regressive politics coexist with progressive politics online, and often compete with each other.

> *Young people do not watch TV; older generations watch TV, and the political talk shows and analyses there are very confrontational, they are not neutral, they are very patriotic… Navalny showed how social media can make people to participate in political protests… the audience of political media is growing, and the Left is also growing; but structural problems of the social media reflect how politics are developing there… the most popular social media for politically engaged audience is YouTube; many popular channels, feminist ones, and communist ones too.*
>
> *A lot of the leftist channels and groups that appear in social media are of low quality; they offer narcissistic consumption possibilities. Even when they are popularizing certain kinds of knowledge, it usually comes in the form of simplified and onesided 'takes'. So, YouTube videos, I see as an unsuitable medium for treating problematic topics that have to be elaborated further, or, that are too inconvenient for the purposes of a polarized discussion.*

Regressive politics associated with anti-feminist perspectives and alt-right ideas and discursive practices are also growing through social media in Russia. Feminist social media networks and YouTube channels are attacked by equivalent alt-right channels, manifesting misogynic and right-wing positions. Ridiculing, slandering, and cyberbullying practices are frequent against feminist social media, producing a highly volatile and polarized discursive environment.

As noted in a critical analysis of the reactionary, anti-feminist commentary of an alt-right vlogger against a popular feminist YouTube page (called nixelpixel):[3]

> *the vlogger uses offensive slurs - "slut", "ugly", "fat", "faggot", "trap". His arguments on feminism don't have any base and ground. He merely uses memes and "funny" comments to ridicule feminist's statements, without giving any examples on what actions of feminists show that they want to dominate society, and without explaining what is wrong with intersectional feminism. Instead, statements like "feminists hate men and free speech" and the comparison of feminists with fascists are regularly repeated in these videos, typical of alt-right speech tropes. Further, the vlogger doesn't fact check his claims, as his arguments on female circumcision is totally wrong, because even in Moscow there is a lot of hospitals where they do female circumcision. [Further] the vlogger argues that feminism doesn't care about men, and devalued the women's experiences of sexism, making it seem as a whim of crazy women.*
>
> Zakharova, 2019

Opposition(s) and Minor Public Spheres

It seems like in Russia we don't have such clear distinction between left and right polit-ical orientation in media. The important difference that split journalists in two camps is their relations with the government. There are pro-government media and independent media (or pro-opposition). So the media that are clearly more oriented to the left values are quite niche.

When [the journal] Skepsis started in the early 2000's, the vacuum that it sought to fill is what existed between a Stalinist left, without class analysis, and a right-wing, meaning liberalism, market-driven politics and nationalism. We tried to create quality, non-academic analysis to reflect from a leftist perspective on current affairs.

The predominant oppositional politics and media in Russia are liberal; these advance progressive and democratic social demands, associated with freedom of speech, transparency and accountability of formal politics, and deliberative practices. Such demands though are often accompanied by anti-leftist, free market and westernizing aspirations (Budraitskis, 2022). The left is caught in both a tactical symbiotic position with the centrist liberals and in an antagonistic relationship with them as well.

There are different liberal media; some are used as political instruments, this is the case of Navalny's work; others work as traditional media. It is not possible to compete with them, but you as a journalist can try to publish something there, we contribute with articles on the cultural sphere. Some political censorship exists from the editors; they have cut articles they deemed as "non-objective"; so a leftist position is not objective, but to be liberal for them is being "objective".

Diverse events, associated with local protests (such as struggles against pension reforms, environmental struggles related to the construction of highways or the construction of new dumpsites, the protection of old buildings from real estate), broader protests connected with the anti-corruption agendas foregrounded by the journalistic and political work of Alexey Navalny and his associates, different elect-oral battles taking place in Russia, formulate terrains of joint struggles among the oppositional forces. The left has its own divisions regarding issues of ideology and strategy. While part of the left abstains from collaborating with the liberals, another part is developing conditional alliances while advancing critique towards liberals. In that sense, various events of social importance and political struggles are often optimized to produce counter-hegemonic, leftist politics. At the same time, more fundamental questions associated with the identity and the practices of the contem-porary Russian left are also enunciated by respondents:

A lot of the left in Russia is western-orientated; there is something artificial about it. They try to import western leftist agendas and western ways, making them seem like they are learning court manners, to appear integrated and Westernized [...] I maintain a third-world perspective, associated with 1970's leftist analyses; Russia has more in common with the non-Western world. Of course things are quite contradictory, and you have cities in Russia like Moscow which are part of the first world. But overall, I do not see the West as cannon to follow. A certain [Western]core-centric left tends to ignore the darker side of (capitalist) progress, as the evil necessary for local social progress, focusing instead on social achievements such as the welfare state of the post WWII era. What I meant is that there is an equivalent of a middle-class gaze in an international sense, obviously countries are not "international classes", that the left has to overcome. It is even more important for Russia, because far from being an element of abstract global analysis, it leads to a delusion relative to the possibilities of Western-style leftwing politics. And whether this kind of politics is desirable, it is a separate issue.

From such a point of view, the impasse of the Russian left is also connected to its latent disconnection from the Russian context and to its bearing of a certain degree of Western-centrism. A different analytical and strategic focus, related to a more decentered and non-Western perspective, is suggested here.

Conclusions

In this paper, I proposed the understanding of Russia beyond the liberal deadlock, which seems to formulate a civilizational benchmark of Western standards to measure and sustain global hierarchies. As I argued, liberal accounts often attribute the shortcomings of the Russian democracy overall to its Soviet legacies, which are usually deemed totalitarian. One-dimensional accounts of the Soviet Union, drawing on liberal notions such as those described above and associated to the rather inconsistent notion of "totalitarianism", are used to explain Russia today (Wood, 2018), sustaining the Cold War dichotomy between the free and the totalitarian states, disregarding the legacies and continuities of colonialism and imperialism exercised by the West across the world (Amin, 2016). Instead, I addressed the current political context and legacies of Russia through critical accounts that look at issues such as the development of neoliberalism in the country, and the rise of an anti-political culture, which, despite its intense presence in Russia, is by no means foreign to Western political cultures (Rancière, 2007). Viewing the Russian context from the framework of global capitalism and its effects on the majority of the population, allows the developing of an understanding of Russia beyond the delimiting lens of authoritarianism versus democracy conceptual framework, by looking at the commonalities and challenges that working people face today globally.

My respondents and the media projects that I took under consideration for this study were mainly associated with the post-Soviet and noninstitutional Russian left. Though growing, it still remains at the margins of political life. Although social media provide a space not fully controlled by the state, their corporate and consumerist structure also compromises politics and the advance of political communication. From a proletarian public sphere perspective, the specific limits are further associated with broader sociostructural constraints delimiting the advance of working class struggles and cultures. The Russian specificities in that sense can also be indicative of broader challenges that the left is faced with across the world today. The difficulty for the Russian left to grow is connected to the harsh material inequalities of contemporary Russia, the coercive and ideological practices of the current Russian federal government, and the lasting impact of post-socialist sociopolitical and ideological trajectories that grew in the Russian social context, notably social depoliticization, disengagement, and a general lack of belief in the potentials of social change, reinforced by the absence of broad counter-hegemonic, and emancipatory social imaginaries, narratives, and political formations. Reflecting on Lauren Berlant's "cruel optimism" (2011) thesis, concerning the realities of neoliberal societies, respondents noted that Russia is instead more defined by a "cruel pessimist" structure of feeling, reinforced by both the material realities of Russian neoliberal capitalism and the coercive practices of the Russian political establishment. The situation emerging after the 24th of February 2022 brings forth new variables and challenges for the Russian public spheres and the Russian left that require further research.

Notes

1 This study was completed before the Russian military invasion in Ukraine in 24 February 2022. The invasion and the escalation of the military conflict following has deteriorated the position of left-wing and independent media in Russia further, accelerating censorship and persecution practices towards critical media, journalists, and civil society agents and movements opposing the war.
2 Owned by wealthy businessmen, Garage and V-A-C Foundation are some of Moscow's prominent cultural institutions, hosting a variety of cutting-edge art exhibitions, conferences, discussions, while facilitating publications on the arts and on social and cultural theory. Alongside them, various similar (but smaller) institutions, like Strelka in Moscow, and other ones can also be found in main Russian cities. These institutions have received worldwide attention, are part of the international arts and cultural sphere, and attract a broad and international audience of artists, scholars, and connoisseurs, among others. Sociopolitical issues often formulate important parts of these institutions' agendas; thus ecology, cultural identity, poverty, gender and sexuality are regularly featured in the periodical exhibitions, as well as in the conferences held by these institutes.
3 www.youtube.com/channel/UC2GQig8tlmGFq2Wp2tj_Jbw

References

Amin, S. 2016. *Russia and the Long Transition from Capitalism to Socialism*. New York: Monthly Review Press.

Baysha, O. 2014. *The Mythologies of Capitalism and the End of the Soviet Project*. London: Lexington Books.

Berlant, L. 2011. *Cruel Optimism*. Duke University Press.

Bolin, G. 2017. *Media Generations: Experience, Identity and Mediatised Social Change*. London: Routledge.

Bozovic, M. & Djagalov, R. 2022. Post-Soviet Aesthetics. In: Lye, C. & Nealon, C. (eds) *After Marx Literature, Theory, and Value in the Twenty-First Century*. Cambridge University Press, 143–160.

Buck-Morss, S. 2002. *Dreamworld and Catastrophe: The Passing of Mass Utopia in East and West*. Cambridge: MIT Press.

Budraitskis, I. 2022. *Dissidents among Dissidents: Ideology, Politics and the Left in Post-Soviet Russia*. London: Verso.

Chupin, I. & Dauce, F. 2017a. The Practice of Political Journalism: Comparing Russia, France, and Germany. *Laboratorium*, 9(2): 5–11.

Chupin, I. & Dauce, F. 2017b. Termination of Journalists' Employment in Russia: Political Conflicts and Ordinary Negotiation Procedures in Newsrooms. *Laboratorium*, 9(2): 39–58.

Coleman, S. & Ross, K. 2010. *The Media and the Public: "Them" and "Us" in Media Discourse*. Chichester: Wiley-Blackwell.

Filimonov, K. 2021. *The Performance of Participation in Russian Alternative Media: Discourse, Materiality and Affect in Grassroots Media Production in Contemporary Russia*. Uppsala Universitet (Unpublished PhD Thesis).

Fisher, M. 2009. *Capitalist Realism: Is There No Alternative?* London: Zero Books.

Fuchs, C. 2016. Red Scare 2.0: User-Generated Ideology in the Age of Jeremy Corbyn and Social Media. *Journal of Language and Politics*, 15(4): 369–398.

Fuchs, C. 2017. *Social Media: A Critical Introduction*. London: Sage.

Habermas, J. 1992. *The Structural Transformation of the Public Sphere: Inquiry into a Category of Bourgeois Society*. Cambridge: Polity.

Herman, E. & Chomsky, N. 1988. *Manufacturing Consent: The Political Economy of the Mass Media*. New York: Pantheon Books.

Macgilchrist, F. 2011. *Journalism and the Political: Discursive Tensions in News Coverage of Russia*. Amsterdam/Philadelphia: John Benjamin Publishing Company.

Matza, T. 2018. *Shock Therapy: Psychology, Precarity, and Well-Being in Postsocialist Russia*. Durham: Duke University Press.

McChesney, R. 2009. *The Political Economy of Media. Enduring Issues, Emerging Dilemas*. New York: Monthly Review Press.

McLaughlin, G. 2020. *Russia and the Media: The Makings of a New Cold War*. London: Pluto Press.

McNair, B. 1991. *Glasnost, Perestroika and the Soviet Media*. London and New York: Routledge.

Morozov, V. 2015. *Russia's Postcolonial Identity: A Subaltern Empire in a Eurocentric World*. Basingstoke: Palgrave McMillan.

Morris, J. 2016. *Everyday Post-Socialism: Working-Class Communities in the Russian Margins*. London: Palgrave McMillan.

Morris, J. 2017. From Betrayal to Resistance: Working Class Voices in Russia Today. *Journal of Working-Class Studies*, 2(1): 45–57.

Negt, O. & Kluge, A. 2016. *Public Sphere and Experience: Analysis of the Bourgeois and Proletarian Public Sphere*. London: Verso.

Pape, U. & Smirnova, A. 2018. Transforming the Public Sphere: The Case of Moscow's City Libraries. *Cultural Studies*, 32(5): 772–799. DOI:10.1080/09502386.2018.1428648

Prozorov, S. 2009. *The Ethics of Postcommunism: History and Social Praxis in Russia*. Basingstoke: Palgrave McMillan.

Rancière, J. 2007. *On the Shores of Politics*. London: Verso.

Steinberg, M. D. 2002. *Proletarian Imagination: Self, Modernity and the Sacred in Russia, 1910–1925*. New York: Cornell University Press.

Wood, T. 2018. *Russia without Putin: Money, Power and the Myths of the New Cold War*. London: Verso.

Yurchak, A. 2005. *Everything Was Forever, Until It Was No More: The Last Soviet Generation*. Princeton and Oxford: Princeton University Press.

Zakharova, V. (2019). Anti-Misandrist Communities and Cyberbullying of Feminist-Activists. Unpublished final student paper for the Media, Culture and Critique MSc course, at the Media Department, NSE-HSE, Moscow.

8

RADICAL DATA JOURNALISM

Sandra Jeppesen

Introduction

The datafication of everything pervades public discourse produced by corporations, governments, mainstream media, local media, social media, and even alternative media. How do radical journalists use big data, public data, or alternative datasets to produce news that integrates intersectional anti-capitalist perspectives? This is particularly cogent in the era of COVID-19 where the public is avidly following a daily outpouring of data, including tables, charts, maps, infographics, data visualizations, and so on. Data in public discourse tend to be thought of as depoliticized because numbers and statistics have a presumed objectivity; however data and statistics are not neutral. Data have long been used to further specific, often authoritarian, political, social, and economic objectives, reproducing systemic racialized, classed, gendered, colonial, and heteronormative oppressions. These uses are explicitly and implicitly contested by radical data journalists.

However, radical data journalism is not without its contradictions, as it both depends on and calls into question the datafication of everything. Although data are known to be biased, activist use of data in the form of infographics, maps, and so on can serve to legitimate radical data journalism for audiences. Radical data journalism thus appears simultaneously to enter into the mainstream media claim to objectivity and transparency in reporting through the use of statistics, and the sharing of public datasets upon which reporting is based. But at the same time, radical journalists call this logic into question by unraveling the data and its presumed objectivity. The promise and peril of radical data journalism will be critically mapped in this chapter to explore its potential for the future of social transformation and democratic discourse.

DOI: 10.4324/9781003221784-8

Big Data

We are living in an era of widespread datafication and big data, in which data are the quantified building blocks of knowledge and technological epistemologies created through processes of abstraction, categorization, and measurement. The term 'big data' refers to massive blocks of data obtained through datafication processes often online through citizen engagement such as browser searches, social media participation, online shopping, gaming, health tracking, smartphone GPS tracking, and so on. Big data are also collected through the platform economy (Uber, Airbnb, Skip the Dishes, Etsy, etc.) and platform labor conducted there. But "big data not only refers to very large data sets and the tools and procedures used to manipulate and analyze them, but also to a 'computational turn' in thought and research" (Hintz et al., 2018, p. 6). Increasingly epistemologies are constructed through reference to data structures which in turn shape society and emergent social norms. "Big data is a social, cultural, and technological phenomenon—a complex amalgamation of digital data abundance, emerging analytic techniques, mythology about data-driven insights, and growing critique about the overall consequences of big-data practices for democracy and society" (Lewis & Westlund, 2015, p. 447). One of the issues regarding big data is not just the power it has to measure reality, but also the fact that "big data shapes the reality it measures" (Hintz et al., 2018, p. 6). As van Dijck and Poell (2013) have found, social media, through the algorithms and big data they produce, can shape the outcomes that they purport to then measure. For radical data journalists, who have followed this computational turn, the objective becomes attempting to tease out the measurement from the social construction, the data from the social reality, and the systemic oppressions produced through, by and in data systems from the purportedly neutral stories they are imagined to tell.

Datafication

Big data's explosion has resulted in the intensification of data's influence in our lives and in society from local to global through what is called datafication. "We need to understand datafication, therefore, not merely as a technical development, but as a trend advanced by the amalgamation of different cultural, political and economic forces that both shift and entrench power relations" (Hintz et al., 2018, p. 49). In other words, datafication is a process related to the production of not just data, but rather, "the wider *transformation of human life* so that its elements can be a continual source of data. The beneficiaries of this are very often corporations, but also states and sometimes civil society organisations and communities" (Mejias & Couldry, 2019, p. 2; italics in original).

Datafication has an immediacy in that technological systems produce massive amounts of data in real time, influencing events, interpretations, thinking, and so on, in the very moment they are taking place. Datafication thus has the "ability to add a real-time data dimension to mass media's notion of liveness. Facebook, LinkedIn, and particularly Twitter process large quantities of users' behavioral data every second" (van Dijck & Poell, 2013, p. 10). This notion of 'liveness' means that not just live footage or live reporting but also live data features prominently in journalism and influences everyday life. However, a key issue with big data and the intensification of datafication is that it is not a transparent and accountable process to the casual user of dominant data-producing systems that include platform labor, web browsers, online shopping, smartphones, fitness trackers, and social media. "The invisibility of datafication processes prompts questions about the actual relationship between data and users: are (real-time) data flows indeed a reflection of real live activities, or are they the result of manipulative monitoring and steering?" (van Dijck & Poell, 2013, pp. 10–11). These data flows are now so deeply embedded in our lives that we are said to live in a datafied society.

The Datafied Society

In the datafied society, "large domains of human life became susceptible to being processed via forms of analysis that could be automated on a large-scale" (Mejias & Couldry, 2019, p. 2). This large-scale automation of human life takes place through mechanisms that are largely hidden from public view. Despite this hiddenness or invisibility, the "mass collection and processing of data have become central to contemporary forms of governance and commercial life" (Hintz et al., 2018, p. 8), being used, in other words, by the state and corporations, thus influencing humans in both citizen and consumer roles. For radical data journalists, citizen journalists, and citizens more generally, "in a datafied society, we must view monitoring and data collection as practices that pervade all forms of social organization, encompassing both state and corporate actors, and operating in a transnational and global context" (Hintz et al., 2018, p. 9). New epistemological formations arise in the global context where citizens, platform users, and journalists are subject to knowledge production that is increasingly under the purview of large corporations in the inequitable structures of the tech sector, creative cities, and the creative knowledge labor sector (Leslie & Catungal, 2012). These epistemological formations might be considered 'data epistemologies' defined as the construction of social knowledge shaped by big data. In other words, we gain knowledge of friendship, how to cook, social norms for dating, creative sharing, and so on, through engagements with internet sites—curated through datafication—as social relations, food preparation, intimate relations, creativity, and other activities once considered fundamentally human are now carried out through algorithmic systems that are both directed by and collecting big data in near-real time.

Data Epistemologies

Data epistemologies are important to consider as we think about what it means to be a radical data journalist, contesting dominant political frames and epistemological assumptions within journalism. Through data epistemologies, "a wider normalization of data-extracting infrastructures [is] accompanied by the internalization of widespread justifications for their premise" (Hintz et al., 2018, p. 108), creating opportunities for data citizenship. As such, data structures become a new space for understanding and claiming citizenship rights through reclaiming digital data and challenging the biased knowledge it tends to produce. This builds on notions of digital citizenship that include aspects of political engagement, membership in communities, and the facilitation of political participation (Hintz et al., 2018, pp. 28–29). Moreover, data citizenship depends on data literacy that extends beyond individual actions, focuses on the complexities of online digital spaces and ecosystems, and provides opportunities for data education and skill-building among citizens (Carmi et al., 2020) to resist the authoritarian power structures that can be embedded in big data.

Radical data journalists can engage in resistance; however, they are dependent on big data, with their journalism perhaps even legitimated by the use of apparently objective statistics, while critiquing the very systems that produce the data being analyzed. "Situating the nature and advancement of datafication in wider hegemonic practices and power structures leads to an active politicization of data, which is a necessary step to begin to challenge the prevalence" (Hintz et al., 2018, p. 142) of data hegemony, surveillance capitalism, data colonialism, and so on. As radical data journalists produce knowledge as truth, "big data and related approaches present new facets for understanding the epistemology of transforming raw information into journalistic truth" (Lewis & Westlund, 2015, p. 453). This takes place through three epistemological aspects of journalism—its form or medium, its production through journalistic practices, and its acceptance as knowledge by news audiences. All three of these have undergone shifts in the quantitative turn to data journalism in both the mainstream and radical media sectors. Below we map out the definition of data journalism, and then explore its function in these two sectors.

Data Journalism

Uses of big data raise epistemological concerns regarding how journalists produce knowledge in the quantitative turn in journalism toward data journalism (Coddington, 2015). For example, "the manner in which media organizations like *The Guardian* and *The New York Times* handled the large amounts of data released by WikiLeaks is one of the major steps that brought the term [data journalism] into prominence" (Gray et al., 2012, p. 17). Despite a long history of journalists analyzing datasets, today "data journalism is having a social, cultural, technological, political and economic moment in journalism" (Hermida & Young, 2019).

As mentioned, journalists have long used datasets derived from sources such as census data, survey data, institutional data, economic data, lifestyle data, demographic data such as births and deaths, and so on to provide context for stories. The history of data-driven journalism goes back at least as far as Computer-Assisted Reporting (CAR) which "was first used in 1952 by CBS to predict the result of the presidential election. Since the 1960s, (mainly investigative, mainly US-based) journalists have sought to independently monitor power by analyzing databases of public records with scientific methods" (Gray et al., 2012, p. 18). CAR might be best understood as a computational technique for analyzing data, whereas data journalism "pays attention to the way that data sits within the whole journalistic workflow" (Gray et al., 2012, p. 21).

Data journalism therefore is not just a data practice but also a journalism practice. "Data can be the source of data journalism, or it can be the tool with which the story is told—or it can be both" (Gray et al., 2012, p. 3). As such, practitioners can approach their work from techno-critical and/or socio-critical perspectives, with hackers and data analysts favoring the former and critical journalists favoring the latter (Lehtiniemi & Ruckenstein, 2019). Data journalism's technological and social aspects are imbued with the three epistemological moments mentioned above—production, representation, and audiences—in which interpretation of data-as-story plays a role in knowledge production.

With respect to news production, the first epistemological concern, data journalism can be understood simplistically as a straightforward blend of the technological and journalistic. It can thus be defined as "the new possibilities that open up when you combine the traditional 'nose for news' and ability to tell a compelling story with the sheer scale and range of digital information now available" (Gray et al., 2012, p. 2). But data journalists do not simply analyze data as a scientist or mathematician would; rather, they bring to bear long-established practices of journalism, such as news gathering, the quest for truth, multiple sourcing, and so on. Data-driven journalism from a journalistic point of view, then, "is the process through which journalists make sense of data—some big, some small—to find angles and details for the story" (Tandoc & Oh, 2017, p. 1002).

However, from a data point of view, the data analyzed in data journalism is not neutral, but may have been vulnerable to manipulation by algorithms, training data used to develop algorithms, social biases creeping into coding of algorithms, and so on (O'Neil, 2016; Tufekci, 2015). Algorithms have been shown to reproduce race, gender, social class, and other biases (Milner & Traub, 2021; Noble, 2018; Sandvig et al., 2016; Wachter-Boettcher, 2017). Once in the hands of data analysts, the data are also prey to selection bias, observation bias, and so on (Bergstrom & West, 2021). In addition, we must examine the typical sources of data used in journalism, as "data journalism is one part in the ecosystem of tools and practices that have sprung up around data sites and services" (Gray et al., 2012, p. 21). Data journalism, without being technologically deterministic, is influenced by the specific technological production and availability (or lack thereof) of specific kinds of datasets that might shape not just the content but also the types of data available in the first place.

Data journalists also sometimes work with hackers or data technologists who can support them in negotiating some of the technological complexities of retrieving datasets and understanding data science (De Maeyer et al., 2015, p. 432). What the data journalist does with the data, and how these large datasets may be interpreted by journalists, is another question, as they investigate to uncover hidden stories in the data. In short, the training data, coding bias, algorithmic bias, and interpretive interventions by data journalists can all serve as moments in which meaning is being constructed in particular ways.

This question links to representation, the second epistemological concern in data journalism, as data are a key consideration in representations of stories. Once the storied numbers have been crunched, they need to be imbued with yet another layer of meaning, then translated into a story and represented to an audience. Data journalists thus now require a tripartite skill set: they are required to "demonstrate high levels of data collection, analysis, and multimedia presentation skills" (Tandoc & Oh, 2017, p. 1003). Hermida and Young (2019, p. 68) argue similarly that data journalism consists of a 'triskelion' of "the assemblage of journalism, data and technology" (Hermida & Young, 2019, p. 68). Combining data-set tools for data visualizations and multimodal representations, "multimedia and visual components are effective in aiding the comprehension of complex information, lending themselves usefulness for data-driven stories to present patterns found in the data" (Tandoc & Oh, 2017, p. 1003). As data contributes to the production of visuals, "newspapers have evolved from using only photographs to also including information graphics ('infographics')" (Tandoc & Oh, 2017, p. 1001), an increasingly popular form of data visualization that purportedly makes stories easier to read. Data journalists must be able to produce data visualizations and representations that are accessible to a broad audience.

Finally, this leads to the third epistemological concern, audiences. Data journalism needs to be understood and interpreted by audiences, the assumption being that viewers and readers are adept at parsing data visualizations that are intended to make it easier for audiences to understand the story. However, this is not always the case. Instead, audiences with limited media literacies are being asked to do increasingly heavy lifting to understand complex data charts, graphs, maps, and so on, as data journalism is becoming a dominant form of news production in many mainstream media outlets. These visualizations may be helpful to some, but they also lend themselves to a range of pitfalls that can bias audience interpretations and affective responses. Bergstrom and West (2021) provide examples of several of these pitfalls, as follows. Disproportional ink occurs when segments in a pie chart or other visualization may imply proportions visually that do not correspond to the data. Skewed x and y axes may have inappropriate, disproportionate, or inconsistent numbering, exaggerating or concealing findings. Bar charts that don't start at zero can create false assumptions by implying low numbers. Negatively drawn graphs decrease rather than increasing along the y-axis, creating mistaken impressions. And finally, bin manipulations can be incorporated in which the division of numbers into bins for each chart in a bar graph is inconsistent (Bergstrom & West, 2021, pp. 134–179). While data visualizations seem neutral because they are based on statistics, instead they create moments where audience interpretive and epistemological biases may arise.

Data journalism is thus prone to these three steps in the process of reporting in which data epistemologies intervene. Attentiveness to data epistemologies may also differ in mainstream and radical data journalism.

Mainstream Data Journalism

Data journalists "are often regarded as forerunners of the journalism of the future" (Appelgren & Lindén, 2020, p. 62). As Hermida and Young (2019, p. 69) have found, disparities in resourcing of news outlets can influence their capacity to undertake data journalism:

> Data journalists in well-resourced media organizations that are investing in the field have been able to leverage technologies and tools to advance new practices and conventions that enhance the journalistic imagination. In contrast, the materiality of data journalism acts as a constraining factor in newsrooms where a lack of institutional backing has contributed to a reliance on third-party, and often free, tools that require little or no training.

Their study pays particular attention to technologies and computational thinking applied in data journalism, as well as the influence of non-human actors, such as platforms and algorithms. Similarly, Tandoc and Oh (2017, p. 1003) consider how "big data journalism [has] not only influenced reporting but also changed the format of the news story." These two studies highlight how mainstream data journalism is both influenced by (through big data sources, algorithms, etc.) and influences (through data visualizations, infographics, etc.) the data technologies and epistemologies of contemporary news reporting.

Mainstream media data journalism is a growing global phenomenon, with *The Guardian* in the UK identified as one of the frontrunners (Bradshaw, 2010; Rogers, 2010; Tandoc & Oh, 2017). Mainstream data journalism has been studied in the USA, with *The New York Times* well known for data journalism and visual investigations, and the *Houston Chronicle* also acknowledged for the use of Freedom of Information requests for public data (Clark & Rodríguez, 2021). Data journalism takes places increasingly globally, and has been documented and researched in Africa (Cheruiyot et al., 2019), China (Zhang & Feng, 2019), Canada (Hermida & Young, 2017), and several countries in Europe including Italy, Finland, Norway, the Netherlands, Belgium, and Sweden (Appelgren & Nygren, 2014; De Maeyer et al., 2015; Lehtiniemi & Ruckenstein, 2019; Porlezza & Splendore, 2019; Widholm & Appelgren, 2020).

Building on Hermida and Young's observation that data journalism might expand the journalistic imagination, we argue that data journalism offers the potential to allow reporters access to information regarding less-covered issues, marginalized perspectives, or excluded voices that might be harder to access through personal interviews. On the one hand, journalists may not know whom to contact, and the trust required for an interview may be missing; on the other hand, the data representing marginalized groups may be publicly available. In addition, while people who can serve as sources may be judged as legitimate or illegitimate based on inferences about their social status, employment position, or other markers such as race, education, gender, linguistic facility, and so on, data are presumed to be neutral such that all data should be considered equal. The opportunity to use data analytics to reveal corruption, expose oppression, represent marginal communities, and so on should thus be seen as presenting an equal opportunity once social markers and status are removed from the equation via non-judgmental data. As with the internet's democratic promise, one might be optimistic that data analysis holds the promise of democratizing affordances and representing marginalized perspectives.

However, in their analysis of *The Guardian Datablog*, an early example of data journalism by a mainstream news outlet, Tandoc and Oh (2017) have found that prominence (not marginalization) was the most common signifier of news value, unchanged from more traditional journalistic practices.

> In traditional news, the value of prominence is linked to the concept of legitimacy, in that the inclusion of well-known personalities is thought to increase the perceived legitimacy of the article. But in doing so, traditional news becomes complicit in perpetuating the influence of those in power.
>
> *Tandoc and Oh, 2017, p. 1009*

At the same time, although both data sources and human sources from the government were found to bedominant, it was by a small margin, with the availability of data from international sources, social media, crowdsourcing, and so on only "slowly breaking journalism's overreliance on the government for information subsidies" (Tandoc & Oh, 2017, p. 1009). While journalists seldom appeared to comment or provide opinions on the data stories and visualizations they presented, we cannot conclude that this makes data journalism more objective. Indeed, as they note, "data is rarely objective" (Tandoc & Oh, 2017, p. 1010), and reporting produced by subjective data will be at least as biased as the data and sources from which it is derived.

Where does data bias come from? Data, as produced, are an interpretation of a situation, influenced by those who decided who or what to count or quantify, how to shape the datasets, how datasets are made available, searchability of data, and so on. This is particularly salient with social media data, a predominant contributor to big data research and data journalism. Neumayer, Rossi and Struthers (2021) have identified four moments in which social media data analysis can introduce interpretive frameworks or structures that may render communities and subjects visible, quasi-visible or invisible, with visibility serving as an index of bias. These include the intentionality of those generating the data, the technology and tools shaping the datasets, the form of these datasets and the ways in which they are made accessible to (or withheld from) journalists or researchers, and the meanings and imaginaries assigned to the data which are closely linked to the world they are imagined to describe (Neumayer et al., 2021, pp. 5–7), in other words, the data imaginaries. *Data imaginaries* can be defined as ways in which individuals, communities, and societies imagine or conceive of their relationship to the datasets produced by social media and other big data sources, including their internalized perception of how big data may be able to either represent or invisibilize something important to them and their communities.

Rieder (2018, p. 90) refers to this as a "Big Data imaginary," a discursive device that encodes not just the computational potential for datasets to be massively produced and statistically analyzed but also the promise that the resultant analysis will narrate and reinforce conceptions of reality that can tell us who we are as a society. However, the term Big Data "acts as a powerful rhetorical device designed to boost support and ensure public consent" (Rieder, 2018, p. 90) to both have data extracted and be subjected to its descriptors of reality. What is further problematic is that big data "incorporates a set of values and beliefs that threaten to undermine key democratic principles" (Rieder, 2018, p. 90). Data imaginaries thus play into mainstream data journalism in ways that tend to ensure hierarchies of information and domination are reinforced rather than challenged.

Moreover, the cost of datasets can create a journalistic digital data divide. "Since the resources available to acquire data access are unevenly distributed this will likely produce a prioritization of those research topics that are mainly of interest to the 'data haves'" (Neumayer et al., 2021, p. 6), rendering media outlets that have fewer resources, including radical journalism outlets, into 'data have-nots' who may face barriers to producing data journalism. Harlow and Salaverría (2016, p. 1004) refer to this divide as the "increasing gap between the information-rich and the information-poor." This gap means that big data and the related "resources, and leadership willing and able to deploy them, are a main determining factor of the ability of data and computational journalists" (Hermida & Young, 2017, p. 168) to produce credible data journalism. Thus mainstream media data journalists continue to be implicated in "journalism's boundary work as manifested in news values, routines, and norms" (Tandoc & Oh, 2017, p. 998) that do not just legitimate their own practices, but also run the risk of reinforcing social, political, economic, and cultural hierarchies through data divides and journalism practices combined.

Therefore, while we understand that mainstream data journalism practices have the advantage of countering the escalation of 'churnalism,'[1] at the same time, big data analytics tend to limit the range, voice, diversity, and topics of news journalism, instead introducing, reinforcing, or amplifying already-existing social biases (Tandoc & Oh, 2017, p. 1000). As data journalists increasingly engage a widening range of the data scraping, analytic tools and big datasets available today, "like any source, [big data] should be treated with skepticism; and like any tool, we should be conscious of how it can shape and restrict the stories that are created with it" (Gray et al., 2012, p. 3).

Despite newsroom changes caused by the advent of big data, datafication, and the datafied society, and the concomitant potential for democratizing journalistic practices and representations, mainstream data journalism is still deeply implicated in the gatekeeping and boundary policing of journalism, tending to perpetuate biases amplified by big data. These have been called into question increasingly by independent, autonomous, citizen, social movement, and other forms of radical journalism. The next two sections will provide a brief overview of radical journalism, followed by a preliminary mapping of the concerns of radical data journalism, referencing a case study featuring radical data journalism on Airbnb in Athens by a radical journalist with *Athens Live*.

Radical Journalism

Radical journalists challenge the media practices of news values, the objectivity and transparency claims of traditional news journalists, and other routines and norms (Anderson & Schudson, 2019). For example, radical media producers can sometimes write from a standpoint within their own communities, producing insider reports on marginalized communities often overlooked by mainstream journalism (Jeppesen, 2016). They can be more transparent in disclosing their relationships to sources, disclosing how they are implicated in the story, linking to related sources, and building relationships with social movements (Downing, 2008; Harlow & Salaverría, 2016). While data journalists claim transparency by providing access through links to raw datasets, it is unknown whether these datasets are useful to the general public, and some scholars have argued that the term 'raw data' is an oxymoron (Gitelman, 2013). As Tandoc and Oh (2017, p. 1010) note, journalistic "operationalization of objectivity and transparency are too simple at best, when these are complex and multi-layered concepts," and the addition of big data into the mix does not render journalism more objective or simplistic.

Radical journalists can advocate for social justice and are sometimes called media activists (Meikle, 2018; Treré, 2019). Moreover, radical journalists can shift the practices and norms of reporting, cultivating a shared sense of co-production in journalism, focusing on building trust and consent within the interview relationship (Jeppesen & MARG, 2018, p. 10). Finally, radical media activists typically work outside of the stability of full-time journalism positions in newsrooms, in precarious or gig economies, despite often having a professional journalist or communications education credential, as they do not want to be constrained by corporate news exigencies, journalistic constraints they believe lead to a lack of diversity in reporting due to technological and corporate media convergence power structures (Atton, 2002; Cohen, 2016; Patterson et al., 2016; Zobl & Drüeke, 2012).

With the advent of digital ubiquity, digital journalism start-ups—some mainstream and some more radical—have begun to crop up. These start-ups "tend to diversify their revenues by experimenting with activities that traditionally have not been associated with journalism, such as content syndication, e-commerce, advertorials, consultancy work, events planning or reader donations" (Appelgren & Lindén, 2020, p. 63). These strategies have some overlap with the political economy of radical journalism, on the one hand, relying on creating alternative media through freelancing that feeds funds back into the media project or sustains the media activist, organizing events to build relationships with and within marginalized communities, and reliance on crowdfunding or sustainer donations for sustainability. (Harlow & Salaverría, 2016; Jeppesen & Petrick, 2018). On the other hand, radical journalism projects may be distinct from commercialized digital start-ups, avoiding e-commerce, advertising, advertorials, and other explicitly capitalist funding models, instead linking their oppositional political content to the political economy of their funding, labor, and organizational structures (Jeppesen & Petrick, 2018). Nonetheless, while contemporary radical journalism does engage with the production of all media genres (radio, podcasts, print, comics, video, film, documentaries, soundscapes, etc.) (Jeppesen, 2019), there is an increasing reliance on digital affordances for content creation, dissemination, and funding among radical journalists, including the digital affordances of big data and its related data epistemologies.

Radical Data Journalism

Radical data journalists can challenge the boundary work of traditional journalists who attempt to circumscribe the field of journalism by policing who can be considered a journalist and establishing "boundaries to classify who is part of the journalistic field" (Tandoc & Oh, 2017, p. 1003), as discussed above. Moreover, increasingly, "scholarship on innovation in journalism revolves around boundary work, where new actors enter journalism as peripheral actors" (Appelgren & Lindén, 2020, p. 63). Radical hackers from the techno-critical or data science perspective and radical journalists from the socio-critical or journalistic perspective have started working together to challenge this boundary-policing through interventions in alternative critical media production. Working at the crossroads of the growing entanglements among data justice activists (Kidd, 2019; Milan, 2017; Vera et al., 2019; Dencik et al., 2022), civic technologists (Baack, 2018; Cheruiyot et al., 2019), and digital journalists (Harlow & Salaverría, 2016; Widholm & Appelgren, 2020), radical data journalists can play a key role in pushing data journalism toward realizing its potential for social transformation. "Harnessing data at the periphery of traditional journalism" (Appelgren & Lindén, 2020, p. 63), these practitioners pose important questions regarding "alternative online media's part in re-conceptualizing the role of journalism and its relationship to activism" (Harlow & Salaverría, 2016, p. 1002), a relationship that is fundamental to radical data journalism.

Radical data journalists can thus be understood to address a host of issues in both radical journalism and mainstream data journalism. First, in data journalism, social media platforms and the invisibilities they produce (Neumayer et al., 2021) are a key concern that radical data journalists are attentive to. In examining data journalism, "what emerges is a material landscape in which a handful of tools and platforms exercise disproportionate power over journalistic norms and practices" (Hermida & Young, 2019, p. 69). Radical data journalists, working in the intersectional contexts of meta-issue movements (Jeppesen, 2021a, 2021b), are careful not to rely too heavily on tools and platforms that might contribute to data asymmetries and journalism inequities across race, class, gender, sexuality, disability, colonialism, and more.

At root these inequalities may be linked to the lack of objectivity and transparency of data collection and related data-epistemology processes. "Data collection, analysis, and release can also be prone to manipulation. This becomes all the more dangerous when such manipulation becomes more subtle, hidden under pages of seemingly objective data points" (Tandoc & Oh, 2017, p. 1011). Ordinary citizens may be unaware of the vast range of data types being collected when they use digital devices that generate data, meaning that "the proliferation of ways information can be and is collected in a datafied society cements the fundamentally asymmetrical power relation that exists" (Hintz et al., 2018, p. 113). The transparency of data collection is also itself asymmetrical. "We, in our digitally mediated daily interactions, are integrated in systems that render our lives increasingly transparent to a range of organizations whose activities are not necessarily transparent to us" (Hintz et al., 2018, p. 105; see also Andrejevic et al., 2015; Lyon, 2010). If we consider capitalism and the intersectional systems it connects with and fundamentally shapes, we can understand that material "surveillance has historically operated along racial, gendered and class lines, made ever-more salient in a datafied society" (Hintz et al., 2018, p. 112). This then "problematizes the idea that data-driven 'mass surveillance' implicates us all equally as individuals" (Hintz et al., 2018, p. 112). Rather, data obtained through data collection, mass data surveillance, or dataveillance are not equitable but rather reinforce already existing inequalities along intersectional lines, re-oppressing marginalized groups that can be considered the 'data poor' (Milan & Treré, 2020), 'information poor' (Harlow & Salaverría, 2016), or 'data have-nots' (Neumayer et al., 2021). Radical data journalists therefore work not only to contest journalistic representations of marginalized groups, but also to ensure data justice is incorporated in the inputs, processes, and outcomes of their epistemological data practices.

Succinctly put, "good data journalism helps to combat information asymmetry" (Gray et al., 2012, p. 7). With radical data journalism linked to social justice and data justice movements, there are two ways of approaching data activism—proactive and reactive (Milan, 2017). Reactive data activism, on the one hand, consists of taking action against data transgressions by corporations or states, such as protecting against attacks on net neutrality, data privacy, open data, and data sovereignty (Milan, 2017; Pohle, 2020). Proactive data activism, on the other hand, consists of using or generating datasets to render injustices visible through digital data traces, data visualizations, data mapping, and so on in order to contest them (Chenou & Cepeda-Másmela, 2019; Kidd, 2019; Milan, 2017). Radical data journalists tend to engage in proactive data justice, using or generating datasets for journalistic purposes that are in turn joined to their social justice objectives.

The ecosystem of radical data journalism incorporates key social actor roles, such as hacker and programmer journalists (Parasie & Dagiral, 2013), who can create interactive journalism (Usher, 2016), as well as citizen journalists who increasingly use data to render marginalized communities visible and challenge hegemonic data narratives and data imaginaries (Reilly, 2020). Data journalists "tend to describe their use of technology as different from mainstream media, for example, using data journalism techniques, such as creating databases and infographics and making documents publicly available" (Appelgren & Lindén, 2020, p. 62). With professional and non-professional journalists working together on radical data journalism, including data-set development, data scraping, data analysis, data visualizations, and writing, "the metajournalistic discourse that arises from these collaborations may challenge how news is produced and consumed" (Appelgren & Lindén, 2020, p. 63). Radical data journalists engage in these technological challenges while maintaining their commitments to community and public service data journalism, journalism as a public good, and the digital media communications commons (Jeppesen et al., 2013; Kidd, 2013; Milberry & Anderson, 2009; Widholm & Appelgren, 2020). They do so through two key processes: using existing datasets and creating datasets from below.

The first process in radical data journalism is the use of existing data to engage in critical analysis that generates stories from below, to find the missing stories left out of mainstream media and data journalism, and to amplify marginalized groups through data analytics. This process is based on the premise that what you see depends on where you look (Bergstrom & West, 2021). Datasets from dominant big data sources such as the state and corporations can be examined in ways that are attentive to inequalities. Radical data journalists thus engage in "the constructive use of data for social and political purposes" (Hintz et al., 2018, p. 131), revealing data gaps, illustrating absences and invisibilities within datasets, or revealing oppressive practices of dominant groups (Milan, 2017). As such, we can understand the myriad ways in which data activists "have applied alternative forms of data use and thereby subverted the dominant purposes and power relations of datafication" (Hintz et al., 2018, p. 132); we can also understand the ways in which these practices are also taken up by radical data journalists.

Key approaches in this process include developing the data commons, public data, or open access data (COVID-19 Canada Open Data Working Group, n.d.; Parasie & Dagiral, 2013; Tufekci, 2014) whereby the public can access big datasets freely and openly at no cost. The resultant "entanglements of civic tech and data journalism" (Appelgren & Lindén, 2020, p. 63) are important, whereby tech activists facilitate access to datasets and work with radical data journalists on social justice reporting, examining existing datasets with an eye toward revealing structural and systemic oppressions across intersectional axes (Bowe et al., 2020; Data for Black Lives, n.d.; D'Ignazio & Klein, 2020; Kent, 2020). This can include data feminism and methods to challenge data racism and colonialism. "The work of data feminism is first to tune into how standard practices in data science serve to reinforce these existing inequalities and second to use data science to challenge and change the distribution of power" (D'Ignazio & Klein, 2020). Data feminism, moreover, challenges the stereotype that women are not good at math and science, as feminist data analysts play a key role in challenging intersectional data domination.

> Underlying data feminism is a belief in and commitment to *co-liberation*: the idea that oppressive systems of power harm all of us, that they undermine the quality and validity of our work, and that they hinder us from creating true and lasting social impact with data science.
>
> *D'Ignazio and Klein, 2020*

Radical data science and data journalism from below thus use existing datasets to generate counter-narratives that privilege marginalized voices and can be used to advocate against racial, colonial, and gender data oppression for intersectional social change.

A second key process used in radical data journalism is the creation of new datasets from below to create stories that are more authentic to the communities omitted from mainstream datasets altogether. Many communities find themselves rendered absent or invisible in big datasets, such as non-binary, Indigenous peoples, people with disabilities, and so on (Neumayer et al., 2021). It has, for example, been found that gender data are often invisible or non-existent in dominant datasets (Wachter-Boettcher, 2017; Zou & Schiebinger, 2018). It has further been observed that social media platforms are "primarily concerned with capital accumulation and profit, and predominantly, if not entirely, engineered to maximize advertising revenue and consumption" (Hintz et al., 2018, p. 9), a focus that can lead to data invisibility for those who choose not to participate in social media, or who are deemed unimportant in generating profits for platforms. A further risk of dominant datasets is that,

> because of their availability and ease of access, big datasets might become a new platform for elite perspectives to dominate the news. A counterargument to this is that news organizations and even ordinary people are becoming more and more capable of generating their own datasets.
>
> *Tandoc & Oh, 2017, p. 1010*

As Treré and Milan have found in their study of Covid-19 representations from the global south or low-income countries, the "data poor" have proven increasingly adept at generating datasets to fill these gaps (Milan & Treré, 2020).

An example of radical data journalism for social change is an article by critical data journalist Sotiris Sideris, co-founder of the critical journalism start-up *Athens Live*. In his article, "Mapping The Dominance of Airbnb on Athens," Sideris (2018) explains that in order "to understand the impact of Airbnb on housing in Athens, [he] downloaded and analyzed a dataset compiled by the independent, non-commercial monitoring service 'Inside Airbnb', which tracks the flow of ads on the online platform." Using data from 2009 to 2017, the article presents several types of data visualizations, including graphs, bar charts, maps, line graphs, timelines, and bubble graphs. Together these illustrate how Airbnb has created a prevalence of ghost hotels in which entire apartment buildings that were once rented to Athens residents are now being rented as Airbnb units, serving as hotels but not regulated through the hotel industry. This erodes the availability of affordable housing for local residents, driving up the cost of rent, and serving as "a symbol for quick value extraction" through short-term rentals (Sideris, 2018). Sideris (2018) also notes that "Airbnb provides NO PUBLIC DATA to help understand the use of their platform and the impact on cites around the world." Therefore, he had to rely on a dataset generated by an individual called "Tom Slee [who] regularly scrapes the Airbnb site to produce maps and analysis of Airbnb use around the world" (Sideris, 2018).

The dataset used in the analysis was generated through a capitalist sharing economy that facilitates platform labor and generates big data. These data, however, are only ephemerally available to the public. Therefore, the data must be captured by a data scientist who scrapes and archives the live data on a regular basis, making them available to the public to compensate for the fact that Airbnb does not. This radical data journalism article, through the archiving work of 'Inside Airbnb', "utilizes public information compiled from the Airbnb web-site including the availability calendar for 365 days in the future, and the reviews for each listing. Data is verified, cleansed, analyzed and aggregated" (Sideris, 2018). The dataset is thus both a big dataset from a capitalist corporation and a dataset generated and archived by grassroots data workers as open data. The data journalism article can then be used by housing activists to demand better regulation of Airbnb, to provide input into political decision making, and to advocate for housing justice, calling into question power imbalances that privilege wealthy property owners and foreign travelers over local citizens' housing. It can additionally be used to advocate for more transparent and open data from platforms that increasingly add proprietary datasets to their proprietary black box algorithms, reducing transparency and increasing data and power asymmetries.

Conclusions

As this chapter has argued, following Hintz and colleagues, "there is the need to interrogate how the increasing production and use of data doubles by corporate and government bodies may affect us as algorithms adjudicate more and more consequential decisions in our lives" (Hintz et al., 2018, p. 6). We do not want to be technologically pessimistic or deterministic, as technologies do not determine outcomes for social change or hegemonic structures. Rather, "new technologies develop in the context of existing practices" (Hermida & Young, 2019, p. 70). Radical data journalism brings together the existing practices of radical journalism, data justice, and data-driven journalism to use big datasets and develop alternative datasets to produce data journalism with social justice objectives.

But we must also avoid being technologically optimistic in imagining that data are explicitly a tool for liberation.

> While such dominant data imaginaries greatly configure thought and action in the datafied society, they are underpinned by materialities prevalent in the infrastructure of the digital environment that significantly shape possibilities for how and to what extent citizens might challenge the datafication paradigm.
>
> *Hintz et al., 2018, p. 128*

Big data is still subjective and does not automatically produce objective journalism. Journalists cannot presume they are "letting the data speak for itself" (Tandoc & Oh, 2017, p. 1003) as this is not a sufficiently nuanced understanding of how data reveals or hides stories and biases. Data journalists must intervene in finding the story, choosing which data to explore, narrating the story, creating the data visualizations to tell the story, and so on, with each step offering opportunities for epistemological bias.

The audience is also crucial.

> As digital citizens, we utilize the opportunities for online interactions, digital cultural exchanges, online activism and citizen journalism, but we also discuss and, if necessary, resist or circumvent challenges such as internet censorship and surveillance, and we claim the right to use digital infrastructure and conduct digital acts.
>
> *Hintz et al., 2018, p. 122*

In this context, radical data journalists are intervening in particular ways as digital citizen journalists who must choose, develop, and analyze datasets carefully to tell authentic stories from below if they are to make claims for not just data equality but also equality and co-liberation across multiple intersectional social, economic, digital, and data divides.

Note

1 Journalism based solely on corporate or government press releases that serve as information subsidies produced by well-funded public relations offices which makes journalism less expensive and faster to produce by catering to the pressures of the 24-hour news cycle.

References

Anderson, C. W., & Schudson, M. (2019). Objectivity, Professionalism, and Truth Seeking in Journalism. In K. Wahl-Jorgensen & T. Hanitzsch (Eds.), *The Handbook of Journalism Studies* (2nd ed., pp. 88–101). Routledge.

Andrejevic, M., Hearn, A., & Kennedy, H. (August 1, 2015). "Cultural Studies of Data Mining: Introduction." *European Journal of Cultural Studies* 18(4–5), 379–394. https://doi.org/10.1177/1367549415577395.

Appelgren, E., & Lindén, C.-G. (2020). Data Journalism as a Service: Digital Native Data Journalism Expertise and Product Development. *Media and Communication*, 8(2), 62–72. https://doi.org/10.17645/mac.v8i2.2757

Appelgren, E., & Nygren, G. (2014). Data Journalism in Sweden. *Digital Journalism*, 2(3), 394–405. https://doi.org/10.1080/21670811.2014.884344

Atton, C. (2002). News Cultures and New Social Movements: Radical Journalism and the Mainstream Media. *Journalism Studies*, 3(4), 491–505. https://doi.org/10.1080/14616700 22000019209

Baack, S. (2018). Practically Engaged. *Digital Journalism*, 6(6), 673–692. https://doi.org/10.1080/21670811.2017.1375382

Bergstrom, C. T., & West, J. D. (2021). *Calling Bullshit: The Art of Skepticism in a Data-Driven World*. Random House.

Bowe, E., Simmons, E., & Mattern, S. (2020). Learning from Lines: Critical COVID Data Visualizations and the Quarantine Quotidian. *Big Data & Society*, 7(2). https://doi.org/10.1177/2053951720939236

Bradshaw, P. (2010, October 1). How to be a Data Journalist. *The Guardian*. http://www.theguardian.com/news/datablog/2010/oct/01/data-journalism-how-to-guide

Carmi, E., Yates, S. J., Lockley, E., & Pawluczuk, A. (2020). Data Citizenship: Rethinking Data Literacy in the Age of Disinformation, Misinformation, and Malinformation. *Internet Policy Review*, 9(2). https://policyreview.info/articles/analysis/data-citizenship-rethinking-data-literacy-age-disinformation-misinformation-and

Chenou, J.-M., & Cepeda-Másmela, C. (2019). #NiUnaMenos: Data Activism from the Global South. *Television & New Media*, 20(4), 396–411. https://doi.org/10.1177/1527476419828995

Cheruiyot, D., Baack, S., & Ferrer-Conill, R. (2019). Data Journalism beyond Legacy Media: The Case of African and European Civic Technology Organizations. *Digital Journalism*, 7(9), 1215–1229. https://doi.org/10.1080/21670811.2019.1591166

Clark, A. M., & Rodríguez, J. (2021). Big Data and Journalism: How American Journalism Is Adopting the Use of Big Data. *Novum Jus*, 15(1), 69–89. https://doi.org/10.14718/NovumJus.2021.15.1.4

Coddington, M. (2015). Clarifying Journalism's Quantitative Turn. *Digital Journalism*, 3(3), 331–348. https://doi.org/10.1080/21670811.2014.976400

Cohen, N. S. (2016). *Writers' Rights: Freelance Journalism in a Digital Age*. McGill-Queen's University Press.

COVID-19 Canada Open Data Working Group. (n.d.). *About Us*. COVID-19 Canada Open Data Working Group. Retrieved November 13, 2021, from https://opencovid.ca/about/

Data for Black Lives. (n.d.). *About Us*. Data for Black Lives. Retrieved May 14, 2021, from https://d4bl.org/about.html

De Maeyer, J., Libert, M., Domingo, D., Heinderyckx, F., & Le Cam, F. (2015). Waiting for Data Journalism. *Digital Journalism*, 3(3), 432–446. https://doi.org/10.1080/21670811.2014.976415

Dencik, L., A. Hintz, J. Redden, & E. Treré (2022). *Data Justice*. London: SAGE

D'Ignazio, C., & Klein, L. F. (2020). *Data Feminism*. MIT Press.

Downing, J. (2008). Social Movement Theories and Alternative Media: An Evaluation and Critique. *Communication, Culture & Critique*, 1(1), 40–50. https://doi.org/10.1111/j.1753-9137.2007.00005.x

Gitelman, L. (Ed.). (2013). *Raw Data Is an Oxymoron*. MIT Press.

Gray, J., Chambers, L., & Bounegru, L. (Eds.). (2012). *The Data Journalism Handbook: How Journalists Can Use Data to Improve the News*. O'Reilly Media.

Harlow, S., & Salaverría, R. (2016). Regenerating Journalism. *Digital Journalism*, 4(8), 1001–1019. https://doi.org/10.1080/21670811.2015.1135752

Hermida, A., & Young, M. L. (2017). Finding the Data Unicorn. *Digital Journalism*, 5(2), 159–176. https://doi.org/10.1080/21670811.2016.1162663

Hermida, A., & Young, M. L. (2019). *Data Journalism and the Regeneration of News*. Routledge.

Hintz, A., Dencik, L., & Wahl-Jorgensen, K. (2018). *Digital Citizenship in a Datafied Society*. Polity.

Jeppesen, S. (2016). Direct-Action Journalism: Resilience in Grassroots Autonomous Media. *Journal of Applied Media and Journalism Studies*, 5(3), 383–403. http://www.ingentaconnect.com/content/intellect/ajms/2016/00000005/00000003/art00005

Jeppesen, S. (2019). Radical Media. In R. Kinna & U. Gordon (Eds.), *Routledge Handbook of Radical Politics* (pp. 341–359). Routledge.

Jeppesen, S. (2021a). Intersectional Technopolitics in Social Movement and Media Activism. *International Journal of Communication, 15*(0), 23. https://ijoc.org/index.php/ijoc/article/view/15766

Jeppesen, S. (2021b). *Transformative Media and Social Movements*. UBC Press.

Jeppesen, S., Kruzynski, A., Sarrasin, R., & Breton, E. (2013). The Anarchist Commons. *Ephemera Journal, 14*(4), 879–900. http://ephemerajournal.org/contribution/anarchist-commons

Jeppesen, S., & MARG. (2018). Intersectionality in Autonomous Journalism Practices. *Journal of Alternative and Community Media, 3*(1), 1–16. https://joacm.org/index.php/joacm/article/view/1034

Jeppesen, S., & Petrick, K. (2018). Toward an Intersectional Political Economy of Autonomous Media Resources. *Interface: A Journal for and about Social Movements, 10*(1–2), 8–37.

Kent, A. J. (2020). Mapping and Counter-Mapping COVID-19: From Crisis to Cartocracy. *The Cartographic Journal, 57*(3), 187–195. https://doi.org/10.1080/00087041.2020.1855001

Kidd, D. (2013). Indymedia.org: A New Communications Commons. In M. McCaughey & M. D. Ayers (Eds.), *CyberActivism: Online Activism in Theory and Practice* (pp. 43–66). Taylor & Francis.

Kidd, D. (2019). Extra-Activism: Counter-Mapping and Data Justice. *Information, Communication & Society, 22*(7), 954–970. https://doi.org/10.1080/1369118X.2019.1581243

Lehtiniemi, T., & Ruckenstein, M. (2019). The Social Imaginaries of Data Activism. *Big Data & Society, 6*(1). https://doi.org/10.1177/2053951718821146

Leslie, D., & Catungal, J. P. (2012). Social Justice and the Creative City: Class, Gender and Racial Inequalities. *Geography Compass, 6*(3), 111–122. https://doi.org/10.1111/j.1749-8198.2011.00472.x

Lewis, S. C., & Westlund, O. (2015). Big Data and Journalism: Epistemology, Expertise, Economics, and Ethics. *Digital Journalism, 3*(3), 447–466. https://doi.org/10.1080/21670811.2014.976418

Lyon, D. (2010). Surveillance, Power and Everyday Life. In P. Kalantzis-Cope & K. Gherab-Martín (Eds.), *Emerging Digital Spaces in Contemporary Society* (pp. 107–120). Palgrave Macmillan.

Meikle, G. (2018). *The Routledge Companion to Media and Activism*. Routledge.

Mejias, U. A., & Couldry, N. (2019). Datafication. *Internet Policy Review, 8*(4). https://policyreview.info/concepts/datafication

Milan, S. (2017). Data Activism as the New Frontier of Media Activism. In G. Yang & V. Pickard (Eds.), *Media Activism in the Digital Age* (pp. 151–163). Routledge.

Milan, S., & Treré, E. (2020). The Rise of the Data Poor: The COVID-19 Pandemic Seen from the Margins. *Social Media + Society, 6*(3). https://doi.org/10.1177/2056305120948233

Milberry, K., & Anderson, S. (2009). Open Sourcing Our Way to an Online Commons: Contesting Corporate Impermeability in the New Media Ecology. *Journal of Communication Inquiry, 33*(4), 393–412. https://doi.org/10.1177/0196859909340349

Milner, Y., & Traub, A. (2021). Data Capitalism and Algorithmic Racism. *Demos*. https://www.demos.org/research/data-capitalism-and-algorithmic-racism

Neumayer, C., Rossi, L., & Struthers, D. M. (2021). Invisible Data: A Framework for Understanding Visibility Processes in Social Media Data. *Social Media + Society, 7*(1). https://doi.org/10.1177/2056305120984472

Noble, S. U. (2018). *Algorithms of Oppression: How Search Engines Reinforce Racism*. NYU Press.

O'Neil, C. (2016). *Weapons of Math Destruction: How Big Data Increases Inequality and Threatens Democracy*. Crown.

Parasie, S., & Dagiral, E. (2013). Data-Driven Journalism and the Public Good: "Computer-Assisted-Reporters" and "Programmer-Journalists" in Chicago. *New Media & Society*, *15*(6), 853–871. https://doi.org/10.1177/1461444812463345

Patterson, A. N., Howard, A., & Kinloch, V. (2016). Black Feminism and Critical Media Literacy: Moving from the Margin to the Center. *Meridians: Feminism, Race, Transnationalism*, *15*(1), 40–65.

Pohle, J. (2020). Digital Sovereignty. A New Key Concept of Digital Policy in Germany and Europe. Konrad-Adenauer-Stiftung. https://www.econstor.eu/handle/10419/228713

Porlezza, C., & Splendore, S. (2019). From Open Journalism to Closed Data: Data Journalism in Italy. *Digital Journalism*, *7*(9), 1230–1252. https://doi.org/10.1080/21670 811.2019.1657778

Reilly, K. (2020). The Challenge of Decolonizing Big Data through Citizen Data Audits. *BigDataSur*. https://data-activism.net/2020/04/bigdatasur-the-challenge-of-decoloniz ing-big-data-through-citizen-data-audits-1-3/

Rieder, G. (2018). Tracing Big Data Imaginaries through Public Policy: The Case of the European Commission. In A. R. Saetnan, I. Schneider, & N. Green (Eds.), *The Politics of Big Data: Big Data, Big Brother?* (pp. 89–109). Routledge.

Rogers, S. (2010, July 27). Wikileaks' Afghanistan War Logs: How Our Datajournalism Operation Worked. *The Guardian*. http://www.theguardian.com/news/datablog/2010/ jul/27/wikileaks-afghanistan-data-datajournalism

Sandvig, C., Hamilton, K., Karahalios, K., & Langbort, C. (2016). Automation, Algorithms, and Politics | When the Algorithm Itself Is a Racist: Diagnosing Ethical Harm in the Basic Components of Software. *International Journal of Communication*, *10*(0), 19. https:// ijoc.org/index.php/ijoc/article/view/6182

Sideris, S. (2018, August 23). Mapping the Dominance of Airbnb on Athens. *Athens Live*. https://medium.com/athenslivegr/mapping-the-dominance-of-airbnb-in-athens-4cb9e 0657e80

Tandoc, E. C., & Oh, S.-K. (2017). Small Departures, Big Continuities? *Journalism Studies*, *18*(8), 997–1015. https://doi.org/10.1080/1461670X.2015.1104260

Treré, E. (2019). *Hybrid Media Activism: Ecologies, Imaginaries, Algorithms*. Routledge.

Tufekci, Z. (2014). Engineering the Public: Big Data, Surveillance and Computational Politics. *First Monday*. https://doi.org/10.5210/fm.v19i7.4901

Tufekci, Z. (2015). Algorithmic Harms beyond Facebook and Google: Emergent Challenges of Computational Agency. *Colorado Technology Law Journal*, *13*, 203.

Usher, N. (2016). *Interactive Journalism: Hackers, Data, and Code*. University of Illinois Press.

van Dijck, J., & Poell, T. (2013). Understanding Social Media Logic. *Media and Communication*, *1*(1), 2–14. https://doi.org/10.17645/mac.v1i1.70

Vera, L. A., Walker, D., Murphy, M., Mansfield, B., Siad, L. M., Ogden, J., & EDGI. (2019). When Data Justice and Environmental Justice Meet: Formulating a Response to Extractive Logic through Environmental Data Justice. *Information, Communication & Society*, *22*(7), 1012–1028. https://doi.org/10.1080/1369118X.2019.1596293

Wachter-Boettcher, S. (2017). *Technically Wrong: Sexist Apps, Biased Algorithms, and Other Threats of Toxic Tech*. Norton.

Widholm, A., & Appelgren, E. (2020). A Softer Kind of Hard News? Data Journalism and the Digital Renewal of Public Service News in Sweden. *New Media & Society*. https://doi. org/10.1177/1461444820975411

Zhang, S., & Feng, J. (2019). A Step Forward? Exploring the Diffusion of Data Journalism as Journalistic Innovations in China. *Journalism Studies*, *20*(9), 1281–1300. https://doi.org/10.1080/1461670X.2018.1513814

Zobl, E., & Drüeke, R. (Eds.). (2012). *Feminist Media: Participatory Spaces, Networks and Cultural Citizenship*. Transcript.

Zou, J., & Schiebinger, L. (2018). AI Can be Sexist and Racist—It's Time to Make It Fair. *Nature*, *559*(7714), 324–326. https://doi.org/10.1038/d41586-018-05707-8

9
THE CHALLENGE OF FAR-RIGHT MEDIA

Eugenia Siapera

Introduction: Positioning Radical Journalism

The role of the media in reproducing the status quo is extensively discussed and convincingly demonstrated in various studies. Political economic critiques have identified the role of journalism and media in creating a hegemonic consensus (Gramsci, 1971) and operating as an ideological apparatus socialising people into accepting the current state of affairs (Althusser, 2012 [1970]). Studies have shown that the involvement of the media in reproducing forms of oppression can be attributed not only to organisational factors, such as, for example their orientation towards elite sources and 'primary definers' (Hall et al., 2013), but also to their structural position as an industry selling readers to advertisers (Smythe, 2012). Sociological factors, such as, for example the class allegiance of most journalists who are themselves middle class (Johnstone, 1976) are also important determinants of media outputs. Authors have further explored the cultural aspects of media power, famously understanding them as a culture industry (Adorno and Horkheimer, 1997) and as a spectacle (Debord, 2012).

In the first instance, therefore, radical journalism is formulated against the bourgeois media and their definitional power. Its starting point is that the current social, political and economic organisation of society is not legitimate because it rests on unequal and unjust distribution of resources among classes of people. Because of this, radical journalism follows an antagonistic trajectory standing in opposition to the political establishment and its media. It seeks to delegitimise the status quo and lead to a different political, social and economic organisation, which guarantees freedom and equality for all. Radical media and journalism therefore aim to highlight the various forms of oppression, as, for example in the antiracist, radical feminist, and LGBT rights magazines that flourished during and after the civil rights movement of the 1960s. They seek to identify the operations of power structures

DOI: 10.4324/9781003221784-9

and the ways in which the establishment is looking to distract, justify or repress attempts to bring forward fundamental changes in the direction of equality, justice and freedom for all. Finally, they aim to mobilise people for action, through disseminating calls for action, participation in protests, strikes, occupations and the like.

Radical journalism and media stand in close alliance and aim to represent the interests of the working class in all its diversity, using critique and agitation to advance its political goals of social justice and equality. Critical pedagogy, class consciousness and radical praxis are therefore key elements of radical journalism. Deconstructing the dominant ideology as it appears in the media in order to aid understanding of current historical, political, economic and socio-cultural developments is a key tactic for radical media. In contrast to liberal journalism's role of legitimating the polity through 'objective' and detached critique and discussion of political decisions, radical journalism actively pursues a politics of emancipation, social justice and equality, through taking the side of the oppressed and imagining new ways of coexisting through a plurality of forms. In pursuing their goals, radical media are in opposition not only to the bourgeois mainstream media but also to the repressive media of the far right (Downing, 2000). The present chapter focuses on the relationship between radical media and the media of the far right.

If we accept the left-right political spectrum, the far right would be close to the end of the continuum, which can be understood, for the purposes of this chapter, as more authoritarian, more nativist, nationalistic and racist than more moderate varieties of the right. Without wishing to flatten important debates on the ideological diversity between different strands of the far right or the differences between far, extreme, populist and radical right (see Mudde, 1996), for the purposes of the current chapter, I adopt a simplified definition based on Mudde (2002), focusing on three elements: authoritarianism and focus on law and order, and support for the police and the military; nativism and nationalism, based on variants of 'blood and soil' belongingness; and racism, building on and entrenching ideologies of white supremacy. Crucially, these ideas focus on the political plane as far-right positions leave the economic plane mostly intact. When they do touch upon economics, it tends to be as a call against globalisation in support of ethno-nationalism rather than against capitalism as such (Sommer, 2008). Their core distinction is between 'us' and 'them' defined in ethno-nationalist terms in stark contrast to the left core belief of a fundamental antagonism between labour and capital.

As expected, the contents of the far-right media universe (including news outlets print and digital, blogs, social media accounts and channels) put forward racist and exclusionary positions against minority ethnic communities and those designated as 'other'; cultivate a politics of suspicion and distrust; and pursue a politics of division between 'them' and 'us', friends and enemies (see inter alia Atton, 2006; Berlet et al., 2015; Wahlström et al., 2021; Siapera and Papadopoulou, 2021; Winter, 2019). Further research on the media of the far right has provided important insights into their relationship with the mainstream media and the political establishment in the nations where they are found (Holt, 2019; Figenschou and Ihlebæk, 2019; Nygaard, 2020). There are some indications for the emergence of a far-right news infrastructure which includes like-minded media operating in complementary ways and which contributes to their normalisation as news and journalistic outlets (Heft et al., 2020).

The rise of the far-right media and their consolidation in the public sphere have not been discussed from the perspective of radical journalism. There is little doubt that if this rise and consolidation are taken to represent an increase in power for the far right, this is bad news for emancipatory radical politics and media. This chapter sets out to unpack the challenges they represent for radical media and their quest for social justice, freedom and equality.

Far-Right Media and Their Challenges

While the tradition of radical journalism has a long history and is internally diverse, it is often simplified as one of two extremes in 'horseshoe'-type of theories. The horseshoe metaphor, attributed to Jean Pierre Faye (2006), holds that rather than following parallel trajectories that never intersect, extreme right and extreme left ideologies eventually converge. Schematically, this is represented as a horseshoe whose bent edges end up meeting. In this scheme, the far right will eventually become the same as the far left as their ideas, tactics and worldviews converge. The first challenge that the rise of far-right media poses for radical media therefore comes not from the far right itself but from centrist ideologies that espouse varieties of the horseshoe theory of the 'two extremes', framing radical journalism and media as extreme. Secondly, the tactics used by far-right media have been shown to include media criticism and critiques of the political establishment (Figenschou and Ihlebæk, 2019), tactics that are part of the trajectory of radical journalism. On the one hand, this lends support to horseshoe arguments; on the other hand, it presents radical journalism with a dilemma: to what extent can it keep using tactics usurped by the far right? This is the second challenge radical journalism faces from the far-right media. Thirdly, the far right have successfully pushed some of their key demands on the media and political agenda as we have seen with the issue of migration. The third challenge for radical journalism therefore is to reclaim the political agenda and defuse the influence of the far right. This section will discuss in more detail these challenges and identify their implications for radical journalism.

Horseshoe Theories and Alternative Media

While in his book, Faye referred to the Molotov-Ribbentrop non-aggression pact of 1939, in contemporary politics, horseshoe type theories re-emerged in 2016, in the aftermath of the US election and in the 2017 French election. Bernie Sanders' supporters were accused of failing to support Hilary Clinton against Trump, while Jean-Luc Mélenchon refused to endorse Emanuel Macron (Freeman, 2017). Commentators postulated that in fact the far right and the 'hard left' have more in common than the liberal centre, which they "both despise with equal vigour" (Patrikarakos, 2017: non paginated). More recently, the ideological confusion of new movements such as the 'Yellow Vest' movement, which took a left wing form in France, Italy and the UK but a far-right guise in Canada, Germany and parts of the UK (May, 2019) seemed to support the conflation of the far right with left positions. A similar ideological confusion can be found in parts of the anti-vaccination and COVID-19 protest groups, where traditional left concerns with civil liberties, bodily autonomy and protections from state over-reach have been conflated with far-right calls for 'freedom' and 'anti-tyranny', as encountered, for example in the Canadian 'freedom convoy' movement, "a far right movement masquerading as a working class revolution" (Lim and Rigato, 2022: non-paginated). Despite criticisms and the lack of empirical support for the horseshoe and 'two extremes' approaches, they seem to have a strong grip on the mainstream centrist imagination (Choat, 2017; Berlatsky, 2018).

In addition, this view is implicit in some academic writing on the media, which refers to the general category or field of alternative media, of which both far-right and left media are part. The issue of the inclusion of far-right media as part of the universe of alternative media has been highlighted by critics of the term alternative media, such as John Downing (2000). Downing (2000) argues that far-right media do not share important attributes of radical media, and in particular some of their key features, such as their openness to sustained debate. Similarly, for Couldry (2002), far-right media cannot be seen as alternative media because they sustain community through closure. Drawing on Couldry (2002) and Downing (2000), Atton (2006) examined the website of the far-right British National Party (now defunct) as 'a species of alternative media' (p. 585). His analysis showed that it cannot be seen as equivalent to, or part of, alternative media insofar as it promotes communities of closure, discourages debate and contestation of positions and lacks the 'democratised creativity' that is typically found in progressive or radical media (Atton, 2006: 586).

Despite these authors' arguments, recent work on far-right media understands and describes them as alternative media, indirectly lending credence to horseshoe-type arguments. In particular, Haller et al. (2019), Holt (2019), Holt et al. (2019), and Figenschou and Ihlebæk (2019b, Ihlebæk and Figenschou 2022) define and examine far-right media as alternative media. Unlike Downing (2000) and Atton (2002) who made the point that radical alternative media cannot be defined on the basis of content alone, Holt et al. (2019) assume a 'non-normative' and 'non-ideological' definition that revolves around the degree to which the contents of these outlets represent "a proclaimed and/or *(self) perceived corrective*" to the dominant mainstream (non-paginated, italics in the original). Additionally, alternative media in this definition rely on alternative publishing routines and form part of an alternative media system. The extent of how alternative they are, or their degree of separation from mainstream media is determined by their own proclamations, as well as by audiences and by the mainstream media themselves. This is why Holt et al. (2019) refer to their definition as relational. They further understand the alternative-mainstream relationship not as a dichotomy but as a continuum placing different media at different points. In a similar vein, Haller et al. (2019) argue that alternative media should include all those media whose contents are a response to their perception that their perspective is not represented or treated unfairly by the mainstream media. In his book on right-wing alternative media, Holt (2019) refers to their 'anti-systemness', defined as the degree to which they are ideologically anti-systemic, i.e. the degree to which they share or oppose the values of the political order within which they operate (c.f. Capoccia, 2002).

While this body of research has focused on understanding the far-right-wing media milieu, theorising it outside of the ideological parameters of their contents, and through adopting implicitly the right-wing media's own proclamations, results in conflating or bracketing the differences between the radical and (far) right media, thereby supporting the 'two extremes' approaches. In this theorising, alternative is seen as a matter of degrees of distance from the mainstream, so that, for example an anarchist publication is treated in the same manner as a fascist publication, since they would both reject the values of the current political order. But this kind of equivalence does not really offer any insights into either of these types of media. Moreover, in this line of theorising, if a right-wing publication claims it is against the system, and its readers agree it is against the system, then it is seen as being alternative even if it supports the same relations of production and exclusions that structure mainstream society and its institutions. In its quest to theorise right-wing media, this 'non-normative' and 'non-ideological' approach is, on the one hand, unable to capture the complex dynamics that structure both the (far) right and radical left media and their position in relations of production; on the other hand, it reproduces the ideological position that the political centre is the only legitimate political system.

From the point of view of radical left media, the challenge of this kind of theorising that comes from the centre is that it pushes them to a defensive position, where they are called to justify their existence and to differentiate themselves both from the mainstream and from the far-right media. In their work Figenschou and Ihlebæk (2022) discuss some the boundary struggles that mainstream journalism engages in in trying to keep the far-right media from gaining professional legitimacy. While such boundary work is undoubtedly taking place between mainstream and far-right media, the centrist positioning of radical left media as another variant of alternative media challenges radical left media to engage in their own form of boundary work in order to preserve and legitimate their position. This is a challenge that needs to be addressed because ultimately radical media are looking to appeal to broader publics. The road to a broad appeal requires this sharpening of the boundaries between emancipatory radical media and both the mainstream and the far-right media, along with the reclaiming of non-centrist positions as legitimate. In part, this has to involve critical tactics. As we will discuss below, however, the issue of tactics presents its own challenges.

Critique as Tactic

The use of critique is an essential part of advancing demands and instituting changes. In his influential work *Critique and Crisis*, Koselleck (1998) has shown that critique was at the heart of the move from absolute monarchy to more democratic forms of political rule in the 18th-century Europe. In his account, criticism entails judgement and differentiation; it involves a test for the validity, beauty, authenticity, truth or rightness of a circumstance, an event, an object and so on (Koselleck, 1998: 103). It represents the main form of the public use of reason. Historically, critique emerged in a context of sociopolitical crisis, first with the medieval religious wars and subsequently with the French Revolution, but it is also these crises that required critique as a way out of crisis. For Koselleck, the dialectic of critique and crisis is characteristic of modernity. Critique therefore is not merely the privilege, right or tactic of a specific political faction but also a defining attribute of our historical epoch, which is an epoch of 'permanent critique' (Foucault, 1991: 42). Foucault outlines critique not only as revealing a domain of possibility but also as entailing the potential of a reversal (Foucault, 1996). Crucially, critique implies a call to action: once a judgement is made, an action can be identified and potentially followed (Koselleck, 1998).[1] The potential and pitfalls of critique have been well documented by Koselleck, who shows how by subjecting everything to criticism, critique hubristically assumes the place of the all-seeing sovereign, failing to identify limits and be subjected itself to critique. In this process, critique deteriorates into self-delusion and hypocrisy. Historically, during the Enlightenment this process led not only to the crisis that was resolved by the French Revolution but also to the terror that followed it. This excursus is important to show the historical location and implications of critique: it is not an inconsequential discourse but a political action with consequences – an indirect assumption of power as Koselleck put it, and one which is historically linked to the emergence of the bourgeois world.

In an abstract and schematic manner, critique operates by publicly putting under test specific claims, demonstrating their validity (or lack of) and in this manner convincing others and triggering action and change. Convincing others to act through critique is the means by which self-conscious agency is developed: people identify their own capacity to act collectively in seeking to change social, political, economic or cultural aspects that have failed the test of criticism. This is why the arena of the media is crucial for the purposes of critique: on the one hand, they can determine agendas and disseminate critical ideas and discourses widely. On the other hand, by undermining their institutional function as mediators of ideas and discourse, the ideas are themselves undermined too: if the media are illegitimate, then their ideas are illegitimate too by proxy. This makes media criticism a crucial arena for struggle.

This is evident in the sustained attack against mainstream media by the far right. In their study of Swedish far-right media, Figenschou and Ihlebæk (2019a) identified three main forms of media criticism: that mainstream journalism is biased, partisan or deceitful; that it excludes certain voices; and that it is not representing the concerns of everyday people. In these far-right media, mainstream journalism is seen as part of an elite, left wing, 'politically correct' consensus imposed on society, while it fails to live up to its own standards of objectivity and neutrality. Other research has identified a more dangerous element to this media critique in which the press is referred to as lying. For instance, the term *Lügenpresse*, which was used in Nazi Germany, is encountered once more in today's public sphere, occasionally accompanied by verbal or physical attacks (Koliska and Assmann, 2021). As Figenschou and Ihlebæk (2019a) have shown, far-right media criticism does not approach the media sphere as a system or structure, but rather superficially focuses on journalistic performance. This is evident in the way in which critics justify and validate their claims which takes place mainly through reference to experiential claims, such as that they were 'victims' of the mainstream media, or (former) insiders or 'ordinary citizens'. These then lead them to formulate actions, for example to boycott or expose mainstream media or to provide 'alternative facts'. Similar criticisms are encountered in the USA, where mainstream media are criticised for elitism, liberal bias and enforcement of a 'politically correct' or 'woke' consensus, although paradoxically such attacks were often mobilised not by 'ordinary people' but by Donald Trump, and his references to 'fake news' and media as 'the enemy of the people' (Carlson et al., 2021). Such claims are also reported in media systems as diverse as Greece (Siapera and Papadopoulou, 2021) and Germany (Fawzi, 2019; Haller and Holt, 2019).

There is some evidence that this kind of anti-elite or populist media criticism correlates with negative attitudes and mistrust of the media (Fawzi, 2019). Carlson et al. (2021) suggest that declining trust in the media in the USA can be attributed at least in part to persistent media critiques. Moreover, they argue that such critiques undermine the epistemic authority of journalism and its social role. Holt et al. (2019) point out that media criticism is pushing mainstream professional journalism into a boundary struggle, seeking to defend their professional practice and norms while also excluding far-right actors from the profession. Taking these into account it is clear that the far-right criticism has been successful in the sense that it has made mainstream media reflect upon their practice. But it also has an effect on the radical left media. In particular, the mobilisation of critical tropes that approximate left positions on the media pre-empts and neutralises radical left media criticism. Even the term mainstream media, which Phelan (2022) argues only entered the public sphere in the 1980s as part of an academic critique of the media, now stands as a signifier for far-right critiques when a few years ago it was part of the critical arsenal of the left. The far-right usurpation of left critical tropes or more broadly what Corcuff (2021: non-paginated) calls 'ideological tinkering', a bricolage of concepts developed in very different ideological contexts, has the effect of eroding the symbolic boundaries between left and right ideologies. This in turn feeds into the 'two extremes' theories discussed earlier.

The challenge and tactical question for radical journalism is, when and if it should mobilise media critiques. On the one hand, it is forced to defend mainstream media, especially when it comes to issues such as factually correct information and deplatforming of racist, misogynist and other hateful actors. On the other hand, it is forced to defend its own use of criticism against mainstream media. These tensions are very clear in the context of the UK and the BBC. The BBC is the target of criticism by right-wing media, which sees it as carrying a liberal 'woke' bias (GBNews, 2021); by the conservative government, which constructs it as expensive, bureaucratic and 'not good value for money', looking to privatise it (Waterson, 2022); and by left media which views it as supporting the status quo (Topple, 2022). There is little doubt that these critiques have weakened the public service broadcaster. While this may have been the intended outcome of both the conservative government and the right-wing media, the left critique aimed to strengthen its identity and independence as a public service broadcaster. In these terms, critique as a tactic for progressive change did not succeed for the left.

If anything, we can see the limits of critique in at least two ways. Firstly, at the level of action, critique must be attendant to the political climate and adjust its short-term tactics accordingly. In these terms, while the propensity of radical media is to criticise both liberal and right-wing media, using critique as a tactic in political struggle means paying attention to the political climate, which in turn may require a different approach. For example, tactically, it may be more important to support a public service broadcaster or some forms of independent liberal journalism in the context of repeated attacks and the threat of physical violence. While these are issues to be resolved in the struggle, the point here is that critique needs to be used judiciously and to be aware of its limits.

Secondly, at a more abstract level, critique cut off from a specific position in relations of production can easily be manipulated and put to the service of reactionary goals. As Benjamin (1970 [1934]) argued, for radical media the goal should not only be propaganda but also political organisation, exemplified through, on the one hand, organising and producing media that stands in opposition to both the far-right (fascist) media and to the bourgeois (liberal) media; and on the other hand, for those who write and produce these media and their critiques to reflect on their own position in the process of production. Stripped from these, critique becomes at best self-delusion and hypocrisy, as Koselleck (1988) found, and at worst a reactionary tool, entailing what Foucault (1996) referred to as reversal: the reversal of important gains in the struggle for emancipation.

Thirdly, the discussion of how critique is mobilised in an ideologically confused context, to which it contributes directly, alludes to the dialectic of critique and crisis that Koselleck identified in his discussion of early modernity. In Koselleck's historical account, the proliferation of critique almost inevitably leads to crisis, and, conversely, crisis almost inevitably produces critique. The present historical period, in which crisis follows another crisis, from the 2008 financial crisis to the crisis of the pandemic, in the context of environmental crisis and impending collapse, is without a doubt a critical one. In the period that Koselleck discussed, critique precipitated the political crisis that reached its peak in the French revolution. We do not yet know what the future holds for the present crises, but we can read the far-right media critiques as part of this dialectic. The radical media are challenged by the far-right critiques to address them appropriately and to interpret them as a symptom of the critique-crisis dialectic. At the same time, the challenge of the far-right media critiques must not obscure left struggles for visibility and for thematising matters of concern. This leads us to the third challenge posed by the far-right media: shaping the mainstream media agenda.

Far-Right Media Agenda Setting

One of the most poignant ironies of the rise of far-right media and their criticism must be the mainstream media response. While radical media have been persistently posing questions of race and racism, colonialism and imperialism, global capitalism and imperial wars that trigger human movements, mainstream media have remained largely unresponsive. For example, their preferred way of dealing with questions of racism and cultural diversity associated with waves of migration has been to deny, sensationalise and obscure, often through constant debate about race and migration (Lentin and Titley, 2011, 2012; Georgiou and Zaborowski, 2017; Titley, 2019; Georgiou, 2020). In addition, racialised others rarely find a voice in the media sphere; even when their voices are incorporated, the process is rife with contradiction and ends up naturalising symbolic borders which migrants and refugees are not permitted to cross (Georgiou, 2018; Chouliaraki et al., 2017). As Horsti (2016) notes, migration has been hypervisible in the media yet refugees and migrants are largely silenced. It is within this context that the far-right focus on migration and/in the media presents an irony: the mainstream media agenda has always foregrounded migration and racialised others as a threat to the nation. Despite this, they are attacked by far-right media as ignoring concerns over migration raised by 'ordinary people' (Figenschou and Ihlebæk, 2019). The irony is that the mainstream media appear responsive to this kind of criticism but not to the left attempts to hold them accountable for racist representations, othering and exclusion. How did the far-right media succeed in pushing their interpretations into the media agenda? I argue that it is not so much a case of the far-right media 'infiltrating' the mainstream, although some of their frames might do. Rather, it is a symptom of the links between liberal and right ideologies, whose difference is one of degree rather than kind – the far right is therefore less a pathology of the normal and more a pathological normalcy, to use Mudde's (2010) terms. The challenge for radical journalism might therefore be to identify and prise open these connections when and where they are encountered and to shift the agenda towards socio-economic issues that focus on relations of production and the fundamental antagonism between labour and capital in all its guises.

Empirically proving direct agenda setting effects is not easy, because most methods are looking to establish a direct route of influence from the far-right media to the mainstream. Often, however, this route is much more convoluted, and follows an indirect line that passes from media to political actors and back again. Additionally, the political context and culture in specific national media systems are important mediating factors. For example, Nygaard (2020) found that mainstream media in Norway and Denmark showed some support for far-right media and their views. In these countries, far-right populist political actors are accepted as legitimate. In contrast, in Sweden, where such actors are seen as 'deviant', support for far-right media was minimal. In Nygaard's work, there were limited, if any inter-media agenda setting effects, where far-right media themes were directly picked up by mainstream media. However, far-right media were given publicity and attention and thereby a platform, even if negatively. Similarly, von Nordheim et al. (2019) found that mainstream press in Germany differed in its coverage of the refugee 'crisis' of 2015–2016 compared to a far-right publication, concluding that, on the whole, the mainstream coverage "refrained from systematically catering to xeno-phobic prejudices" (p. 51). Von Nordheim et al. argue that their findings suggest that far-right media react to but do not drive the media agenda. Nevertheless, both Nygaard (2020) and von Nordheim et al. (2019) point to the ways in which con-troversial far-right actors and their views are given publicity by mainstream media.

Focusing more closely on the issue of migration coverage, von Nordheim et al. (2019) report that while mainstream media covered the refugee 'crisis' from a var-iety of angles, the far-right media used mainly 'us' and 'them' frames, did not pro-vide any European or international context and framed refugees as culturally alien, inassimilable 'others'. However, other studies on the mainstream media framing of the refugee 'crisis' report different findings. In a comparative study of European mainstream media coverage of the 'crisis', Georgiou and Zaborowski (2017) iden-tify three temporal phases in the framing: careful tolerance, ecstatic humanitar-ianism and fear and securitisation, with the latter mobilising xenophobic narratives. Similarly, Krzyżanowski et al. (2018: 1) refer to a persistent 'exclusionary rhetoric of othering'. Even the framing as 'crisis', which was common across all mainstream media, is significant, because it adds alarmist connotations and justifies extraor-dinary responses and urgent measures. Krzyżanowski et al. draw attention to the close connections between politics and media, and argue for the need to context-ualise the framing in terms of ongoing political developments, such as, for example, Islamophobia that emerged during the 'war on terror' and the securitisation of borders. They point to the politisation of migration, which makes it an issue on which politicians and other political actors necessarily take a stance, often one of being 'in control' or 'strong'. The close connection between media and politics means that the media follow the negative politicisation of migration. At the same time, the political sphere itself is mediatised, that is, increasingly dependent on the media, leading to shifts in politics, such as from policy making and representation to attention seeking and visibility, which makes political actors prone to simplifi-cation and sensationalisation. The politicisation of migration and the rise of far-right actors can therefore account for the already negative mainstream coverage of migration rather than the hijacking of the media agenda by the far-right media.

While Krzyżanowski et al. (2018) refer to structural aspects of the relation-ship between politics and media, there are also ideological connections between the mainstream and the far right. Cas Mudde (2010) has argued that instead of considering the far right as a pathology of normal politics it may be more appro-priate to view it as a 'pathological normalcy', that is, less of a perversion of the normal and more its extension and logical follow up. Pointing to important ways in which key ideological tenets of the far right (nativism, nationalism, authoritarianism and law and order) overlap and intersect with mainstream ideological positions of nation states, Mudde (2010) shows that the far right is not alien to the key values of liberal democracies. Using evidence from attitude studies, he demonstrates empirically that the key tenets are shared by European publics, albeit to a more modest degree. This leads him to the conclusion that such ideas are not antithetical to the values and constitutions of liberal states. They are typically fairly widespread but expressed in more moderate forms. In these terms, the difference between liberal democracies and the far right is not one of kind but one of degree. Their key set of issues and positions on corruption-immigration-security are shared by a significant part of the population in Europe. The far-right political struggle therefore is one of issue saliency: if people become concerned by immigration or security they will turn to the far right and its positions.

These insights are crucial in order to understand the agenda-setting role played by the right-wing media: if migration is already on the media agenda then the far right is favoured, even if the media representation is more moderate; if it isn't, the far-right media speak of corruption, silencing of the concerns of ordinary people, and 'failing' mainstream media. In fact, they do this anyway, as Figenschou and Ihlebæk (2019a, b) have shown. This is the challenge for radical media and journalism: interjecting in this agenda by taking a positive position on migration entails the danger of adding to what Titley (2019) refers as debatability: the endless production of discourse on migration and race, adding more layers of signification and entering into definitional struggles that, to the extent that they focus on migration cut off from its political economic context, end up playing at the hands of the far right. Not talking about migration, on the other hand, risks making radical journalism irrelevant, since this is a salient agenda issue and a key political debate. It is difficult to eschew this dilemma. However, in line with the radical political agenda of social justice, freedom and equality, radical journalism could, and occasionally does, operate in ways that foreground the voices and experiences of migrants, building solidarities and connecting struggles, all the while pointing to the possibility for a different social, political and economic organisation. The Roar Magazine issue 8 *Beyond the Border* (2018)[2] is an example of such an attempt. On the other hand, competing for visibility and salience in mediatised and platformised public spheres (De Blasio et al., 2020) means that such attempts may never scale. While far-right media, their simplifications and loud accusations profit from the mediated structures of the public sphere, the work that radical media are or should be doing is unlikely to reach broader publics. While this may be a perennial issue for radical media (Khiabany, 2000) the operations of the far right and its media and their direct and indirect contributions to the public agenda exacerbate the problem, while pulling radical media towards reacting to this agenda rather than creating another one that may shift the debate.

Conclusion

The rise of far-right media has alarmed mainstream media not only because their monopoly is undermined but also because they often find themselves at the receiving end of intense and sustained attacks. While the relationship between the mainstream and far-right media has been examined, the challenges they pose for emancipatory radical journalism are less well known. This chapter constitutes an attempt to provide an initial discussion of three important challenges. The first challenge comes from the liberal centre and dismisses both emancipatory radical journalism and far-right journalism as two extremes which will eventually converge. This positions radical journalism in a defensive position and requires that sharper boundaries be drawn. The second challenge concerns the role of critique and its use as a tactic by both the far-right and radical journalism and media. As critique is not only a tactic but also a defining characteristic of modernity, its role is complex and ambivalent. For radical journalism and media, mobilising critique without reflecting on their own position and role in relations of production risks the deterioration of critique into self-delusion and hypocrisy or, worse, to be put in the service of reactionary ends. The third challenge comes from the apparent success of the far right to influence the mainstream media agenda. Focusing on the key issue of migration, the discussion here showed that it is not so much a case of the far right infiltrating the mainstream as it is an occasion of convergence between the mainstream and the far right. The challenge for radical journalism is to shift the agenda towards drawing connecting lines between migration, global exploitation and constant imperialist wars.

The discussion here remained conceptual and abstract. The goal of the chapter was to schematically outline some of the provocations that the far right and its media have set for emancipatory media in order to make clear some of the stakes involved. This theoretical discussion cannot offer any political solutions. Ultimately, any responses to these challenges will be formulated in political struggle. For now, it is important to show that the far right does not only impact the mainstream media but presents important challenges for emancipatory radical media as well.

Notes

1 Koselleck refers to Friedrich Schiller, the philosopher and playwright, who pointed out that it is not enough to unmask the unjust and despotic politicians of his time, but also to undermine them or else "be vanquished by them" (in Koselleck, 1998: 103).
2 Available at: https://roarmag.org/wp-content/uploads/2018/09/ROAR_Issue_8_Beyond_the_Border.pdf

References

Adorno, T. W., & Horkheimer, M. (1997). *Dialectic of enlightenment* (Vol. 15). London: Verso.
Althusser, L. (2012). Ideology and ideological state apparatuses (notes towards an investigation). In Durham, M. G., & Kellner, D. M. (Eds.), *Media and cultural studies: Keyworks* (pp. 80–87). Malden, MA: Wiley.
Atton, C. (2006). Far-right media on the internet: Culture, discourse and power. *New Media & Society, 8*(4), 573–587.

Benjamin, W. (1970 [1934]). The author as producer. *New Left Review, 1/62* (July–August), available at: www.marxists.org/reference/archive/benjamin/1970/author-producer.htm

Berlatsky, N. (2018). Let's put an end to 'horseshoe theory' once and for all. *Pacific Standard*, February 9, available at: https://psmag.com/social-justice/an-end-to-horseshoe-theory

Berlet, C., Christensen, K., Duerr, G., Duval, R. D., Garcia, J. D., Klier, F., Koronaiou, A., Lagos, E., Mason, C., Mazurski, L., & Mihailovic, A. (2015). *Digital media strategies of the far right in Europe and the United States*. Boulder, CO: Lexington Books.

Capoccia, G. (2002). Anti-system parties: A conceptual reassessment. *Journal of Theoretical Politics, 14*(1), 9–5.

Carlson, M., Robinson, S., & Lewis, S. C. (2021). Digital press criticism: The symbolic dimensions of Donald Trump's assault on US journalists as the "enemy of the people". *Digital Journalism, 9*(6), 737–754.

Choat, S. (2017). 'Horseshoe theory' is nonsense – the far right and far left have little in common. *The Conversation*, May 12, available at: https://theconversation.com/horseshoe-theory-is-nonsense-the-far-right-and-far-left-have-little-in-common-77588

Chouliaraki, L., Georgiou, M., Zaborowski, R., & Oomen, W. A. (2017). The European 'migration crisis' and the media: A cross-European press content analysis. Final Report, London School of Economics and Political Science, available at: www.academia.edu/33647366/The_European_migration_crisis_and_the_media_A_cross_European_press_content_analysis

Corcuff, P. (2021). *La grande confusion: Comment l'extrême droite gagne la bataille des idées*. Paris: Éditions Textuel.

Couldry, N. (2002). Alternative media and mediated community. Paper presented at the 23rd International Association for Media and Communication Research Conference, Barcelona, July 21–26.

De Blasio, E., Kneuer, M., Schunemann, W., & Sorice, M. (2020). The ongoing transformation of the digital public sphere: Basic considerations on a moving target. *Media and Communication, 8*(4), 1–5. doi: 10.17645/mac.v8i4.3639

Debord, G. (2012). *Society of the spectacle*. Bread and Circuses Publishing.

Downing, J. D. (2000). *Radical media: Rebellious communication and social movements*. Thousand Oaks, CA: Sage.

Fawzi, N. (2019). Untrustworthy news and the media as "enemy of the people?" How a populist worldview shapes recipients' attitudes toward the media. *The International Journal of Press/Politics, 24*(2), 146–164.

Faye, J. P. (2006). *Le siècle des ideologies*. Paris: Armand Colin.

Figenschou, T. U., & Ihlebæk, K. A. (2019a). Challenging journalistic authority: Media criticism in far-right alternative media. *Journalism Studies, 20*(9), 1221–1237.

Figenschou, T. U., & Ihlebaek, K. A. (2019b). Media criticism from the far-right: Attacking from many angles. *Journalism Practice, 13*(8), 901–905.

Foucault, M. (1991). "What is enlightenment?". In Rainbow, P. (Ed.), *The Foucault reader* (pp. 303–319). New York: Pantheon.

Foucault, M. (1996). What is critique. In Schmidt, J. (Ed.), *What is enlightenment? (Eighteenth-century answers and twentieth-century questions)* (pp. 382–398). Berkeley, CA: University of California Press, doi:10.1525/9780520916890-029

Freeman, H. (2017). Le Pen is a far-right Holocaust revisionist. Macron isn't. Hard choice? *The Guardian*, April 25, available at: www.theguardian.com/commentisfree/2017/apr/25/le-pen-far-right-holocaust-revisionist-macron-left

GBNews. (2021). Has the BBC gone so woke it is now a threat to free speech? December 2, available at: www.youtube.com/watch?v=Pt39OWNsEl8

Georgiou, M. (2018). Does the subaltern speak? Migrant voices in digital Europe. *Popular Communication, 16*(1), 45–47.

Georgiou, M. (2020). Racism, postracialism and why media matter. *Ethnic and Racial Studies, 43*(13), 2379–2385.

Georgiou, M., & Zaborowski, R. (2017). *Media coverage of the "refugee crisis": A cross-European perspective.* Strasbourg: Council of Europe.

Gramsci, A. (1971). *Selections from the prison notebooks* (Hoare, Q. & Smith, G. N. Trans.) NewYork: International Publishers.

Hall, S., Critcher, C., Jefferson, T., Clarke, J., & Roberts, B. (2013). *Policing the crisis: Mugging, the state and law and order.* Basingstoke: Macmillan International Higher Education.

Haller, A., & Holt, K. (2019). Paradoxical populism: How PEGIDA relates to mainstream and alternative media. *Information, Communication & Society, 22*(12), 1665–1680.

Haller, A., Holt, K., & de La Brosse, R. (2019). The 'other' alternatives: Political right-wing alternative media. *Journal of Alternative and Community Media, 4*(1), 1–6.

Heft, A., Mayerhöffer, E., Reinhardt, S., & Knüpfer, C. (2020). Beyond Breitbart: Comparing right-wing digital news infrastructures in six western democracies. *Policy & Internet, 12*(1), 20–45.

Holt, K. (2019). *Right-wing alternative media.* London: Routledge.

Holt, K., Ustad Figenschou, T., & Frischlich, L. (2019). Key dimensions of alternative news media. *Digital Journalism, 7*(7), 860–869.

Horsti, K. (2016).Visibility without voice: Media witnessing irregular migrants in BBC online news journalism. *African Journalism Studies, 37*(1), 1–20. doi:10.1080/23743670.2015

Ihlebæk, K. A., & Figenschou, T. U. (2022). Knock, knock! Right-wing alternative media is at the door: Institutional boundary work in a hybrid media environment. In Ferucci, P., & Eldridge II, S. (Eds.), *The institutions changing journalism* (pp. 17–30). London: Routledge.

Johnstone, J. W. (1976). *The news people: A sociological portrait of American journalists and their work.* Chicago: University of Illinois Press.

Khiabany, G. (2000). Red Pepper: A new model for the alternative press? *Media, Culture & Society, 22*(4), 447–463.

Koliska, M., & Assmann, K. (2021). Lügenpresse: The lying press and German journalists' responses to a stigma. *Journalism, 22*(11), 2729–2746. https://doi.org/10.1177/14648 84919894088

Koselleck, R. (1998). *Critique and crisis: Enlightenment and the pathogenesis of modern society.* Cambridge, MA: MIT Press.

Krzyżanowski, M., Triandafyllidou, A., & Wodak, R. (2018). The mediatization and the politicization of the "refugee crisis" in Europe. *Journal of Immigrant & Refugee Studies, 16*(1–2), 1–14.

Lentin, A., & Titley, G. (2011). *The crises of multiculturalism: Racism in a neoliberal age.* London: Bloomsbury Publishing.

Lentin, A., & Titley, G. (2012). The crisis of 'multiculturalism' in Europe: Mediated minarets, intolerable subjects. *European Journal of Cultural Studies, 15*(2), 123–138.

Lim, M., and Rigato B. (2022). Close to home: The Canadian far right, COVID-19 and social media. *The Conversation,* April 3, available at: https://theconversation.com/close-to-home-the-canadian-far-right-covid-19-and-social-media-178714

May, R. (2019).The YellowVest phenomenon and the radical right. *Open Democracy,* February 25, available at: www.opendemocracy.net/en/can-europe-make-it/yellow-vest-phenome non-and-radical-right/

Mudde, C. (1996).The war of words defining the extreme right party family. *West European Politics, 19*(2), 225–248.

Mudde, C. (2002). *The ideology of the extreme right.* Manchester: Manchester University Press.

Mudde, C. (2010). The populist radical right: A pathological normalcy. *West European politics, 33*(6), 1167–1186.

Nygaard, S. (2020). Boundary work: Intermedia agenda-setting between right-wing alternative media and professional journalism. *Journalism Studies, 21*(6), 766–782.

Patrikarakos, D. (2017). Could the French far left propel Marine Le Pen to victory? *Spectator Magazine,* May 3, available at: www.spectator.co.uk/article/could-the-french-far-left-propel-marine-le-pen-to-victory-

Phelan, S. (2022). Why legitimate criticism of the 'mainstream' media is in danger of being hijacked by anti-vax and 'freedom' movements. *The Conversation,* March 3, available at: https://theconversation.com/why-legitimate-criticism-of-the-mainstream-media-is-in-danger-of-being-hijacked-by-anti-vax-and-freedom-movements-178166

Siapera, E., & Papadopoulou, L. (2021). Hate as a 'hook': The political and affective economy of 'hate journalism'. *Journalism, 22*(5), 1256–1272.

Smythe, D. W. (2012). On the audience commodity and its work. In Durham, M. G., & Kellner, D. M. (Eds.), *Media and cultural studies: Keyworks* (pp. 230–256). Wiley.

Sommer, B. (2008). Anti-capitalism in the name of ethno-nationalism: Ideological shifts on the German extreme right. *Patterns of Prejudice, 42*(3), 305–316.

Titley, G. (2019). *Racism and media.* London: Sage.

Topple, S. (2022). The BBC continues to push pro-Boris Johnson propaganda, *The Canary,* February 10, available at: www.thecanary.co/uk/analysis/2022/02/10/the-bbc-continues-to-push-pro-boris-johnson-propaganda/

von Nordheim, G., Müller, H., & Scheppe, M. (2019). Young, free and biased: A comparison of mainstream and right-wing media coverage of the 201516 refugee crisis in German newspapers. *Journal of Alternative & Community Media, 4*(1), 38–56.

Wahlström, M., Törnberg, A., & Ekbrand, H. (2021). Dynamics of violent and dehumanizing rhetoric in far-right social media. *New Media & Society, 23*(11), 3290–3311.

Waterson, J. (2022). BBC licence fee to be abolished in 2027 and funding frozen. *The Guardian,* January 16, available at: www.theguardian.com/media/2022/jan/16/bbc-licence-fee-to-be-abolished-in-2027-and-funding-frozen#:~:text=The%20culture%20secretary%2C%20Nadine%20Dorries,for%20the%20following%20three%20years

Winter, A. (2019). Online hate: From the far-right to the 'alt-right' and from the margins to the mainstream. In Lumsden, K., & Harmer, E. (Eds.), *Online othering* (pp. 39–63). Cham: Palgrave Macmillan.

INDEX

For Product Safety Concerns and Information please contact our EU
representative GPSR@taylorandfrancis.com
Taylor & Francis Verlag GmbH, Kaufingerstraße 24, 80331 München, Germany

www.ingramcontent.com/pod-product-compliance
Lightning Source LLC
Chambersburg PA
CBHW070344270326
41926CB00017B/3980